W9-CDN-985

The Great Super Cycle

The Great Super Cycle

Profit from the Coming Inflation Tidal Wave and Dollar Devaluation

David Skarica

WILEY

John Wiley & Sons, Inc.

Published by John Wiley & Sons, Inc., Hoboken, New Jersey.
Published simultaneously in Canada.

For general information on our other products and services or for technical support, please contact our Customer Care Department within the United States at (800) 762-2974, outside the United States at (317) 572-3993 or fax (317) 572-4002.

Wiley also publishes its books in a variety of electronic formats. Some content that appears in print may not be available in electronic books. For more information about Wiley products, visit our web site at www.wiley.com.

Library of Congress Cataloging-in-Publication Data:

Skarica, David.
   The great super cycle : profit from the coming inflation tidal wave and dollar devaluation/David Skarica.
     p. cm.
   Includes bibliographical references and index.
   ISBN 978-0-470-62418-0 (hardback); 978-0-470-94024-2 (ebk);
   978-0-470-94023-5 (ebk)
     1. Investments—United States.   2. Investment analysis—United States.
3. Business cycles—United States.   4. Inflation (Finance)—United States.   5. Dollar, American.   6. Debts, Public—United States.   I. Title.
   HG4910.D53 2010
   332.60973—dc22

                                2010032267

Printed in the United States of America

10 9 8 7 6 5 4 3 2

To my late grandfather, Miroslav Skarica, who had the courage to start a new life in the new world and give me the opportunity to write this book and the late great Jon Templeton who taught me how to be a true contrarian and spot value and big time long term trends.

Contents

Preface

Economic Armageddon

*How Super Powers Fall and Empires End
and Why It Is Not the End of the World*

Wwe all know that bad news sells. I am in the investment
newsletter business. The only people I know who see more
doom-and-gloom types than myself are owners of funeral
homes. The crash of 2008 saw doom-and-gloomers spread over the
globe like a biblical locust swarm. We were all helpless in preventing
those naysayers from invading our homes via our TVs and computers.
They worked their way into every nook and cranny of our screens in a
frenzied feeding of media hysteria. Every expert who had claimed to
have predicted the crash and meltdown (where were they before?)
brashly proclaimed that the crash was not only the end of Wall Street as
we know it but the end of the world. However, you and I are still here.
I am sure you are very weary of this type of thing, even if you are not a
whole lot poorer. Very few gurus have a great track record over the long

term. Many of the people who called the economic crash had been calling it for *years and years*. At some point a downturn was going to happen. As the old saying goes, even a dead clock is right twice a day.

Investment gurus such as David Rosenberg, Gary Schilling, and Robert Precther told us (with some glee on occasions) that the world was going to enter another Great Depression and the Dow would sink back to 5,000. Of course, this did not come to pass and the Dow bottomed around 6,500 in March 2009 before entering a huge rally that took it to over 10,000 by early 2010 (as I am writing this book).

The truth is rarely as devastating as those Nostradamus lovers would like us to believe. On the other side of the coin, remember those who in 1999 were telling us that the Dow was going to 40,000 and we were in some sort of Goldilocks economy? Isn't it ironic that with unemployment in the double digits as I write, we never hear that term anymore! (*Note*: The *Goldilocks economy* was a theory that the economy had entered a perfect combination of high economic growth, low inflation, and low employment, which many pundits in the late nineties were telling us we were in for the long term.)

Things are never as bad as the doom-and-gloomers say and they are never as good as the Goldilocks crowd says. I take a middle ground when I do my research. I make my predictions based on sound reasoning backed by decades of historical precedents.

In the past 10 years, we have seen the stock market go virtually nowhere and lose over two-thirds of its value when adjusted for inflation. Many attribute this to the Iraq war, the disastrous presidency of George W. Bush, higher oil prices, and the financial crisis of 2007–2009. They see the market not going anywhere and see events as part of a stream of random occurrences. However, what they fail to understand is that most of these random events occur within the realm of a Great Super Cycle.

For some reason, markets move in major cycles. It is the cycles that drive these events, not the other way around. Since 1900, the U.S. stock market has seen numerous 15- to 20-year periods where equity prices have been strong and 15- to 20-year periods when they have been weak. In up-cycles, stocks start out cheap; they climb in price; the economy is strong, and eventually this leads to what Alan Greenspan referred to as "irrational exuberance." There are usually new technologies that capture the imagination of investors during this time period, along with peace and low unemployment. This cycle then travels in this direction for too long; the market tops, becomes overvalued, and then collapses and does nothing over a long period of time. This long period of underperformance scares investors out; the market again becomes cheap and the cycle starts all over again.

We all too often blame the key actors during the cycles (e.g., Bush, Obama, etc.). However, they are mere pawns in the larger game of cycle chess. What goes up must come down and it is these periods of cycles (which have always occurred throughout history) that drive markets.

Why Should You Listen to Me?

Why should you listen to me? What makes me different? Do I have a track record? Is it any good? These are basic questions that are never asked about many of the experts that you see in the media.

A bit about myself: I like to believe that I am not like most talking heads on TV or university professors. I have to make my living in the trenches. I write two investment newsletters: *www.addictedtoprofits .net* and *Gold Stock Advisor*. I live comfortably in the Bahamas. If I do not make good calls for my subscribers, I will lose my readership and be forced into eating death-burgers and microwave dinners before the inevitable heart attacks that always kill that lifestyle. Therefore, I must make accurate calls on a consistent basis or go back to freezing my butt off in my native Toronto, Canada.

In 1999, at the tender age of 21, I had my first book, *Stock Market Panic! How to Prosper in the Coming Bear Market*, published by Productive Publications, a small publisher in Canada. The book was not a commercial success (mostly due to my age and my lack of experience and name recognition in the financial industry). However, the predictions in it were remarkably accurate. How was I able to be so accurate? In the late nineties, I pored over the history of bubbles and the cycles of booms and busts. I devoted myself to endless research. I began to fear that the stock market and Internet bull market of the nineties were turning into huge bubbles. This sparked my initial interest in cycle research. This research told me that markets trade in cycles where they do nothing for a long period of time. I discovered that certain assets go into a bull market cycle at the same time as other assets go into a bear market cycle, and so on.

After countless hours of work, I came to the following conclusions and made a number of predictions in *Stock Market Panic!* that I believe have proven to be uncannily accurate.

The book made the following predictions:

- **U.S. stocks were peaking and would be in a bear market for years to come.** This was a valuation readjustment as stocks had to come down from overvalued to undervalued. The Dow, which traded near 10,000 at that time, 10 years later trades near 10,000 and has lost much of its value on an inflation-adjusted basis.
- **The real estate market was a bubble that would burst.** The real estate boom went on longer than I thought it would. I thought real estate would bust with the tech bubble. However, the interest rate cuts and loose money that were initiated by the Federal Reserve to bail out the economy after the bursting of the tech bubble caused a leverage and real estate bubble far greater than I ever imagined. I thought real estate would collapse but even I never envisioned subprime mortgage–backed securities leveraged at 30 to 1 or greater.
- **Bonds would top and interest rates would move much higher, and real estate in rural and exotic areas around the world would outperform urban real estate.** This is the one prediction that has not yet occurred. It looks as if the interest rate market made an important low and bonds an important top in December 2008. However, rates have remained low on a historical basis. But you have to think that, with all of the debt the United States is issuing, rates will ultimately be headed much, much higher. Although some rural and exotic real estate has crashed with the rest of the real estate market, much of it has held up. There is still a willingness by investors to pay a premium to move to exotic locales away from society. In addition, many small Caribbean and South Pacific nations did not use the reckless borrowing methods used in the United States and are positioned favorably to take advantage of future economic recoveries.
- **Inflation would head much higher.** Shawdowstats.com, which is run by John Williams, measures the rate of inflation. To do so, Williams takes into account real inflation (e.g., not the jaded inflation numbers we see released by the government today that try to repress inflation due to the increasing entitlements that the government is

on the hook for) and calculates inflation the way the government did 20 years ago. Williams calculated that inflation in mid-2008 hit 9 percent; this is the highest inflation since the seventies.

- **Gold would become in vogue again and move much higher in price.** Gold, which began the decade hovering around $300 an ounce, climbed to over $1,000 an ounce by the end of the decade.
- **Other commodities—such as oil, wheat, corn, and soybeans— would also be headed much higher.** All of these agricultural commodities saw spikes in price during the 2000s.
- **The U.S. dollar would fall in value**. The U.S. Dollar Index (an index of the U.S. dollar versus a basket of currencies) began the decade trading at 100 and now trades at about 78 as we go to press. This represents a loss of 22 percent.
- **There would be major wars between the United States and the Middle East.** In 2001, the United States began a major campaign in Afghanistan, and in 2003, the United States began a major campaign in Iraq. It is still involved in both.

As you can see, virtually all of the main predictions I made in *Stock Market Panic! How to Prosper in the Coming Bear Market* have come to pass in the past 10 years. As I stated earlier, and as you will read in later chapters, the one prediction that has not yet happened is the collapse of the long-term bond market. I feel very confident this prediction will be realized in the coming years. With the amount of debt the United States is planning on issuing in the coming years, it is fairly obvious that foreigners are going to ask for a higher rate of payment on this debt as it will not be the safe investment it was in past years.

The bottom line is that over the past 10 years I possess a fairly accurate track record. My research has led me to make accurate predictions. Therefore, any investor who wants to make profits during the inflation tsunami needs to read this book.

What Is This Book About?

The Great Super Cycle looks at what we can expect in global economics by looking at the history of political shifts in power. The United States is becoming increasingly socialistic with the government running many of the banks and mortgage and car companies. *The Great Super Cycle* is an intriguing look at shifting economic power and the relationship between Washington and Wall Street.

The underlying theme of this book is that everything moves in cycles, from the megacycle of world powers, to economic cycles that can last for decades, to mini-cycles that usually last 10 to 20 years. The market will move much lower in the coming years in inflation-adjusted terms. Cycles are the most important and also the most powerful tool we have to make money in the coming years. The megacycle that we are in will feature the coming debt bubble, a commodities boom, and a major economic shift from west to east. Some sectors and some countries will benefit from these shifts and will outperform. In this book, I will show you how you can profit from specific key sectors—gold, oil, the growing Asian markets, and offshore accounts. (I believe that more regulation and taxes will make the U.S. economy less competitive and will cause funds to move offshore.)

Accordingly, the dominant theme of this book is this simple but irresistible revelation: Market cycles are the most powerful of all influences that prevail on capital markets. A thorough understanding of market cycles is an essential tool for any investor who wishes to successfully trade and make money in the capital markets. Market cycles are like gravity—you can't see them but they bind your fate regardless.

In the coming chapters, I tell you why, after the tech bubble and housing bubble, the next and final bubble has now turned to debt instruments. This debt bubble is at the heart of our investment philosophy for the next 10 years. The debt bubble will lead to bull markets in commodities, such as oil and gas, wheat, corn, gold, and silver, and a shift of economic power to emerging economies such as China and India. It is this crisis that will lead to opportunity!

Overview

Much of this book focuses on *stock market cycles*. These are the 10- to 20-year bull markets that are followed by 10- to 20-year bear markets. However, the particular bear market cycle in which we currently find ourselves also falls in the context of a larger cycle. The larger cycle will see the end of America's reign as the world's superpower. Economic downturns can often see shifts in power.

For example, the Great Depression hit the United States and Great Britain equally hard. However, the British had to support their Empire, which at one point covered nearly a quarter of the world. The financial constraints of Empire, the Great Depression, and then World War II cumulatively produced a shift from Great Britain to the United States as the world's superpower. We should note, too, that the demise of the United States bears many similarities to the demise of the British nation. Both are English–speaking, democratic capitalistic western nations. Their populations, politics, and policies have much more in common than, say, the British and Romans had.

The Shift from Great Britain to the United States as the World's Superpower

The very simple lessons learned from the rise and fall of empires are usually very similar. A nation usually builds itself based on an advanced legal and political system. Then, from this system, which creates prosperity and wealth at home, the growing world power is able to build up a military and spread its influence around the globe. It then benefits from the reach of its empire. However, the nation usually then becomes dependent on this reach, overextends itself financially, lives beyond its means, becomes indebted, and then is forced to shrink the scale of its global influence. It happened to the British in the mid-twentieth century and this is where the United States is heading.

Britain overextended itself financially, and actually much of the pressures leading to the fall and dismantling of its Empire came from within. We must remember that the first calls for dismantling imperial Britain did not come after the empire was bankrupt post–World War II. Many British just did not feel the justification of ruling the world when so many Britons during the Great Depression were struggling at home. The calls for less empire came when the British themselves wanted more help at home for relief from the Great Depression. Remember that when London crashed in the early twentieth century, it was still London, not Wall Street, that was the financial capital of the world. The Brits wanted the expansion of a welfare state and wanted their resources to be used for the support of British citizens and not the empire. After World War II, the British passed the National Health Act, which brought in a universal government-run health-care system at a time when the British economy was heavily indebted.

We can see the same mentality prevailing in the United States with the recent health-care bill and the call for more social spending at home in light of the Crash of 2008. At some point, like the British, the United States will probably shrink the size and scope of its military around the globe to pay for social expenditures at home.

People marvel at America's current military presence, massive sports stadium expenditures, and massive amounts of wealth and are in awe of the size and strength of the country's economy. In reality, the American Empire is, by historical standards, short-lived and relatively weak. The British Empire, at its peak, ruled a quarter of the world and the British were the preeminent power in the world for most of the seventeenth and eighteenth centuries as well as the first 40 years of the twentieth century. That's a period of over 200 years. Compare that with America, which has been the preeminent power from post–World War II to the present and possibly for another 5 to 10 years to come after the publication of this book. That is all of 70 years or so. The United States is following the path of the British but they found a much quicker path to collapse as a superpower!

Even the French and the Spanish empires, which were ineptly administered and constantly on the brink of bankruptcy, were able to keep intact for roughly 100 years.

Despite amassing the greatest amount of wealth the world has ever seen, Americans were also able to waste it and dispose of it almost as quickly. With the U.S. republic just over 200 years in age, the United States seems to be following Fraser's megacycle (there is that word again: *cycle*) of falling into complacency and back into bondage. Whether the average American is aware of it or not, the United States got complacent because it was the world's sole superpower for so long. (Yes, the United States had the Cold War with the Russian empire, but really the Soviet Union never came close to approaching the economic power of the United States. Even at its peak, the Soviet Union had an economy less than half the size of the United States.) With the continued increase in the size of the welfare state, Americans are falling into dependence upon the government. The United States now has two rivals, mega–emerging economies in India and China, that can seriously challenge its economic superiority.

However, I am not telling you all this to scare you. America's decline in power will not result in the end of the world. Just because you lose your empire or superpower status does not mean that you lose your country. In the long run, the United States may be better off without its empire draining trillions of dollars from its treasury.

In addition, the loss of the empire could be good for the United States because it might get the United States back to the roots of the country's core beliefs, such as individual rights, freedom of speech, limited government, and limited involvement in foreign matters. When the United States followed these beliefs much more closely in the middle of the twentieth century, it was revered for its freedom. There was nowhere near the anti-Americanism that there is today because the younger United States was much more selective in the wars and conflicts it would participate in.

In addition, after France and Britain lost their empires, their cultures thrived. Perhaps America's will, too. It could be argued that in the postwar period Britain has led the world in cultural exports with its superbly skilled movie directors, actors, musicians, and so on. In addition, London is still one of the main financial centers of the world. Similarly, the French have produced great music and writers (think Alexander Dumas). Both also have extremely high standards of living. Regardless of which publication you look at—the CIA's *World Fact Book* or The World Bank—both of these two nations still rank in the top 20 in the world in GDP per capita. Their empires have disappeared, but despite ups and downs, both remain prosperous first-world countries with strong democratic traditions. I suspect that, in the years to come, the United States will be the same. It will not be the ruler of the world, but America will still be a prosperous country playing an important role.

The Land of the Not-So-Free?

With that said, until the United States enters its post-empire renaissance, I see some very difficult times on the horizon. A major problem with the current United States is the loss of freedom. Most notably, its economic freedom is disappearing as government largesse and taxes eat up more of the national economy.

All the talk of U.S. political and economic freedom has become just that—talk. I will not vent or rant about politics in this book. In the next two chapters you will see statistics and facts to back up the brutal trend— that there is an ongoing and serious economic decline of the United States. Here is a quick example just to start. Most nations in Europe and Canada have a simple law that states that if you move from that nation and become a nonresident you are no longer taxed in the nation in which you are nationalized but rather are taxed in the nation you are domiciled in. Therefore, if you are Canadian (as I am) and you become a nonresident (so you are still a citizen but do not live there any longer) and move to a tax-free or low-tax jurisdiction such as the Cayman Islands or Bahamas, you are taxed in that jurisdiction in which you reside. The Caymans and the Bahamas have an income tax which is zero. However, as an American you must still file with the IRS wherever you reside. If your income is $139,000 or greater in the United States, in the five years before you file and you expatriate, you must pay an expatriate tax.

These U.S. policies are a major restriction on residing and working where you like. In the future, this law will hinder many who wish to move to the United States and become American citizens. Individuals who get their American citizenship will always be obligated to pay the government income tax regardless of whether they down the line decide to reside outside of the United States.

This may seem a minor trifle at this time because most Americans choose to reside within the United States. However, it just shows how an American in terms of living abroad is not as free as citizens of other nations of the world. Non-Americans have more global mobility if they choose to move and become a nonresident from their country of origin. They only have to pay taxes in the jurisdiction in which they reside, whereas Americans must pay U.S. taxes on their global income no matter where they reside. This one law, in one respect, is just a small example of how economic freedom is being stifled by the U.S. government as the U.S. nation declines economically.

The Fall of America's Dominance

As stated in the beginning of this chapter, the United States took over from Britain as the world's superpower. However, there was also a bit of luck involved in this shift of power. In the post–World War II period, the United States had a head start—much of the rest of the world was bombed out, flirting with communism, or being freed from imperialism. Asia did not have a manufacturing base and was flirting with communism. Asia's leading economy, Japan, was sifting through rubble. The United States, in contrast, had its industrial base built up due to the expansion in the Military-Industrial Complex during World War II.

However, during the sixties, the United States started to lose its advantage in industry to the Japanese. For example, according to the International Monetary Fund (IMF), the average Japanese per-capita income as a percentage of an American's was 10.31 percent in 1950, meaning that an American made about 10 times what the average Japanese did. By 1990, this had changed to 105.82 percent. This means that in 35 years, the average person in Japan went from making just over 10 percent of what the average American did to making 5 percent *more* than the average American! In lay terms, the average standard of living of a Japanese person from 1955 to 1990 increased at 10 times the pace of the average American! (As a quick side note, the average Japanese person now makes 85 percent of what the average American earns; the economic downturn in Japan in the past 20 years has taken its toll on the Japanese economy.) Japan's economy was in ruins after World War II and it took it a while to rebuild. However, after it did rebuild, Japan caught up to the United States quite quickly.

In 1950, India and China, which were economic powers in the Middle Ages, had been deindustrialized. India's industry was dismantled by the British, who moved manufacturing back to the U.K. during its rule of India. China was ruined by the brutal rule of Mao and communism. Both countries became quite xenophobic and turned within, thereby closing themselves off to foreign investment.

In the past 30 years, that has begun to change. Both of these nations have opened themselves up tremendously (China in 1979 and India in 1991). It is only natural that the rise of these historically powerful nations is going to threaten Americans' standard of living. It is important to remember that before Mao took over the Chinese economy and India was deindustrialized by the British, China and India were two of the leading economies in the world for hundreds if not thousands of years. The twentieth century was a short-term situation, where they were basically out of the global equation. These countries are returning to their historical role of global leaders. Americans did not have to compete with these two giants during the fifties, sixties, and seventies. The reemergence of these two nations as major competitors is a prime reason we have seen declining living standards in the United States over the past 30-plus years.

This Collapse of 2008 Did Not Breed Change, But the Next One Will!

Despite Obama's hollow slogans of change, his administration, in terms of financial and economic policy, has been one of a virtual freezing of the status quo.

Most collapses breed a change in the system, but the 2008 crash did not. Right now there is a convoluted connection between Wall Street and Washington, whether they admit it or not. Hank Paulson, former treasury secretary under Bush, was the former chairman of Goldman Sachs. The $700 billion bailout package to recapitalize the banks did not save the economy as so many said it did. History is full of bank collapses and the like and the world did not end. The financial bailout was a result of the system of cronyism that exists between Wall Street, the White House, the Fed, and Congress, which keeps the average person in the dark. If the system collapsed, it would have been restructured into something new and different to ensure that the current crony system could and would no longer exist.

However, instead, Goldman Sachs and other investment banks were allowed to get funds for free, turn around and speculate in markets near the bottom (as the Fed was pumping billions of dollars into the system), and turn those funds into huge profits. Therefore, instead of changing the system by letting it collapse, the bailout created an even bigger intertwining between Wall Street and all levels of the government.

We can begin a period of sustainable economic growth only when the current system is destroyed. That destruction will come when the debt that has now been shifted from the private sector to the government results in the near-bankruptcy of the nation and the government *cannot* bail out its buddies because it cannot bail *itself* out.

At the end of declines, tough decisions must be made. I cannot agree with everything that FDR did; however, I agree with his decision to fire nearly everyone at the Federal Reserve Board in 1933. This ushered in a new era and helped to end the most severe part of the Great Depression.

I also agree with the tough decision made by Ronald Reagan. In the early eighties, the President allowed Paul Volker to raise interest rates to near 20 percent and cut off the money supply to strangle inflation. This was a tough decision (and in fairness was started under Jimmy Carter in 1979) and many people went bankrupt due to the high interest rates and deep recession of the early eighties. However, this strategy choked off inflation and led to a significant economic boom for the rest of the decade.

For the next major economic boom to start, we must end the current cronyism system and start making tough decisions. Hopefully, this will occur before the nation is on the cusp of bankruptcy.

All of This Is Part of the Long-Term Cycle

Let me state that I am not blaming a political party or free trade, or using any sort of that jingoistic-speak. The decline of the U.S. economy and political power all falls within the context of cycles and megacycles. Like all of the world's superpowers, the United States has gone through its cycle of building its power, overextending itself, and then going into slow decline.

I do not expect that we are going to see a collapse in the United States into third-world status. That is just foolishness. There are great minds in the United States, and a relatively great amount of freedom; it will continue on as a center of technology, culture, and wealth.

However, due to current policies, which are increasing debt at a rapid pace, and the scar that the recent financial crisis has left on the United States, I do see U.S. prosperity decreasing compared to other nations. I see a shift of power going to Asia.

Asia is the creditor; Japan and China own huge amounts of U.S. debt. The United States is now the largest debtor nation in the history of the world. In the forties, the United States was the world's creditor; it even gave an emergency loan to the United Kingdom in 1946 after the war so the United Kingdom could survive. Power shifted from the U.K. to the United States. Now Asia is the creditor, so I see the power shifting there in the coming years.

Interesting enough is the curious fact that ever since the days of the Mongol Empire of the fourteenth and fifteenth centuries, which controlled much of Asia and Europe, prosperity has moved westward like some kind of economic tsunami. After the Mongols, it was the

French and Spanish Empires, followed by the British Empire, and then the United States. Much like we saw a movement in prosperity over the Atlantic from Europe to North America, we are seeing a movement in prosperity westward over the Pacific from North America to Asia.

Remember what I told you earlier: This is not a doom-and-gloom book. The United States is in slow decline. It will not see a significant recovery until it makes the tough decisions, which means ending its empire around the world and cutting government spending. Until that happens, it will slowly deteriorate under a mountain of debt. We will see a shift toward Asia as the economic center of the world.

The Chinese symbol for crisis is the same as the symbol for opportunity: Crisis = Opportunity. Therefore, as the United States declines in the coming debt bubble, there will be great opportunities. When the British Empire fell in the forties and fifties, the global economy boomed. There was merely a shift. Those who positioned themselves to profit from this shift made fortunes.

The same goes today; if you position yourself to the coming boom in Asia, or inflation-related investments, which will prosper as the United States devalues its currency, you will be able to make a fortune. This book will help you to position yourself.

Part One

THE NEXT BUBBLE
AND BOOM

Chapter 1

The Explosion of Debt and the End of the Super Bubble

How We Got Here

The road to bankruptcy is not an easy one. It can take years if not decades or generations to arrive, especially when you look at the United States with its vast resources of wealth. To fritter that away is not an easy thing. However, the amazing thing is how fast the United States has done it. Many other superpowers, such as the Roman and British empires, took hundreds of years to fritter away their wealth and power from when they became superpowers. The United States became the world's superpower during World War II and is on the verge of bankruptcy only 70 years later.

In this chapter, we will show you how the United States has wound up in this condition. We will explore how the country created its debt problem internally by expanding government. We will examine how this has led to inflation. We will see that foreigners allowed and even helped to trigger U.S. reliance on debt to finance its needs. We will also show you why access to this funding may end.

The Start of the Problem

In the 1930s, Franklin Delano Roosevelt began the welfare state with an avalanche of government programs. Many saw these programs as short-term solutions until private spending and the economy bounced back. As such, the U.S. government was still small by modern measures. At that time, the expectation was that government intervention would lessen over time and eventually shrink back to former levels. FDR even tried to get the books back into balance in 1937. It had more to do with the public mentality than economic theories. Despite or perhaps due to the frugality of the public's own spending habits, many did not agree with the federal government living beyond its means for an extended period of time. The U.S. government never really got carried away with spending during the Great Depression. Therefore, the internal spending of the government was still modest as compared to modern government budgets.

The Sixties—The Expansion of the Welfare State

The mid-sixties and early seventies were really the key eras in the turning point of the American economy. In the mid-sixties, we saw a huge expansion in the size of the federal government. The role of the government in the daily lives of Americans increased dramatically in scope.

Some of this was born out of confidence in the government itself. People believed government intervention would result in increased prosperity for the U.S. economy. After all, the expansion of government under FDR seemed to get the economy out of depression in the thirties. Plus, America had now won two world wars against Germany and the space program was a smashing success. And due to the lack of competition in the global economy post–World War II, the

U.S. economy boomed and seemed to have a never-ending source of funds and prosperity.

The major shift came under Lyndon Johnson. Johnson was a war hawk and a social liberal. He decided that he would fight wars against both communism in Vietnam and poverty at home. Programs such as Medicare and Medicaid were put into place. Government spending soared as Johnson increased social spending dramatically to fight the so-called War on Poverty. U.S. voters increasingly realized that they could vote themselves more things from the government.

Programs such as Medicare and Medicaid have turned into a spending nightmare, sucking the life out of the U.S. economy while steadily increasing its national debt. For example, the actual increase in expenditures—compared to the initial estimates at the time—have run anywhere from 500 to 1,500 percent over budget over the past 40 years, depending on the study. (We will discuss this more later in this chapter.)

The United States began to run structural deficits. A *structural deficit* is a deficit that is permanent because the expenditures that cause that deficit are permanent government expenditures (see Medicaid or Medicare) as opposed to a one-time expense (e.g., like a stimulus package). Aside from a few years in the sixties, the United States began to run a budget deficit nearly every year. During the fifties and sixties, the United States had all sorts of extra expenditures, which led to an explosion in spending and deficits. The United States had to pay for wars in South Korea and Vietnam and also make payments for Medicare and Medicaid. Finally, it had to come off the gold standard and there was huge inflation in the seventies to catch up with the printing of money and the spending done in the sixties.

According to www.usgovernmentspending.com (including states and local governments), total government spending as a percentage of GDP was 3.05 percent in 1900. Therefore, total government spending was approximately 3 percent of GDP. By 1940, this had increased to 20.5 percent of GDP. During World War II, due to the military buildup, the total of government spending became half the size of the economy as its spending accounted for over 52 percent of GDP in 1945. After the winding down of the war effort, the total of government spending stayed at a relatively small size throughout the fifties. By 1965, total government spending was just over 26 percent of GDP. This meant that the government made up just over one-quarter of the total economy. This was not the tiny total of 1900, but it was still small total government expenditure, especially when compared to the size of federal governments of other developed nations. The effect of Johnson was immediate; by the end of his term in 1968, total government spending was over 30 percent of GDP.

However, the problem was not so much Johnson's immediate spending but rather the future impact of that spending. Spending that was instituted in the mid-1960s has left a permanent legacy for future generations of the U.S. government. Usgovernmentspending.com estimates that total government spending will be nearly 44 percent of GDP for 2011.

The budget deficit for fiscal 2009 was over 11 percent of GDP at $1.42 trillion. The only budget deficit in the history of the United States that was larger was in 1945, when the United States was expanding spending due to World War II. That year, the budget deficit was just a little over 20 percent of GDP.

Now that we have so much so-called "essential" spending, such as for social programs and military, it would be a major undertaking to reduce the structural deficit and shrink the size of government.

At some point the debt problem will become bad enough that the United States will be *forced* to cut spending as it will not be able to finance its deficits. History teaches us that when a nation falls into or near the brink of bankruptcy—marked by high inflation and unemployment rates and social unrest—it usually takes a significant leader or drastic changes to the economy and government to get it out of such a mess. Things can get ugly as this occurs. For example, when New Zealand came out of fiscal insolvency in the eighties, it deregulated the economy, privatized government-owned industries, and streamlined the economy. The same goes for the United Kingdom in the early eighties, when the British economy became dominated by socialists and union leaders. A showdown eventually culminated in coalminer strikes as Margaret Thatcher "broke" the unions in the United Kingdom in an attempt to rein in their power and get the country back to fiscal responsibility.

However, at the moment there is *no* political will in the United States to cut the deficit. In Britain and other European countries there is a debate at the moment about whether to cut spending and raise taxes because of the debt situation due to the impact of various financial crises. However, in the United States all we hear is talk of fiscal stimulus, more "jobs," health-care reform, public bailouts, how to revive credit growth, and Tiger Woods' libido. There is no talk of tightening belts to deal with the coming debt crisis. (Currently, Tiger's belt loosening and tightening appears to generate more talk than any other issue.)

The coming national debt crisis is the *most* important issue in the United States at the moment. However, virtually no one is talking about it.

The End of the Gold Standard and the Beginning of Inflation

From 1873 to 1934, the United States was on a gold standard. This meant that a certain number of dollars would buy an ounce of gold. The intention of the gold standard, whether it is admitted or not, was that the number of dollars in circulation could not be increased indefinitely. It was intended to create a stable exchange system. For example, if $500 equaled one ounce of gold under the gold standard, it meant that roughly $500 of money should be in circulation for every ounce of gold that the government had in reserves. This system was designed for the sole purpose of keeping governments financially stable. Essentially, governments could not print paper money unless they had the mandated ratio of gold to dollars in their reserves. In other words, the government had to add 10 percent more gold to its reserves if it decided to circulate 10 percent more currency or increase its expenditures by 10 percent. That is the gold standard in theory.

In 1971, the United States went off the gold standard. The system became a completely *fiat* system, meaning the dollar was linked to nothing. The government could print as much money as it wanted with no limitations. The central bank had begun to print more and more money to pay for ventures and the pressure was too much for the pegs at $35 an ounce to hold. This created inflation because they printed more paper money than they had gold in their reserves. After the United States went off the standard, the dollar was linked to nothing.

It is no accident that on this purely fiat money system we have seen a huge increase in government spending and consequently the amount of debt in the economic system. The United States started down that treacherous road of increased government spending with the growing size of the welfare state and later when it had pay for wars in Vietnam and Korea.

The fiat money system has also resulted in financial bubbles, which have been caused by excessively loose monetary policies. From 1933 to 1971, when the United States was pegged to gold, there were no financial bubbles. The Fed during that period of time thought that its mandate was to control inflation—in other words, to stop the punch-bowl from being spiked when the economy and financial markets got overheated. The gold standard helped it to do this by keeping in line the number of dollars that could be in circulation (e.g., if it wanted to go crazy printing, the government would have to add gold or reserves to its vault to justify this printing). However, after 1971, the Fed could print as much money as it wanted. As a result, in the 38 years since the abolishment of the gold standard, there have been no fewer than four major financial bubbles, including:

1. The commodities and inflation bubble of the late seventies
2. The stock market and technology bubble of the late nineties
3. The real estate and leverage bubble of the 2000s
4. The current bond market bubble (and the coming debt and second inflation bubble)

The reason you get these bubbles in a fiat monetary system is simple. The gold standard acts as a discipline mechanism that prevents governments from spending too much and the Fed from printing too much paper money and creating too much credit. When the Fed can print all the money it wants, this creates massive dislocations and therefore creates massive bubbles.

With no discipline on spending programs, spending is unchecked and goes wild.

Domestic Government Spending + Expenditures Abroad = Bankrupt America

As we will learn in this section, government spending on domestic social programs and expenditures overseas is out of control. This is worrisome as the decline of most empires is characterized by an over-extension of spending both at both at home and abroad.

Medicaid and Medicare—The Black Holes of Domestic Spending

Government programs are a perfect example of when monetary policy meets political policy. When the government can print money for these programs and has no accountability for the limits of spending on them, spending gets out of control. Most government programs are well intentioned. Food stamps to feed the poor, health care for those who cannot afford it, benefits for those who have lost their jobs—who can argue with those programs? However, problems develop when vote-seeking politicians, who don't have the real dollars to finance them, implement programs come hell or high water.

The best examples of government spending gone awry are Medicaid and Medicare. It is no coincidence that the huge run-up in health-care costs coincided with the creation of Medicare. Medicare is an insurance program for the elderly with compulsory premiums. Medicaid is a program by which state governments use government monies to pay for health care for low-income individuals. We should note that Medicaid is one reason that state budgets have also exploded since the sixties.

According to Harry Browne, in his book, *Why Government Doesn't Work* (Liamworks, 1995), Medicare was created in 1965 with an estimate that in 1990 its costs would be $3 billion. Adjusted for inflation in 1990 dollars, that would come to $12 billion. The actual cost in 1990 was $98 billion. The estimated cost for the 2010 budget is $453 billion. The payroll tax to help cover these costs has risen from 0.9 percent in the mid-sixties to over 4 percent today. It will have to go even higher in future years to cover future Medicare costs. Medicare would actually be bankrupt except that the government keeps raising payroll taxes to pay for it.

Browne also notes that the pattern for Medicaid is almost entirely the same. When Congress passed Medicaid in 1965, the budget was $1 billion. By 1993, it was $76 billion, and it was $290 billion in 2010. According to www.inflationcalculator.com, something that cost $1 in 1965 would cost $6.87 today for an inflation rate of 586.8 percent in those 44 years. Yet Medicare expenditures have increased by 7,500 percent!

The Cost of War—The Black Hole of Expenditures Abroad

War and defense is playing a part in the deterioration of the U.S. financial situation, but not as much as you would think. As of 2010, the United States will spend $895 billion or 6.14 percent of GDP on its military. Most of this is not even for the wars in Afghanistan or Iraq, but rather to pay for its armed forces, which feature bases in nearly 140 nations.

If the United States cut its military expenditures to normal levels and stopped policing the world, it would help the country's finances. For example, global war expenditures as a percentage of GDP are approximately 2.4 percent according to the Stockholm Peace Institute's *2009 Yearbook*. If the United States were to cut to the global average, it would save the country about $550 billion. With the 2010 deficit running at about $1.45 trillion, that would cut the deficit to $900 billion a year.

So we can see that the military plays a large role in the current fiscal problems of the United States. Pension and health-care expenditures are estimated to be $1.6 trillion combined in 2010, and by 2015, according to usgovernmentspending.com, it will increase to $2.0 trillion (more than doubling the expected expenditures of $900 billion budgeted for the military that same year). This means that by 2015, pension and health-care expenditures will be over 10 percent of GDP, whereas the military will be under 5 percent! Yes, the cost of defense is excessive, but again, only about 13.8 percent of the total government's budget is spent on the military. And this number will shrink in the coming years; 86.2 percent of the government's expenditures are coming from *outside* the military. The decline of the American Empire will in all probability come from within.

The perfect example of a country that was crushed by debt by both its empire and domestic policies is the United Kingdom. After two world wars decimated its coffers, the U.K.'s debt as a percentage of GDP went from just over 30 percent in 1913 to over 250 percent by the mid-forties. The U.K. needed a bailout of $3.5 billion from the Americans just to stave off insolvency after the war and then began to dismantle its empire to cut expenses drastically. Then in 1976, with inflation and spending out of control (a deficit of nearly 6 percent of GDP), the U.K. had to go to the IMF for a £2.3 billion ($3.5 billion) loan as it was unable to raise money on the public markets. This shows us the twofold effect of debt. The first U.K. debt crisis of 1946 led to the collapse of the empire as the easiest thing to cut first was foreign expenditures. The second debt crisis was caused by excessive social spending and out-of-control inflation. This inflation led to super-high government bond yields that the government could not afford to pay.

Can the Government's Debt Be Sustainable?

A unique situation that is saving the United States at the moment is low interest rates. Unlike the U.K. in 1976, the United States is still paying very low interest on its debt. One of the things that cause governments to go insolvent is a spike in bond yields. For example, if interest rates double or triple, it causes interest payments to soar and this development squeezes out spending on other things such as military or social programs. The United States has benefited from being the reserve currency of the world. When the financial crises hit in 2008 and then the Greek crisis hit in 2010, interest rates plunged as investors fled to the so-called safe haven of U.S. Treasuries. At some point, these interest payments are going to rise. Estimates are that in 2010, the U.S. government will spend $309.2 and $384 billion on interest payments. That is about 4.8 and 5.6 percent of GDP. However, by 2015, total government interest payments are expected to double as interest rates and the total government debt rise, to $762.0 billion or nearly 8.8 percent of total government expenditures. These figures are based on government estimates, which almost always assume the rosiest scenarios possible. We must remember that these numbers are also based on total expenditures. Current total expenditures are totally unsustainable. If the budget were to be balanced in 2015, that 8 percent number would probably rise to about 12 to 15 percent depending on the amount of revenue the government took in at that time as total government spending would have to be cut.

We can be sure that economic growth and government revenue will not grow as fast as the government's numbers state. This means more debt and higher interest payments. In addition, I believe that the U.S. long bond and the interest rate market in general are in a bubble (more on this in Chapter 2). I feel that interest rates are headed much higher in the coming years. As just stated, the current low interest rates are the only thing keeping the United States from entering a debt crisis. The reason that Greece went from being solvent in 2009 to a crisis in 2010 was that its bond market woke up and the yield on 10-year Greek bonds went from 4 to 14 percent in 6 months. This increase in interest payments made the rest of the budget insolvent. What happens if the United States sees rates spike like the Greeks in 2010 or the Brits in the mid-seventies? Interest rates would have to spike to attract foreign investors; that development would lead to a totally out-of-control runaway budget deficit and debt crisis. If interest rates were to double or triple from current low levels, the scenario is set for interest payments to represent 20, 30, or maybe even 40 percent of total spending.

If this scenario were to occur, you would see similarities to the fall of other empires. In an interview with *Newsweek*, published on November 28, 2009, Professor Niall Ferguson tells us that France (before the revolution) was spending 62 percent of total revenue on debt service in 1788; the Ottoman Empire was paying 50 percent of its budget on interest by 1875. In the interwar years in the thirties, Britain was paying 44 percent of its budget toward interest. A spike in rates would have the United States at these near-bankrupt levels.

I am not even including the negative effects and increased expenditures from the financial crises. I have not talked about the so-called *emergency loans* to General Motors and Chrysler, or the nationalization of Freddie Mac and Fannie Mae, or the TARP program, or the $700 billion stimulus. What is obvious is that the increased spending and deterioration of the nation's finances has been occurring for years. As the population ages, we will see increases in the need for expenditures for Social Security, Medicaid, Medicare, and the new health-care plan being proposed by Congress. According to an article published in *USA Today* (May 29, 2007), the costs of these unfunded liabilities could ultimately be as high as $59.1 trillion! We must also remember that if Congress is telling us that the new health-care proposal will cost $940 billion over the next 10 years, it will probably end up costing 3 to 5 times that amount or even more and add to the deficit even further. This is not a book to rant about the size of government, nor am I going to preach on why the United States must cut back, and so on. However, the inescapable fact is this: The current growth of U.S. government debt is not sustainable.

The Parabolic Curve

When a move is unsustainable in the markets, it tends to be something that goes straight up in price. This is reflected in diagram form by the infamous *parabolic curve*. A parabolic curve often occurs near the end of a bubble. It is a move straight up on a chart at a near-90-degree angle that is totally unsustainable. NASDAQ stocks in 2000, Japanese stocks in 1989, and U.S. stocks in 1929 are all examples of asset classes that saw parabolic curves and crashes.

Figure 1.1 shows the total U.S. debt as a percentage of Gross Domestic Product (or a percentage of the total goods and services produced in a nation in a given year). This is an important tool to calculate debt. Debt is not all bad. You can use debt to build roads, fight wars, and so forth. In the long run, as long as that debt increases at a slower pace than the economy, your *debt-to-GDP ratio* is going down and is sustainable. If a government runs a deficit at around 1 to 2 percent of GDP and the economy is growing at 3 to 4 percent, its debt in relation to the size of the economy is going *down* and that small amount of debt will not put a stranglehold on a nation.

However, if the debt is growing too fast in relation to the economy, it is unsustainable as revenues and economic activity will not be able to keep up with the amount of debt in circulation. Just look at your own finances. If you grow your income by 5 percent a year, but grow your debt at 10 percent a year, at some point you will not be able to service the debt you have built up and you will go broke.

All bubbles trade the same way. They start on a slow increase. The speed of the ascent begins to quicken as the bubble rolls on and then the bubble experiences the mania or blow-off phase. In technical terms, this is the parabolic curve. This final blow-off phase of a parabolic curve can cause a particular market that is in a bubble to double or triple in just a short period of time. However, the rate of the increase is totally unsustainable and it eventually collapses.

There is only one time in the 200-plus-year history of the United States that the nation has experienced a debt bubble. This was in the mid–1940s, as debt ballooned to help fight the war effort.

Figure 1.1 shows that debt grew slowly in the early part of the twentieth century. Debt as a percentage of GDP grew from 10 percent in 1900 to about 20 percent in 1917, then in the twenties it continued to grow and was in the low 30 percent range at the 1929 stock market top. It then increased at a more rapid rate in the thirties as increased government spending and decreases in revenues began to take their toll on the public finances. By the end of the thirties, the debt-to-GDP ratio stood at nearly 65 percent. It then exploded during the war in a five-year period from 1941 to 1946: Debt as a percentage of GDP more than doubled from 54 percent to 128 percent due to the war effort. Of course, a more-than-doubling like this every five years was totally unsustainable. It was the top of the debt bubble.

When bubbles blow up, they blow up fast. Usually, the last blow-off phase of the bubble is lost within a few years of the bubble. By 1957, the debt-to-GDP ratio had collapsed to 70 percent of GDP; by 1967, it fell even further to 52.83 percent. You can see on the chart in Figure 1.1 the parabolic move upward, followed by this collapse. Debt as a percentage of GDP then bottomed out at 43.53 percent in 1982. That was the end of the 36-year downtrend in debt.

However, the rate of increase was subdued; by 2001, the debt-to-GDP ratio stood at 73.19 percent. That was the start of the bubble; during

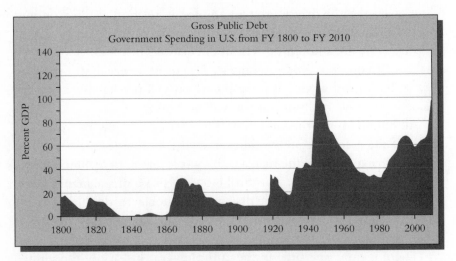

Figure 1.1   Debt as a Percentage of GDP.

In the 1870s, due to the Civil War, the United States saw a mini-debt bubble as the U.S. debt climbed to just over 30 percent of GDP before falling back in the early 1900s. The first major debt bubble was in the 1940s; we are now building for the second debt bubble.

SOURCE: www.usgovernmentspending.com.

the period of 2001 to 2009, the bubble picked up steam in order to pay for the wars in Afghanistan and Iraq, among other things. By 2009, the debt-to-GDP ratio increased to 89 percent of GDP.

We are now entering the blow-off phase. Debt-to-GDP in 2010 is estimated to be over 110 percent of GDP; this marks the first time since World War II that the debt-to-GDP ratio will be over 110 percent. By 2014, it is estimated to be over 125 percent of GDP. Again, if you are like me and you feel that the costs of Medicare and Medicaid will go up faster than the government says due to the aging of the population, and that economic growth will be less robust than the government predicts (highly likely in a post-bubble environment), then this number will be even higher.

Figure 1.2 takes the debt bubble one step further. This takes into account projections made by the CBPP (Center on Budget and Policy Priorities) and shows that debt as a percentage of GDP will hit nearly 300 percent of GDP by 2050 if nothing is done. It is surely an

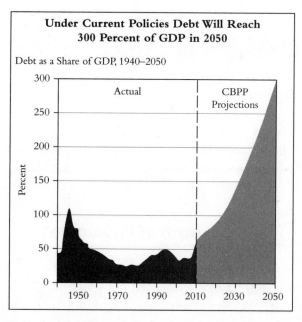

Figure 1.2 Government Debt as a Percentage of GDP (Estimate)
NOTE: CBPP projections based on CBO data.
SOURCE: cbpp.org.

unsustainable bubble to eventually have government debt *three times* the size of the economy.

However, I do *not* think we will reach that level. At sometime in the next 15 years, and more likely in the next 10 years, we are going to reach a point of emergency where the debt bubble will be out of control and will then collapse. It will be a forced collapse. The government will be all but bankrupt and forced to cut expenditures.

Government Underestimates Its Debts

I hate to depress you, but not only is this debt unsustainable but it is even worse when you include the huge growth in unfunded liabilities and government-controlled corporations. As I mentioned previously, the government actually underestimates debt and reports lower numbers.

On top of the typical state, local, and federal government debt that we have used in all our calculations, we must remember that with the bankruptcies of Fannie Mae and Freddie Mac and the government takeover of these institutions (it is an equity stake but in reality a takeover), the government has essentially added $5.3 trillion in mortgage debt to the federal debt. Let's face it: If these mortgages were defaulted en masse, the companies would simply *not* go bankrupt and you would see the government having to absorb this debt. We do realize that not all of this $5.3 trillion of debt is bad debt. But having to take on that sort of debt is scary, indeed.

For argument's sake, however, $5.3 trillion in Fannie and Freddie debt would put the total government debt up from the 2010 estimate of $17.7 trillion to $23.0 trillion overnight!

Huge Growth in Private Debt

Not only has the government seen a huge amount of growth in debt but the private sector has as well. I am not going to get into the nitty-gritty details of the average person's debt, but I will add the private numbers together with the government numbers to show you just how dire the situation has become.

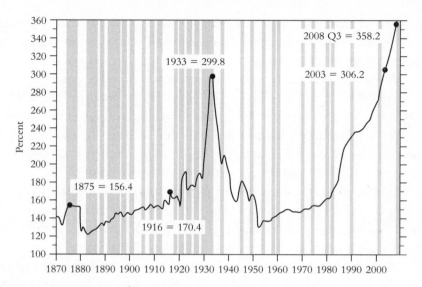

Figure 1.3 Total U.S. Debt as a Percent of GDP
NOTE: Annual, through Q3 2008.
SOURCE: Bureau of Economic Analysis, Federal Reserve, Census Bureau: Historical Statistics of the United States, Colonial Times to 1970.

If you add the private numbers to the public numbers, you get another debt bubble (Figure 1.3).

We can see the first bubble in Total Debt as a Percentage of GDP. This bubble blew off in 1933, 13 years before the public debt bubble did. With the collapse in the economy, this actually peaked in 1933 at a level of 299.8 percent of GDP. This meant that total debt and government debt in 1933 was about 3 times the size of the economy.

Note that Figure 1.3 also traded like most other bubbles. There was a very small increase from 120 percent of GDP in 1870 to 160 percent of GDP in 1919. There was an uptick in acceleration to about 185 percent of GDP in 1929, and then a parabolic blow-off from 185 percent to 299.8 percent from 1929 to 1933 as the economy collapsed during the Great Depression. Again we must remember that these numbers were influenced by the collapse in the economy. Government increased debt from 1929 to 1933, but the GDP shrank.

Government increased its debt from \$33.41 billion in 1929 to \$41.61 billion in 1933, but the economy contracted from \$103.6 billion in 1929 to \$56.4 billion in 1933. Much of that bubble was caused by a decrease in economic activity. Again, if your income is halved but your debt stays the same, your debt as a percent of your income is going to increase.

We can see that this bubble collapsed in the 20 years following. This occurred despite the *huge* run-up in government debt that lasted until 1946. The main reason for this collapse was due to the fact that corporations and individuals deleveraged big-time, cutting their debt during the Depression and into the forties. By the early fifties, total debt as a percentage of GDP had fallen to just over 130 percent of GDP.

At that time, the next bubble began. Until 1980, total debt as a percentage of GDP slowly increased to roughly 160 percent of GDP. It then exploded until 2008, reaching over 358 percent of GDP! Again, this is totally unsustainable and at some point must collapse.

We have already seen the private sector begin to deleverage much like they did in the thirties and forties. However, for argument's sake, let's say that the government sector is 13 years behind the deleveraging just as they were in the 1933-to-1946 period. That would mean that the government would not begin to deleverage or cut its debt until about 2022!

Having a debt that is 3.5 times the size of GDP is totally unsustainable. To again quote professor Niall Ferguson, he indicated in the opening statement he made during a debate at the PanAmericanCenter about the Global Economic Crisis, "Once you end up with private and public debts in excess of three and a half times your annual output (GDP), you *are* Argentina!"

Middle Class in Decline

All of this debt has led to a decline in the standard of living of the American middle class. As the average standard of living has declined, people have used this debt to try to keep their standard of living high.

One of the marks of a great society is building a middle class. During their periods of power, the Romans and British had a large middle class. In the post–World War II period, the United States built the largest middle class in the history of humankind. This was marked with the ability to finance properties via mortgages and cars via loans or leases.

These were managed debts that helped to expand the U.S. economy and in turn increased the standard of living of the average person.

In the eighties, however, as people on the lower and middle end of the income spectrum could not keep up their standard of living, they attempted to maintain their living standard by relying on debt. The savings rate by the year 2000 was in the negative as consumers used debt and stock and housing gains to live on. This was totally unsustainable and it collapsed in the 2000s.

For example, if we break up the nation into five quintiles, the top quintile of income earnings (to 20 percent) followed by the second quintile, followed by the third (middle 20 percent), fourth, and fifth quintile (lowest 20 percent) of income earnings, we can see a real disparity in the past 30 years.

According to a study undertaken by the Congressional Budget Office (CBO) in 2007, the following income adjustments (adjusted for inflation) occurred since 1980:

Top Quintile = increase by 69 percent.
Second Quintile = increase by 29 percent.
Third Quintile = increase by 21 percent.
Fourth Quintile = increase by 17 percent.
Lowest Quintile or 20 percent = increase by only 6 percent.

This decrease in standard of living has helped lead to excessive debt levels of individuals as many in society who have had a hard time keeping up have turned to debt to artificially support their standard of living. It also means that the middle class is making less and therefore paying less in taxes. This leads to less income for the government, which leads to bigger deficits and bigger public debts as well. The entire situation is a vicious circle, which means more debt for the government and the private individual.

The Explosion and Implosion of the Super Bubble

George Soros, the hedge fund manager who gained fame from his Quantum fund's unparalleled returns and as the man who broke the Bank of England in 1992 (making billions from the collapse in the British pound that year), published a book in 2008 entitled *A New Paradigm for Financial Markets*. This book dealt with the credit crises of 2008. Soros is a brilliant mind whose main belief is in a theory he calls *reflexivity*. This complex theory states that financial markets are not always right, but rather they are always wrong and they shoot to the upside too far and then shoot too far to the downside.

Many do not agree with his politics or political views. However, I believe that Soros has figured out the reasoning behind this huge debt bubble.

Soros says that the debt bubble was the Mother of All Bubbles (my words, not his) or the Super Bubble. The Super Bubble was essentially a shift made in the early eighties where markets were opened up through globalization and market fundamentalism. Soros states that the United States abused its position as the reserve currency of the world. Basically, there was a shift toward what Reagan called "the magic of the markets" in the eighties and toward more open global finance. As the United States was the center of global finance, it benefited from this liberalization. Many of the rules of the International Monetary Fund and global finance put strictures on smaller, undeveloped nations (e.g., the size of the deficits they could run, etc.). However, the United States did not need to play by these rules. That benefited the United States and allowed it to live beyond its means as huge amounts of funds flowed into the United States. That is Soros's theory. I agree with most of it. I do, however, need to add my own tidbits.

Super Bubble

As the global economy became freer and there were cheaper labor markets, U.S. products lost their luster (the United States had already started to lose its manufacturing superiority to the Germans and the Japanese in the sixties and seventies).

As many other nations started to come online in the global economy, they had low labor costs. They became great candidates for cheap products. The United States was the largest consumer economy in the world. Its labor was pricing itself out of the global manufacturing community at the same time as there was a market for exporting into the United States. In addition, as the United States now had its currency linked to nothing, developing cheap foreign labor markets would allow it to print as much money as it wanted to without creating huge amounts of inflation. America simply allowed itself to take advantage of cheap labor and products in foreign markets and import lower-cost products, thereby temporarily importing deflation.

Therefore, there were huge shifts of money into the United States to keep interest rates low and support the Super Bubble. This allowed the United States to live beyond its means. It was a beneficial agreement; the Japanese, Chinese, and others could buy U.S. bonds. They funded the U.S. current account and trade deficits (current account = balance of trade + net factor income from abroad + net unilateral transfers from abroad).

Foreigners would buy U.S. bonds to help keep U.S. interest rates low and U.S. spending high. In turn, the United States would buy their goods (mostly from China and Japan) and keep these nations' economies roaring. In addition, the United States would initially import deflation due to the cheap cost of goods because of the abundant cheap labor these nations possessed. Despite the fact that the United States was printing huge sums of money and running up huge debts, it was not seeing huge inflation.

However, the Super Bubble blew up when the United States took this relationship to an extreme and abused it. As U.S. citizens and their government lived way above their means, the *current account deficit* started to get out of control; by the mid-2000s, the current account deficit was growing toward 6 percent of GDP. In addition, the United States had to turn increasingly to debt to fund these finances. During the 2000s, the savings rate actually turned negative for a while, as consumer and government debts continued to explode.

Adding fuel to the fire, the Federal Reserve went crazy printing money and implementing easy monetary policies. After the events of 9/11 and the recession caused by the explosion of the tech bubble, Alan Greenspan panicked. He cut rates to 1 percent to stave off another Great Depression. Greenspan also printed a seemingly endless supply of money and did not raise interest rates until 2004—nearly three years after the economy came out of recession. This easy money led to a gigantic housing boom and leverage boom and debt bubble.

Concurrently, there was a huge demand for U.S. debt to meet the demands of the Super Bubble. In other words, foreigners wanted U.S. debt to keep interest rates in the United States low, which would keep the U.S. consumer spending, who was in turn buying foreign goods. As an example, if rates went down, Americans' equity in their homes would go up; they would feel richer; they could spend more on foreigners' goods; foreigners could pump more money into the United States; and the U.S. consumer could buy more and more! It was the ultimate Ponzi scheme.

This loose credit spread into the subprime market. Wall Street packaged these garbage investments and leveraged them 30 to 1, Moody's and S&P rated them as AAA, and they were sold all over the world.

The subprime market blew up; investment banks exploded; the housing bubble burst; U.S. consumers lost equity in their homes; they could not buy as much stuff from foreigners; and foreigners had less money to pump back into the U.S. economy. It was a vicious circle that fed on itself. The Super Bubble burst. Americans could no longer live beyond their means.

This brings us to a major future problem: The United States is planning to issue trillions of dollars of debt in the coming years to meet its so-called obligations, but foreigners have less reserves and money coming in to buy those Treasuries. There will be less demand for dollars at a time when there are even more of them being issued.

How will the United States pay for all of its debts? It will *print its way out!* The next chapter deals with this phenomenon.

Chapter 2

The Money Printers and the Coming Inflation

The Death of the Bond Bubble

With the credit crunch of 2008, there was a lot of debate between inflation and deflation. The simple question was: Which one of those two evils would rise from the ashes of the financial markets' ruin? I have always felt that the ultimate collapse of the system would result in inflation. *Inflation* is a rise in the general level of prices of goods and services in an economy over a period of time.

Part of the reason why I believe inflation will soar in the coming years is that, unlike the 1920s, when the crash was mainly due to too much leverage in the private sector, this crisis will end ultimately with sovereign defaults as governments overspend to stimulate their economies and keep their welfare states afloat. We have already seen the beginning of this with the European debt crisis affecting countries such as Greece, Portugal, and Spain. When governments go bust, they have two alternatives:

1. Don't pay.
2. Make all payments in full by simply printing money to meet their obligations.

We must remember that in 1929, when the Crash and Depression started, government debt as a percentage of GDP was 32.25 percent. Even during the Great Depression it built up to merely 65 percent of GDP by the end of the thirties.

This time around, U.S. government debt as a percentage of GDP was 83 percent in 2007 *before* the crisis began. Therefore, government debt as a percentage of economic output was higher *before* this crisis than it was *after* the Great Depression.

In addition, many commentators seem not to understand what exactly deflation is. The technical definition of *deflation* is a decrease in the money supply. With the Fed printing money like crazy throughout the financial crisis, we are not seeing this. When the price of a computer or calculator goes down, that is not deflation; that is an improvement in technology that translates into a consumer product being made more cheaply. Improvements cause prices to go down. In addition, valuations in the stock market and housing market going down is not deflation; that is merely the stock market and housing market fluctuating in price as they always do. By all measures we really haven't seen, nor will we see, massive deflation in the coming years.

The main reason we will not see deflation is that history teaches us that the only realistic way out of this crisis is to print money. In this chapter, I analyze the inflation-versus-deflation debate and show you what crisis this is most similar to. The result may surprise you. This comparison will reveal why we should see massive inflation and not deflation when everything is said and done.

The Deflation Argument—Credit Destruction

The deflation argument is very simple. The Deflationists argue that we are seeing a destruction in dollars as debtors default on their loans. When they default on loans, the money essentially disappears as the loan becomes null and void. Deflationists argue that, as subprime and prime mortgages are defaulted on, the mortgage-backed securities they were packaged and rolled into will disappear under a crashing mountain of leveraged-debt instruments. This in turn will cause investment banks to fail and we will experience credit contractions. *Credit contractions* are attempts to minimize or limit the amount of credit that is currently available to consumers. The use of a credit contraction is normally associated with the desire to slow the rate of inflation in the general economy. By creating a state of recession, credit contractions help to slow or even possibly stop any growth of inflation for a period of time. This in turn will create more unemployment as credit becomes unavailable and people have less money to spend. Given that the destruction of credit leads to less spending, this ultimately means that prices must go down as there is less money in circulation to buy goods. For technical geeks, experts say that this is an age of "unsustainable negative savings rates." As consumers curb their spending habits out of necessity, they will begin to save, resulting in a decrease in demand and prices.

They argue that the last time we saw this sort of destruction of credit was during the 1929–1932 period, when investors, who were buying stocks with 95 percent margin, were wiped out and the financial community blew itself up. In response to this crash, the Federal Reserve let the money supply implode and allowed banks to collapse. As the money supply imploded, it meant less money in circulation, which means less purchasing power and lower prices. The Deflationists tell us that equity prices will crumble like in the early thirties and the safest place to be is long-term government bonds as they will at least pay some yield at a time of declining prices. They also argue that the U.S. dollar will rally in price because the destruction of dollars will lead to fewer dollars in circulation.

This is the Deflationists' case in a nutshell.

Why the Deflationists Are Wrong

In my opinion, the Deflationists' argument is dead wrong for the reasons outlined in this chapter.

Reason #1: Deleveraging, Not Deflation

What we saw during the financial crisis of 2008 was not deflation. It was deleveraging. *Deleveraging* is an attempt to decrease debt. The best way for a company (or individual) to deleverage is to immediately pay off any existing debt on its balance sheet. If it is unable to do this, the company (or person) will be in significant risk of defaulting. As we saw in Chapter 1, leverage and debt gradually increased since the early 1980s with the advent of the Super Bubble and the United States abusing its position as the reserve currency of the world by living beyond its means. Not only were consumers living beyond their means but the excess debt filtered into the financial markets.

Many hedge funds and financial institutions borrowed heavily during the boom time. They used as much as 30- or 40-to-1 leverage. Of course, the problem with 30-to-1 leverage is that if your investment loses a mere 3 percent of its value, you lose all of your equity. If it loses 50 percent of its value, you now *owe* about 18 times as much as your initial capital was worth. To better illustrate my point, let's look at an example. Let's say you have $3 million controlling $100 million worth of assets. You have 33.3-to-1 leverage. Let's say you lose 50 percent on that $100 million worth of assets. All of a sudden, you have lost $50 million. Your $3 million is wiped out. But not only that—your total debt is still $97 million. You can sell only $50 million worth and have to come up with the $47 million shortfall to make complete payment. You are ruined.

With all these downsides, why do investors leverage excessively? Simple. People can make huge amounts of money if they gamble right. Let's say your $100 million investment climbs 3 percent to $103 million. You sell your $103 million investment; you pay back your $97 million in loans and you have 6 million in capital and you have doubled your money on only a 3 percent return!

When Lehman Brothers collapsed in 2008, the TED spread spiked to over 400 basis points (it normally trades around a 25-basis-point spread!). What is the TED spread, and why is it important? The *TED spread* is the difference between the interest rates on interbank loans (LIBOR) and short-term U.S. government debt (T-bills). *TED* is an acronym formed from *T-Bill* and *ED*, the ticker symbol for the Eurodollar futures contract. The TED Spread is the difference between the three-month T-bill interest rate and three-month LIBOR. In a nutshell, a 400-basis-point spread (far in excess of the normal 25-basis-point spread) meant that banks did not trust each other and were not lending to each other or other financial institutions such as hedge funds, and so forth.

All of a sudden, people and institutions could not loan back and forth. If you had borrowed on 5-, 10-, or 20-to-1 leverage as either an investment bank or hedge fund, then you had to *deleverage*—that is, you had to sell investments to pay off debt. Plus, if you were a hedge fund, you were getting mass redemptions, so you *had* to sell to pay back your investors.

As a result, everything collapsed in price: commodities, gold, stocks, emerging markets, and so on. Again, this was *not* deflation; this was a massive deleveraging. In my newsletter, *Addicted to Profits*, I called it the "Mother of All Margin Calls." This is because investors were loaded up with the largest amount of debt they'd ever had and they all got a margin call at once to pay back this debt.

Reason #2: The Reaction to the Financial Crisis Has Been Different from That of the 1929 Crash

There are many arguments as to why and how the Great Depression lasted so long with ruinous runs on banks and years of deflation. Some argue it was the excessive credit boom-and-bust cycle. This means two things:

1. The Federal Reserve created money via printing and this helped to create an excessive boom.
2. The Fed then allowed this money circulation to collapse and this helped cause the bust by letting the decline in prices get out of control in a continuous downward spiral.

What they don't note is that the deflation in the 1921 recession was actually worse!

Monetarists such as Milton Friedman argue that the lack of money supplied to banks was a major reason for the deflation and banking failures of the Great Depression. In his legendary book, *A Monetary History of the United States* (paperback: Princeton University Press,

1971) originally published in 1963 (which he co-authored with his wife, Anna Schwartz), Friedman argues that for every three dollars that were held in banks in 1929, only two were left in 1933. He blames the Federal Reserve for bungling the handling of the downturn. Friedman himself stated the following:

> The Fed was largely responsible for converting what might have been a garden-variety recession, although perhaps a fairly severe one, into a major catastrophe. Instead of using its powers to offset the depression, it presided over a decline in the quantity of money by one-third from 1929 to 1933. . . . Far from the depression being a failure of the free-enterprise system, it was a tragic failure of government.
>
> —Milton Friedman, *Two Lucky People*, page 233

The Monetarists such as Friedman believe that in 1930, instead of the Fed giving a hand to the banks and loaning money to them, the Federal Reserve sat on the sidelines and allowed banks to fail. Friedman argues that if the Fed had just given liquidity to the banks, stable banks that should have stood strong would not have failed. As the banks failed, the money supply would decrease and this caused a deflationary spiral.

A deflationary spiral would mean that Americans made less and, as Americans were poorer, they imported less and bought less. At the same time, Britain saw a huge downturn and decrease in economic activity. This was partly because its exports to the United States fell. Gold from Britain was sold into the United States. Britain was on the gold standard, so they could not print; therefore, they lost liquidity as the gold was transferred from Britain to the United States. This transferred gold was an injection of money into the United States and should have added to liquidity as the Fed could have increased the money supply as the amount of gold in its vaults increased. However, the Fed did not act; instead, it hoarded the gold and did not create money on the back of increased reserves to keep banks upright.

In 1931, Britain went off the gold standard.

Ben Bernanke himself is a student of Friedman. Everyone in the Modern Era is scared of entering another Great Depression and will do anything to avoid such a deflationary spiral. So the response has been exactly the opposite. During the first credit scare in August 2007, when we saw a spike in the TED spread and a decline in the stock market, the Federal Reserve cut the fed funds rate (*federal funds rate* is the interest rate at private depository institutions—mostly *banks*). The Federal Reserve from 2007 to mid-2008, even before the crumbling of Lehman Brothers, cut the fed funds rate numerous times from over 5 percent to under 3 percent and printed massive amounts of money.

Then, in the wake of the financial crisis in late 2008, the Fed expanded its balance sheet immensely. Figure 2.1 shows how much money the Fed supplied over this time. Note the spike in the short-term money supply to cover the expansion of the balance sheet (the Fed basically exchanged T-bills for the toxic debt of the banks). It added hundreds of billions of dollars of liquidity to the system.

It is debatable whether this was the correct thing to do. Anna Schwartz, Milton Friedman's wife and co-author in his writings, said in an interview with the *Wall Street Journal* on October 18, 2008, that Bernanke was doing the wrong thing. It was the Monetarists' belief that the Fed

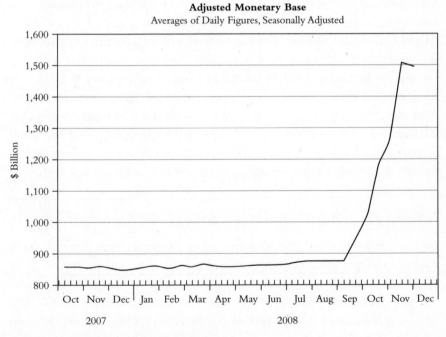

Figure 2.1   Monetary Base of Federal Reserve
SOURCE: Federal Reserve Bank (investinblog.com).

should be giving liquidity to solvent institutions to prevent bank runs. However, they should allow bad institutions to fail.

My point here is not to defend what the Fed has done, or debate whether it was right or wrong. The basic point is that, unlike the early thirties, when the Fed sat on its hands, let banks fail, and let the money supply collapse, the current Fed has done the opposite. It has done everything to prevent banks from failing and has printed massive amounts of money. So the Deflationists are *wrong*; this is not like the thirties and we are not seeing monetary deflation. In addition, printing of money always causes *inflation*.

From a fiscal standpoint as well, the government's response has been much more aggressive than anything seen during the Great Depression. Again, all authorities are scared to death of repeating the soup lines of the thirties. Even in 1933, the year after Roosevelt was elected to office, the Total Government Deficit as a percent of GDP was 3.27 percent; in 1934 it was 3.11 percent.

From 1933 to 1936, as Roosevelt ramped up the New Deal to get the economy out of depression, the largest deficit the government ever ran was 4.76 percent of GDP. In 1940, Roosevelt cranked up spending to get the economy out of the recession of the late thirties, and even that year the government deficit was just 3.02 as a percent of GDP.

By comparison, the deficit for 2009 was 11.02 percent of GDP and for 2010 it is estimated to be 8.54 percent of GDP, significantly higher than the spending of the thirties. We have had a $700 billion stimulus package and the government now says that it plans to spend the $200 billion it got back from the TARP program on new-jobs programs.

They are throwing everything but the kitchen sink at this thing.

Reason #3: The Deflation Numbers of 2008 Were Skewed

In 2009, we saw a lot of talk of deflation. However, a lot of this was a statistical anomaly. During the first part of the recession and crisis, from 2007 to mid-2008, we saw the prices of many commodities skyrocket. We saw gold climb from $650 an ounce to over $1,000 per ounce. We saw oil spike from just over $60 an ounce to over $147 a barrel. Natural gas climbed from just over $5.25 to $13.69 per contract; gasoline climbed from $1.80 to $3.63 per contract. Corn climbed from $3.75 to over $7.50 a bushel. Wheat went from $4.00 a bushel to over $12.50 a bushel and soybeans from $8.00 to over $16.00.

The fuel for these increases was provided by the Fed via its loose monetary policy. When the Fed first started to loosen the strings in 2007, that money flowed into the hot sector, which was commodities. This pushed commodity prices sky high into mid-2008. Figure 2.2 is a chart of the Reuters CCI index; we can see that this index climbed by over 50 percent from a level of 400 in the summer of 2007 to over 615 at its peak in the summer of 2008.

Commodities then crashed with the rest of the market as the institutions that rode the wave of liquidity and the hot sector had to deleverage in late 2008 and sell commodities like everything else. This led to a very favorable comparison for inflation from 2008 to 2009. Oil, which had been $147 a barrel in the summer of 2008, was trading to near $35 by early 2009 and was around $70 a barrel in July 2009. This made the year-over-year comparisons very favorable for inflation for 2009. As commodity prices make up calculations for the Consumer Price Index (CPI), we saw very favorable inflation numbers and even some negative inflation from late 2008 to mid-2009. However, as of late 2009, that anomaly is finished. The year-over-year comparisons for 2010 are going to be compared to the lower commodity prices of 2009; we are going to start seeing inflation tick up again. Unless

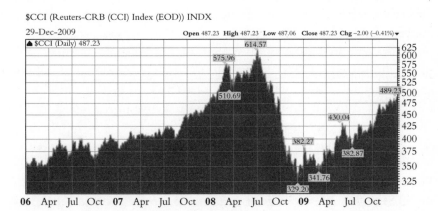

Figure 2.2   Reuters CCI Commodity Index
Source: Courtesy of StockCharts.com (http://stockcharts.com).

there is some sort of major crash (we do not expect there to be one), it looks as if the deflation of 2009 was a temporary phenomenon of the deleveraging of 2008.

Reason #4: There Is No Shortage of Dollars—The Dollar Strength of 2008 and 2010 Was Temporary

During the financial crisis of 2008, and the Euro debt crisis of 2010, the dollar was really strong. There was much talk that the dollar was still the ultimate safe haven. It was emphasized that when there was fear in the worldwide economy, investors still flocked to the dollar to save themselves from financial Armageddon.

Facts do not support these opinions. Here is how things really unfolded. Previously, we talked about the Super Bubble and the huge buildup in leverage. When the Fed cut rates to near zero from 2001 to 2003 and printed money to avoid a bubble-induced depression, it increased the leverage bubble even more. Alan Greenspan even made numerous speeches on the great new world created by all of these fresh financial innovations.

As the leverage increased, the trade was to borrow in dollars, short the dollar, and go long risky assets. Hedge funds all around the world went long commodities, emerging markets, European markets, even U.S. stocks, and so on. However, we previously noted that all of this ended with a huge margin call that was caused by the Lehman collapse. Therefore, when they had to sell stocks and commodities because of this margin call, they also had to reverse their U.S. dollar short trade. In addition, as people sold assets and had to pay back redemptions, most of the redemptions were in U.S. dollars. So, for example, you had to sell your investments in Indian stocks, and then pay back your hedge fund investors; you had to sell these Rupee-dominated investments and buy U.S. dollars, then pay your investors back.

The U.S. dollar rally was not really due to a flight to safety. Rather, it was all part of the massive deleveraging trade we saw in 2008 and Euro Fear Trade in 2010. However, despite the rallies of 2008 and 2010, the U.S. dollar, due to years of printing of money and fiscal deficits, is actually in a long-term downtrend.

Thus, the U.S. dollar is not about to crash; it has already begun to crash. In looking at the U.S. Dollar Index (the U.S. Dollar Index is an index of the U.S. dollar again major foreign currencies) as early as 1982, we can see that the U.S. dollar has fallen from a peak of over 160 in 1985 to about 80 as I write. This is a loss of 50 percent against other major currencies in the world.

I expect it to decline more. When the British pound was the reserve currency of the world, it took five U.S. dollars to buy one pound. In the early eighties, the British pound went down to near par. This meant that the pound, over the course of the twentieth century, fell nearly 80 percent against the dollar. I expect the U.S. dollar to have a similar decline against the rest of the major currencies of the world. If you take the 1985 top of 160 on the Dollar Index and calculate a 75 to 80 percent decline, that would mark the dollar's bottom at around 35 to 40. This is a further 50 to 60 percent decline from current levels.

The Proof Is in the Pudding

As we can see from the previous examples, whereas in both 2007–2009 and 1929 there were credit crunches, that is about where the similarities end. In 1929, the Federal Reserve allowed the money supply to contract and banks to fail. The government was not overly aggressive in its response to the Depression. In addition, government debt problems were not as worrisome or dire in 1929 as they are today. In addition, the global economy was nowhere near as developed in 1929. International finance and economic growth basically revolved around the United States and the British Empire in 1929. Now we have China and India and much of Asia growing at warp speed. While these areas were hit by the credit crunch at first, many of them are rebounding very strongly. The Chinese are already back to near 9 percent growth and India reported a stronger than expected rate of over 8 percent for the third quarter of 2009 and may grow at that rate for 2010.

The bottom line is that the crisis of 2008 led to a deleveraging of debt and a debt crisis, but it is not a deflationary depression. In addition, the response to this crisis is to print more money. This will lead to inflation.

The Coming Inflation

The crisis to which this most recent one is most similar is not that of the 1930s. Rather, we must go to a different part of the world to see the most similar credit crunch of the past. We must go to the banana republics of South America.

The Seventies Credit Boom and Eighties Hyperinflation in South America

The seventies are usually associated with negative connotations in economic terms: stagflation, high unemployment, oil crises. Despite what you might think, much of Latin America experienced a huge boom in the seventies. In Brazil, some refer to the early seventies as the "magic economy." For example, the Brazilian economy experienced growth rates of nearly 10 percent per year from 1970 to 1974.

In the seventies, South American nations borrowed huge amounts of money for industrialization and development of infrastructure. Much of this money came from the petrol nations of the Middle East. With oil prices soaring in the seventies, they were rich in cash and looking to invest it.

According to studies on the South American debt crisis, loans at South American banks increased at an average annualized rate of 20.4 percent from 1975 to 1982. This lending caused Latin America to more than quadruple its external debt from $75 billion in 1975 to $315 billion in 1982.

However, a funny thing happened on the way to the Super Boom in Latin America. Paul Volcker head of the U.S. Federal Reserve, decided that he was going to help kill inflation in the early eighties. He jacked up interest rates; he cut the money supply. Interest rates spiked; the U.S. dollar rallied; commodity prices fell; the U.S. economy temporarily went into a severe contraction. Oil collapsed from a high of $40 per barrel in 1980 to as low as $6 in 1986. The petrol dollars dried up. In addition, rising interest rates made it increasingly difficult for South American countries and banks to pay back the huge loans they had taken on. The lifeline to the loans in South America dried up. The South American economies stopped functioning. Most of South America entered into a massive credit crunch.

From 1980 to 1985, the per-capita income in South America decreased by 9 percent on average. The total economic growth (while the rest of the world started an economic boom in 1982) in the region was a mere 2.3 percent, according to the Institute for Latin American Studies paper entitled, "The Debt Crisis in Latin America." In the summer of 1982, the Mexicans all but admitted that they would not be able to repay their debt.

However, South America did not enter a deflationary spiral as loans spiraled out of control. Instead, they resorted to printing money to get out of this crisis and pay back the loans.

Figure 2.3 is the inflation rate of Mexico in the 1980s. Note that when you examine the numbers in this figure they are all based on *yearly averages*. Intra-year numbers, at any given moment during the peak of the inflation bubble in South America, would produce rates that were *much* higher in the mid- to late-eighties (often in the thousands or tens of thousands of percent).

In 1982 and 1983, according to the International Monetary Fund, Mexico experienced inflation rates of 110.90 and 72.92 percent. After prices stabilized in 1984 and 1985, Mexico had a second bout with inflation in 1986 and 1987. Mexico experienced inflation rates of

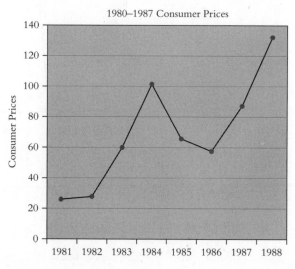

1980–1987 Consumer Prices

Figure 2.3   Mexico: Inflation Rate, 1980s
Source: International Monetary Fund (data).

49.33 and 52.87 percent. In cumulative terms, Mexico's Consumer Price Index, which stood at 26.47 in 1980, was trading at over 131.82 by 1987, an increase of 500 percent!

Figure 2.4 is Argentina's inflation rate in the 1980s. Argentina saw inflation rates of 57.72, 108.64, and 82.30 percent from 1981 to 1983. It then saw a second round of inflation in the late eighties with inflation rates reaching 45.78, 161.13, and 797.92 percent in 1989! By some estimates the maximum rate was over 4,000 percent by early 1990. The Argentina Consumer Price Index, which stood at 100.79 in 1980, stood 10 years later at 3079.45, a resultant increase of 3,000 percent in prices throughout the 1980s!

Brazil saw huge inflation in the eighties as well—10 of the 13 years from 1981 to 1993 saw double-digit inflation. The Brazilian Consumer Price Index, which began 1980 at a level of 90.34, stood at 2947.33 in 1990, an increase of over 3,200 percent in 10 years!

As you can see in Figure 2.5, Bolivia was perhaps the hardest hit in terms of inflation. From 1980 to 1985, the Bolivian CPI increased from

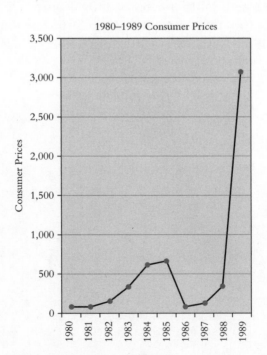

Figure 2.4   Argentina: Inflation Rate, 1980s
Source: International Monetary Fund (data).

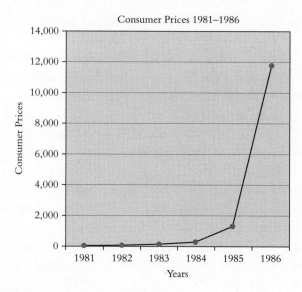

Figure 2.5   Bolivia: Inflation Rate, 1981–1986

SOURCE: International Monetary Fund (data).

a level of 47.05 to 11,749.63 percent in 1985, an increase of over 24,971 percent! Bolivia saw yearly increases of 364.96 and 816.97 percent. At its peak in 1985, Bolivia saw an inflation rate of approximately 20,000 percent (it should be noted that while researching Bolivia, I saw so many different numbers on the official inflation rate that finding true numbers became an impossible and ridiculous task). Some said the top rate was 15,000 percent; some had it as high as 50,000 or 60,000 percent.

The problem with all of these numbers is that they are so high and so out of control that it is hard to know the exact amount of inflation in South America in the 1980s. We do know, however, that it was high—very high!

The U.S. Situation Is More Like South America than the 1930s

The situation at the moment is much more similar to the inflationary busts of South America in the eighties than to the Great Depression of the thirties or the Japanese recession of the nineties. One reason is that the credit bubble of the seventies led to the inflation bubble of the eighties in South America. I believe that the credit bubble of the past 20 years in the United States will lead to an inflation bubble for the next 10 years.

Another reason relates to the state of the nation. Both the United States in the thirties and the Japanese in the eighties were huge creditors. Both nations possessed huge foreign exchange reserves. During the Great Depression, as we noted earlier, gold moved from Britain to the United States. In 1946, even after the spending during the war, the United States was able to give the British an emergency loan to keep the British afloat.

The United States was a creditor nation. The United States had high savings rates in the thirties as did Japan. When both your government and citizens are huge savers, there is little incentive to print money and create massive inflation. The reason, quite simply, is that by introducing inflation, you wipe out the savings of both the government and your citizens.

However, when you are like the United States in the late 2000s or South America in the eighties, and governments are heavily indebted, the easiest solution is to print this debt away. Who can blame them? The U.S. savings rate is very low (about 4 percent at the moment, and for years it was zero); many Americans have negative equity in their homes. As we pointed out earlier, the total debt as a percentage of GDP is over 350 percent. There is a very strong incentive for the government to inflate its way out.

The U.S. Government Will Be *Forced* to Print Its Way Out of the Debt Crisis

As I stated above, printing money is one of the few options that may be left to the United States. The United States benefits from still being the reserve currency of the world. Unlike many developing nations that have to borrow in U.S. dollars or foreign currencies, the United States owns nearly all of its debt in U.S. dollars. Therefore, when push comes to shove, it can print that debt away. Of course that is a worst-case scenario, as the United States does not want to worry its foreign investors.

Over the years as the Super Bubble built up, foreigners built up their holdings of U.S. debt to keep rates low to keep the U.S. consumer

Table 2.1   U.S. Trade Deficit

Trade deficit 2007:	−$258.5 billion
Trade deficit 2008:	−$268.0 billion
Trade deficit 2009:	−$188.5 billion (est.)

spending. However, as just stated, now that the United States is buying fewer foreign products, foreigners now have less money to put back into Treasuries at a time when the U.S. government has to issue more of them.

Table 2.1, from the U.S. Census Bureau's own numbers, shows the U.S. trade deficit with the rest of the world and illustrates this point.

Note that the trade deficit has gone from well over $250 billion in 2007 and 2008 to under $200 billion during the recession of 2009. This means that, as the trade deficit shrinks and China's trade surplus shrinks, China has fewer excess dollars to put back into the U.S. Treasuries. The basic law of supply and demand is that the United States is issuing more Treasuries at a time that there is less foreign money to buy these Treasuries. Therefore, supply cannot meet demand. Bond prices will go down and interest rates will rise.

Many countries are now steering away from the U.S. dollar. In November 2009, the Indian Central Bank shocked the monetary world by stating that they were buying 200 tonnes of gold from the IMF. The Chinese, in numerous statements in the past year, have expressed their worries about the U.S. financial situation. Brazil and China, in a recent trade agreement, made a deal to use multiple currencies, including the Chinese Yuan. When Tim Geitner, Treasury Secretary, during a speech made in China on June 1, 2009, stated that the Chinese holdings of U.S. Treasuries were safe, laughter erupted from the crowd. It is a sad day when the Treasury Secretary of the most powerful country in the world becomes a laughing-stock by the expedient of praising U.S. money.

This is not just talk or a laughing matter. Foreign countries are putting their money where their mouth is. Table 2.2 shows the foreign holdings of U.S. Treasuries.

When we look at the figures in Table 2.2, they appear fine on the surface. But look a bit deeper, and it isn't pretty.

Table 2.2 Major Foreign Holders of Treasury Securities (in Billions of Dollars) Holdings at End of Period

Country	May 2010	Apr 2010	Mar 2010	Feb 2010	Jan 2010	Dec 2009	Nov 2009	Oct 2009	Sep 2009	Aug 2009	Jul 2009	New 5/ Series Jun 2009	Old 5/ Series Jun 2009	May 2009
China, Mainland	867.7	900.2	895.2	877.5	889.0	894.8	929.0	938.3	938.3	936.5	939.9	915.8	776.4	801.5
Japan	786.7	795.5	784.9	768.5	765.4	765.7	754.3	742.9	747.9	727.5	720.9	708.2	711.2	677.2
United Kingdom 2/	350.0	321.2	279.0	233.5	208.3	180.3	155.5	108.1	126.8	104.3	97.1	90.8	213.6	163.9
Oil Exporters 3/	235.1	239.3	229.5	218.8	218.4	207.4	208.3	209.0	205.9	209.8	209.9	211.8	191.2	192.9
Carib Bnkng Ctrs 4/	165.5	153.2	148.3	144.5	143.7	128.4	123.4	114.3	116.7	125.2	138.7	135.3	191.9	195.2
Brazil	161.4	164.3	164.4	170.8	169.1	169.3	165.8	164.9	153.6	146.0	146.8	148.5	139.8	127.1
Hong Kong	145.7	151.8	150.9	152.4	146.6	148.7	142.1	137.8	128.0	120.5	111.1	95.7	99.8	93.2
Russia	126.8	113.1	120.1	120.2	124.2	141.8	151.4	145.9	145.1	144.9	141.3	143.3	119.9	124.5
Taiwan	126.2	126.9	124.8	121.4	119.6	116.5	115.4	115.6	115.1	112.9	114.4	114.0	77.0	75.7
Canada	85.0	82.1	77.0	67.1	54.7	52.8	50.7	44.8	42.3	30.2	24.1	23.0	18.4	11.0
Switzerland	84.4	80.0	78.8	81.8	84.4	89.7	89.6	85.3	82.7	82.0	81.9	85.7	72.0	63.7
Luxembourg	76.3	77.6	84.6	77.9	79.1	88.4	80.2	79.5	87.5	83.0	80.8	92.9	104.3	96.2
Germany	55.4	54.3	53.7	49.9	49.0	47.8	48.7	47.9	48.8	50.1	51.2	48.9	53.8	55.1
Ireland	48.0	45.7	43.3	38.7	39.2	43.6	43.1	42.6	37.0	40.8	42.9	50.6	46.3	50.6
Thailand	46.3	46.9	43.5	42.1	33.3	33.3	29.6	28.0	27.9	31.4	29.3	27.5	29.7	26.8
Singapore	40.6	42.4	45.5	42.6	41.3	39.2	37.5	36.3	39.4	43.1	43.4	41.9	40.9	39.7
Korea, South	37.8	38.7	40.1	39.8	39.7	40.3	40.2	43.3	39.9	39.8	38.7	37.4	36.3	37.4
France	36.4	38.8	38.7	32.5	35.9	30.5	40.4	29.1	25.0	28.0	17.5	18.9	26.0	25.9
Mexico	34.1	33.1	36.1	33.9	34.4	36.8	31.9	26.5	27.8	33.2	33.4	35.2	29.5	31.5

India	29.3	31.0	32.0	31.6	32.7	32.5	34.5	35.8	38.8	41.5	41.8	42.2	39.3	38.8
Egypt	28.0	21.1	21.4	21.7	19.4	18.9	19.4	14.3	14.9	14.5	12.7	11.5	17.3	18.6
Turkey	27.6	27.9	28.7	27.3	27.5	28.1	29.4	30.3	28.1	28.5	27.1	27.3	26.9	28.3
Poland	23.4	24.6	23.4	22.6	22.3	22.9	21.9	21.9	21.5	21.3	20.9	20.5	5.6	5.0
Italy	20.8	20.3	20.5	20.9	21.3	21.1	21.6	21.6	20.0	19.3	19.8	19.1	16.7	16.7
Israel	20.1	19.9	22.0	18.9	16.8	13.8	15.1	14.5	16.9	16.2	15.5	16.6	18.1	19.0
Belgium	17.6	18.5	17.1	17.0	17.4	17.3	17.4	16.9	17.2	17.7	17.8	17.9	15.7	15.7
Netherlands	17.6	19.6	19.2	20.4	20.7	20.4	21.0	20.5	22.0	22.0	22.2	19.6	18.9	16.4
Colombia	15.7	15.7	16.2	16.0	16.0	17.3	17.2	18.3	18.3	17.9	16.4	13.3	11.9	12.1
Norway	15.2	15.0	14.6	13.6	12.3	12.1	8.5	7.3	7.6	7.1	11.3	11.1	28.7	28.3
Philippines	14.4	15.0	14.6	12.5	11.3	11.7	11.7	11.4	11.4	11.9	10.9	11.2	11.6	11.8
Australia	14.1	17.9	14.4	14.4	15.4	16.3	13.7	12.8	12.3	12.5	12.1	12.2	9.9	9.0
Sweden	13.4	15.3	16.3	16.0	15.7	15.2	15.5	15.3	14.4	12.7	12.5	12.5	16.4	13.0
Denmark	12.8	9.7	9.6	9.8	8.9	8.5	7.8	7.7	7.1	5.3	5.5	5.3	5.5	5.4
Chile	12.0	12.0	11.9	12.3	12.5	12.4	12.1	12.4	12.8	12.9	13.4	14.2	14.3	14.7
Spain	11.6	13.0	13.5	13.4	13.7	13.7	13.1	13.1	12.3	12.8	11.6	11.1	5.5	4.7
Malaysia	10.5	10.9	11.0	10.9	11.0	11.7	11.8	11.7	11.7	11.9	12.5	12.4	11.7	12.3
All Other	150.1	145.4	140.3	138.9	138.5	142.2	146.1	150.3	152.2	155.7	158.2	157.2	130.9	133.6
Grand Total	3963.6	3957.8	3885.0	3752.2	3708.6	3691.5	3674.9	3575.9	3575.3	3531.0	3505.7	3460.3	3383.3	3292.5
Of which:														
For. Official	2697.2	2721.6	2709.4	2677.1	2681.1	2706.3	2734.3	2714.5	2699.2	2689.8	2675.9	2625.5	2295.3	2287.1
Treasury Bills	473.4	505.0	507.3	503.4	508.5	534.3	586.6	598.0	597.7	607.3	606.6	571.9	571.9	586.2
T-Bonds & Notes	2223.8	2216.6	2202.0	2173.8	2172.6	2172.0	2147.7	2116.5	2101.5	2082.5	2069.3	2053.6	1723.4	1700.9

SOURCE: U.S. Treasury Department (www.ustreas.gov/tic/mfh.txt).

- In October 2008, at the depths of the financial panic, foreigners owned $2.06 trillion of U.S. Treasuries. As of October 2009, they owned $2.38 trillion or an increase of about $322 billion. That looks like strong buying.
- However, when you look inside the numbers, it is not a pretty picture. We must remember that the U.S. federal government ran a deficit of $1.42 trillion in the same time period. This means that foreign increases in debt holdings accounted for merely a little over 22.6 percent of the total amount issued.
- As of October 2008, foreigners held just over $360 billion of short-term securities and $1.70 trillion of long-term Treasuries. The math tells you that foreigners held long-term versus short-term Treasuries at roughly a 4-to-1 margin. In the past year, though, the nature of their purchases has changed a great deal. Foreigners increased their long-term holdings from only $1.70 trillion to $1.78 trillion, a small increase of $80 billion. However, they increased their short-term holdings from $360 billion to $598 billion or roughly $238 billion. Therefore, in the past year, they have reversed course buying short-term over long-term Treasuries at a 3-to-1 margin.
- This means that foreigners are not investing in U.S. debt as they had been before. When they buy, they buy much more short-term Treasuries. In effect, they are just "parking" money rather than investing it. They are just holding it short term before they look to put it somewhere else. It also shows a lack of desire to buy the long-term bond at under 4 percent.
- I think the most interesting note is the nature of China's holdings. China is the largest holder of U.S. Treasuries, owning over $895 billion worth. This number is up from $684.1 in 2008. However, since July 2009, the Chinese have been *net sellers* of U.S. debt. In July 2009, they owned nearly $940 billion and by March 2010 this number was down to $895 billion. This is being done at a time when the United States has issued hundreds of billions of dollars' worth of additional debt.
- This shows us that the rate of foreign buying cannot keep up with the rate of U.S. debt issuance.

Figure 2.6 shows the percent of total debt that foreigners have held since the mid-1980s. As you can see, foreigners bought more and more

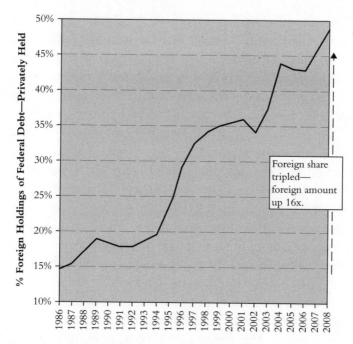

Figure 2.6   Foreign Holdings of Federal Government
SOURCE: Grandfather Economic Report (www.mwhodges.home.att.net).
DATA: Department of Treasury.
NOTE: T-bill and T-bond debt (held by "public") = 49 percent of total. In 2008,
$3.1 trillion foreign holdings (China = 22 percent; Japan = 19 percent),
up from December 1992, $0.5 trillion; December 1986, $0.2 trillion.

U.S. debt since the 1980s, which kept interest rates low. However, now with the Super Bubble bursting, they can no longer keep up with these rates of purchases.

In my opinion, this means that the only realistic way in which the United States will be able to meet its debt obligations is by printing money to buy debt. This is known as *monetizing the debt*. This is extremely inflationary. It should be noted that the Federal Reserve already started such a program in 2009 when it bought some long-term Treasury bills.

Another major problem is not just the debt but rather the makeup of the debt. Most countries, when they issue debt, try to issue longer term securities. Why? Because if they run into financial problems and are forced to simply print away their debt, they can erode their currency slowly over a number of years rather than causing a complete collapse.

Many European nations that experienced defaults (such as Spain and France in the nineteenth century) or hyperinflation (such as Germany) learned from these mistakes. According to Niall Ferguson, at page 171 of his book, *The Cash Nexus*, in stats he got from Ecengreen and Wyplosz, Germany has only about 3.9 percent of its debt in short-term notes, the U.K. only 29.6 percent, the Netherlands 4.9 percent, and France 42.4 percent (all numbers are circa the mid-nineties). (*Short term* means maturity of less than 5 years on bonds.)

According to Ferguson, the United States has about one-third of its debt in maturity of less than one year and 72 percent of its debt has a maturity of less than five years! During the financial crisis, when the United States has had to issue trillions of dollars of new debt, it has been doing most of it in short-term maturities. At some point, the United States *will not* be able to pay it back; the United States will reissue it and will have to print to cover the payment of the debt. As most of this debt rolls over within five years, the Federal Reserve will print a massive amount of money in a short period of time to repay the debt and pay the interest. This means that at some point there will be a *huge* spike in inflation in the United States.

What Does All This Mean?—Inflation, the Death of the Dollar, and the Popping of the Long-Term Bond Market Bubble

We can see from this chapter that the United States now has an unsustainable amount of debt that it both possesses currently and will be issuing in the future. Foreigners are *not* going to be able to purchase this debt, due to the combination of the bursting of the Super Bubble and a lack of willingness to support U.S. fiscal irresponsibility. This lack of demand at a time of great supply should put a lot of upward pressure on U.S. interest rates in the coming years.

In addition, the deterioration of the creditworthiness of the U.S. government itself will also put upward pressure on rates.

As the United States issues all of its debt in its own currency, it has the luxury of printing money to pay off the debt. However, this is massively inflationary, and will most likely push up interest rates.

As a result, the final financial bubble will burst. In the early 2000s, we saw the NASDAQ and technology bubble burst. From 2006 to 2009, we saw the housing bubble burst. Now we will see the financial bubble, created by the long-term government bond bubble, burst as well.

Since 1981, long-term government bonds have been in a major up-cycle (remember that when interest rates go down, the price of a long-term government bond goes up). In September 1981, the interest on the 30-year Treasury peaked at over 14 percent. The bull market in bonds commenced until the yield hit a low of 2.52 percent in December 2008. Since then, this yield has backed off to 4.67 percent as I write. Figure 2.7 shows the USB, which is the U.S. 30-year bond. Note the huge spike higher in December 2008. This is similar to the other final Blows Off that we have seen in other financial bubbles.

However, we are just in the midst of the long-term downtrend in bonds and uptrend in rates. Turn the figure of the bond upside down after the 1981 bottom and that is where we are. As the United States continues to run up debts and is then forced to print money to pay for these debts, interest rates will soar.

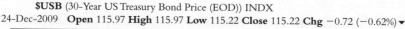

$USB (30-Year US Treasury Bond Price (EOD)) INDX
24-Dec-2009 **Open** 115.97 **High** 115.97 **Low** 115.22 **Close** 115.22 **Chg** −0.72 (−0.62%) ▾

Figure 2.7 Long-Term Bond Prices
SOURCE: Courtesy of (http://stockcharts.com).

This brings us back to Milton Friedman. Friedman was famous for stating, "Inflation is always and everywhere a monetary phenomenon." Translation: Printing money = eventual inflation.

Niall Ferguson added to this commentary further with his comment in *The Ascent of Money*, that inflation is also a political phenomenon. Translation: Printing money + government spending = inflation. As we have discussed, we have both phenomena in play at the present moment.

In Friedman's book, *Money Mischief* (Mariner Books, 1994), he states the following:

> A change in the monetary growth affects interest rates in one direction at first but in the opposite direction later. More rapid monetary growth at first tends to lower interest rates. But later on, the resulting acceleration in spending and still later in inflation produces a rise in the demand for loans, which tends to raise interest rates. In addition, higher inflation widens real and nominal interest rates. As both lenders and borrowers come to anticipate inflation, lenders demand, and borrowers are willing to offer, higher nominal rates to offset the anticipated inflation. That is why interest rates are higher in the countries that have had the most rapid growth in the quantity of money and also in prices—countries like Brazil, Argentina, Chile, Israel, South Korea.

This shows us the current crisis in a perfect nutshell. When the Fed really started to print money rapidly in late 2008, interest rates went *down* as investors fled to bonds with the excess liquidity as the fear of financial meltdown was in the air. However, if Friedman is right, we will see a huge increase in inflation as the printing of money filters throughout the economy and lenders to the United States begin to ask for a further higher rate of return in anticipation of this inflation.

In addition, as the United States prints more and more money, the value of the U.S. dollar will decrease more and more. At some point in the next few years, the U.S. dollar will cease to become the reserve currency of the world and the United States will proceed into massive inflation to pay off its debts.

This will burst the great bond bubble. For those interested in protecting themselves against the bursting of the bond bubble, you can purchase the TBT (the Proshares Ultra 20-Year-Plus Short Bond Fund) or the HTD (the 30-Year Short Fund), which trades in Toronto. Both of these are *double leveraged*, meaning that they should go up twice as fast as bonds go down.

Now What?

Part One of this book has a specific purpose. I am not a doom-and-gloomer and would prefer to tell you right away what you should invest in and why. However, I believe in economic cycles, and that the stock market is not going to do much in the next 10 years. I also believe that inflation will go much, much higher and that interest rates will increase significantly in the coming years. Merely saying it puts you on the level of just about anyone—only convincing proof based on reliable research will guide investors in the turbulent times to come.

The basic arguments to support my predictions in this part of the text (as summarized and articulated in the previous paragraph) are as follows:

1. **Bonds look like a bubble.** The parabolic action in the bond market is indicative of moves that happen near the end of a major move upward.
2. **The bursting of the Super Bubble means funds will not flow as fast into the United States.** The United States abused its position as the world's reserve currency with the Super Bubble system. However, funds will not flow as fast in the coming years and instead will flow into other parts of the world. As the United States becomes increasingly indebted, foreigners will shy away from U.S. debt. The United States will have to print money to buy this debt. This will devalue the dollar and cause inflation.
3. **The United States *will have to* print money because of the makeup of the debt.** The makeup of the debt is very negative for the United States. Most of the debt is short term in nature (five years or less). This means it will have to print money like crazy over a short period of time to pay it off.
4. **Interest rates will spike and the U.S. bond bubble will burst.** As inflation soars and the dollar declines, interest rates on the long end of the curve will have to rise to reflect these trends. The 27-year bond bull market probably ended in 2008 and has

not yet entered into a major bear market. This means much higher interest rates going forward. The law of supply and demand states that as supply outstrips demand, investors will require higher interest rates to sustain any desire in investing in U.S. bonds.

These four arguments reflect and support my belief that ultimately inflation will go up and that the U.S. dollar will go down. In the coming chapters, we will discuss how you can:

- Protect your investments from these developments.
- Prosper from the coming inflation.
- Know which investments will not perform well under such circumstances.

Part Two

RIDING THE SECULAR AND CYCLICAL TIDAL WAVES

Chapter 3

You Cannot Fight the Power of Cycles

Profiting from Secular Moves

B efore writing this book, I pored through hundreds of years of history and discovered a simple but powerful current that courses through the ages similar to the way that all rivers flow inevitably to the ocean. Although this current cannot be resisted, surprisingly, it is ignored by almost all other investment books in the same manner that underground streams pass under our feet completely unnoticed. Accordingly, the dominant theme of this book is this simple but irresistible discovery: Market cycles are the most powerful of all influences that prevail on capital markets. A thorough understanding of market cycles is an essential tool for any investor who wishes to successfully trade and make money in the capital markets. Market cycles are like gravity; you can't see them but they bind your fate, regardless.

The Trend Is Your Friend

There is an old adage on Wall Street that "the trend is your friend." That is really another way of saying that "you do not fight the tape"; you follow the prevailing cycle of the day. Living in the Bahamas as I do, I often go to the beach to swim or take walks. While there, I watch the tide of the ocean come in.

When swimming, you realize that it is a lot easier to swim with that tide coming in than against it going out. That is how investing is; you have to swim with the tide. If you do not, it is like swimming against the current, and that, my friends, is very difficult to do. However, at some point the tide is going to turn, and part of being a good swimmer or investor is not only to go with the tide but to also be able to see the tide turn. If you are caught moving in one direction and the tide turns in the other direction and goes against you, you could get smashed into the shore.

In this chapter, you will learn how to profit from the flow of the tide and then be able to spot the coming turn in it.

But before that, let's get some terminology out of the way.

- A *secular move* is a long-term trend in the stock market or any market. It lasts between 5 and 30 years but usually tends to be in the 10- to 20-year range.
- A *cyclical move* is a short-term move in the market. It happens within the context of the longer term trend (i.e., within the secular move) and it usually lasts anywhere from a few months to a few years.

For example, 1966 to 1982 was a long-term secular bear market in the stock market. The 1973 to 1974 bear market was a cyclical bear market within the context of the long-term secular bear market. The 1974 to 1976 bull market was a cyclical bull market within the context of a secular bear market. This chapter for the most part deals with the long-term secular moves in markets. Chapter 4 deals with cyclical moves.

The Length of Secular Cycles

So, how do you determine when a secular trend is reaching the boiling point? Believe it or not, all you have to do is go to your favorite bookstore. You don't have to buy or read anything; just glance at the bestseller lists.

You don't believe me? Well, in the late nineties and 2000, all of the books on the bestseller list were about holding stocks for the long term, day trading, tech stocks, Dow 40,000, and the like. Anything with a bullish theme sold. In 1980, when the Dow was below 1,000, any book that was negative about stocks, gold, or hyperinflation sold. *Newsweek* ran its infamous "Death of Equities" cover in 1979, right near the end of the great bear market of 1966 to 1982.

So all of the books that sold in the early eighties were negative on equities. However, the real question in 1982 was that, with the Dow trading under 800 and down nearly 75 percent adjusted for inflation over the past 16 years, was it really going to down another 75 percent in the next 16 years? As the famed Jim Rogers would say, one of the most important questions you can ask yourself about an investment is "How much can it go down?" Stocks in 1982 had little downside, whereas stocks in 2000 had a lot of downside. That is the irony about psychology; when everyone feels good, that is usually the time to be selling. When everyone is down in the dumps, that is the time to buy. As the old adage goes, it is always darkest before the dawn!

The lengths of secular cycles are pretty similar to each other. As we saw from the above example, the S&P 500 and Dow Jones Industrial Average have both experienced many major cycles where they have seen valuation contractions and valuation expansions. The periods of secular advances and declines are about 15 years. Since 1900, there have been four specific bear market cycles (assuming we are in the fourth right now), lasting approximately 15 to 20 years in length. On the other hand, there have been three bull markets, lasting between 8 and 18 years. Table 3.1 shows the outline of these cycles on the Dow Jones Industrial Average. The Dow came into existence in 1896, so all performance before that level is based on performance of equities before the Dow came along.

Table 3.1 Bull Market and Bear Market Cycles of the Dow Jones Industrial Average

Years	Average Gain/Loss per Year (%)	Length
Bull Market Cycle		
1815–1835	10.0	20 years
1843–1853	13.7	10 years
1861–1881	12.0	20 years
1897–1906	12.2	9 years
1921–1929	25.2	8 years
1949–1966	14.0	17 years
1982–1999	14.9	17 years
Average	14.6%	14.4 years
Bear Market Cycle		
1835–1843	−0.6	8 years
1853–1861	−3.0	8 years
1881–1897	3.9	16 years
1906–1921	−1.1	15 years
1929–1949	0.8	20 years
1966–1982	−1.4	16 years
2000–????	?	?
Average	−1.4%	13.9 years

Fear and Greed Drive Cycles

Markets are all about fear and greed. Mr. Market is not your friend. He wants you to lose as much money as possible when trading. Cycles are part of the way of doing this. Bull markets are exciting; they sucker people into thinking they can become rich beyond their wildest dreams. Bear markets are scary; they scare people to panic and sell.

A major problem for all investors is filtering out the noise generated by the investment media. Much of the millions and billions of information tidbits generated by company news, investment experts, and media hype are of limited assistance in determining the future long-term direction of the market. These information tidbits are also virtually useless in guiding investors through the inevitable but often devastating turns in the market. With the explosion of the Internet and various communication vehicles, this problem is now worse than ever.

During a bull market, most of the news reported is good. The economy is booming, unemployment is low, inflation is low, and everything seems as good as can be. As an investor, you are willing to buy stocks during these macro influences because all you are hearing is how good things are and how everyone is making money in the market.

During a bear market, it is exactly the opposite. News is terrible, inflation and interest rates are spiking, and unemployment is high. The financial system is often a mess, banks are collapsing, and the economy is sinking.

Ironically, you must go against your emotional urges during these times—you sell on euphoria and you buy on pessimism. John Templeton was famous for saying that you "buy at the point of maximum pessimism." On the flipside of the coin, you could say you "sell at the point of extreme optimism."

Once you understand the logic of cycles, trading and making money from a long-term cycle is a lot simpler than you think.

Check Your Mind at the Door

The long-term cycle is a reflection of psychology. When the bear cycle is starting and the bull market is ending, everyone is bullish on stocks, despite the fact that they are extremely expensive. It's vice versa when the secular bear market is ending and the bull market is starting. At the point of maximum pessimism, no one wants stocks, due to a host of well-publicized reasons: high inflation, weak corporate profits, the bad economy, and the fact that stocks have not done anything in years. When I was bullish on gold in the year 2000, people would point out to me that gold's return over 20 years had been negative and tell me it was a terrible investment for the past 20 years. My response was, "That is why I want to buy it."

The opposite occurs at a time when a major bull market is ending. The news is good, the economy is booming, there is talk of new eras of economic prosperity and the Goldilocks economy, and valuations are stretched. Stocks have been going up for years. For example, in the year 2000, when the Dow Jones Industrial Average was 11,700, up from a low of 777 in 1982, the market had gone up 1,400 percent in

18 years. In the year 2000, did you really think it was realistic to believe it was going to go up another 1,400 percent over the next 18 years?

What is amazing about these cycles is that they have a purpose. From a psychological standpoint, I always think the market wants as many people to be as wrong as possible. Just when things seem like they cannot get any worse, the stock market cycle turns and a major bull market starts. When things seem as rosy as can be, the market sees a long-term top and then declines for the next 15 to 20 years.

The market also seems to be "wrong" at just the perfect time. Just when the secular long-term trend of the economy is going to turn up, the stock market is at dirt-cheap levels (see 1982). Alternatively, just when the secular long-term trend is about to turn down (see the first quarter of 2000), the market is exorbitantly expensive. Basically, the market hits extreme levels at just the wrong time.

A great explanation of why these shifts happen is George Soros's *theory of reflexivity*. In a nutshell, Soros argues that the market is not always correct (like those who preach and believe in the efficient market theory believe). It is just the opposite according to Soros: The market is *always wrong*. So the market is reflexive and then turns in the opposite direction because the market has not accurately reflected the future or current economic outlook. (I find it amazing that one of the greatest speculators of our generation has made his money by buying and relying on the errors and flaws of financial markets!)

The True Reason for Secular Moves—Valuation!

While secular moves are influenced by psychology, fundamentally they are all really about one thing: valuation, or more specifically the Price-to-Earnings Ratio of stocks. The *Price-to-Earnings Ratio* is a measure of the price paid for a share relative to the annual net income or profit earned by the firm per share. It is the most common tool used to value stocks. We see the reflexivity or change in the markets' long-term secular trend when valuations stretch too far in one direction.

The median valuation of the S&P 500's Price-to-Earnings Ratio (P/E ratio) is about 15. (Historically, P/Es of fewer than 12 are considered cheap and P/Es of over 20 are considered expensive.) We must remember that the reason that something has a median is because it spends half the time trading above it and half the time below it.

In 1929, at a top in stock valuations, the P/E ratio of the S&P 500 traded at over 30. Over the next 20 years, the S&P 500 did nothing; by 1949, it actually fell over 50 percent to just over 150 from its top of over 380 in 1929 (it lost nearly 75 percent adjusted for inflation in those 20 years). In 1949, at the secular market bottom, the S&P's P/E ratio was just under 10. That started a 16-year bull market that saw the S&P climb sixfold until 1966.

The basic reasoning that this happens goes back to psychology; when times are good, people dive into stocks and push valuations to extremes. There is a huge amount of euphoria. Anyone and everyone is investing in the market. The market is priced for perfection and "everyone" is in there; there really is not anyone left to push it higher. However, stocks do not go from overvalued to undervalued overnight. It takes a long time.

Undervalued Markets Lead to Major Secular Bull Markets

For example, Figure 3.1 shows the S&P 500 Price-to-Earnings Ratio on a 10-year trailing basis. This means you simply divide the current price of the S&P 500 by the average of the previous 10 years' earnings. The top of the figure is the S&P 500's price on an inflation-adjusted basis and the bottom part of the figure is the 10-year trailing average for the S&P 500's P/E ratio.

Whenever the 10-year average of the Price-to-Earnings Ratio has reached under 10, stocks have been undervalued and usually performed well in the years that followed. For example, in 1921, the 10-year P/E ratio of the S&P 500 was 4.8. Over the next 8 years stocks advanced an average of 17.90 percent per year until their top in 1929.

In 1949, after 20 years of doing nothing and after years of deflation, high inflation, depression, and a world war, the 10-year average of the S&P 500's P/E ratio was 9.1. This undervaluation helped launch the great bull market of 1949 to 1966. From 1949 to 1966, the S&P 500 saw an average gain of 11.40 percent per year.

In 1982, the 10-year average P/E ratio of the S&P 500 was 6.6. Over the next 18 years, until topping in the year 2000, the average gain for the S&P 500 was 14.96 percent a year.

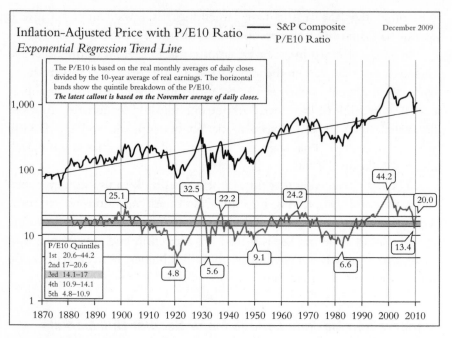

Figure 3.1   S&P Composite: 1871–Present
SOURCE: www.dshort.com.

From the above examples, we can see that all three secular bull markets of the past century have started whenever the 10-year average of the S&P 500's P/E ratio has traded at under 10.

Overvalued Markets Launch Secular Bear Markets

When stocks become overvalued, they do not perform well for long periods afterwards. More specifically, whenever the S&P 500's 10-year average P/E ratio has traded over 20, the market has not performed well during the period that followed.

Stocks became extremely overvalued at the 1929 top with the 10-year average P/E on the S&P 500 climbing to over 32.5. Stocks then crashed into 1932, losing 89 percent of their value and entered a trading range that lasted until 1949. This trading range saw stocks lose over 50 percent of their value in nominal terms and nearly 75 percent of their value in inflation-adjusted terms.

In the mid-sixties, stocks again became overvalued; by 1966, the 10-year average P/E of the S&P 500 was over 24. The market then entered a 16-year trading range, with the market actually losing around 74 percent of its value from 1966 to 1982 when adjusted for inflation.

In 2000, we saw the S&P as overvalued as it ever was. The 10-year average of the S&P 500 was over 44. Part of the reason for this was the heavy weightings that technology brought into the S&P 500 during the tech bubble of the late nineties. Many of those tech companies traded at 1,000 times earnings or had no earnings at all; accordingly these stocks inflated the P/E of the S&P 500. Putting tech companies aside for a moment, most large-cap blue-chips were trading nearly 30 times earnings at that time. After this overvaluation, we experienced the bear market of 2000–2002 and then the bust of 2007–2009, as stocks began to come down to their average long-term valuations.

The Inflation-Adjusted Decline

When you look at some of these moves on the surface it doesn't look too bad. The Dow was 1,000 in 1966 and it was 800 in 1982. The S&P was at about the same level in 1982 as in 1966. However, when we adjust these moves for inflation, it gets ugly. Inflation adjusting is obviously very crucial in determining real gains or losses. In those same 16 years, if your income had not gone up, I am sure you would not have been very happy.

Figure 3.2 is the inflation-adjusted graph of the Dow going back to 1900. We can see the large moves down in the 20 years from 1929 to 1949 and 1966 to 1982. However, what we can also see is the good news going forward. Despite the numerous calls that we see in the current media for more crashes and the like, the erosion of the market since 2000 has already put a lot of the inflation-adjusted secular decline in.

What is even more interesting is Figure 3.3. This is an inflation-adjusted chart of the Dow using shadowstats.com Consumer Price Index (CPI) numbers. Shadowstats.com is a wonderful site run by John Williams (not the music composer!). Williams has stated that CPI figures have understated inflation for years.

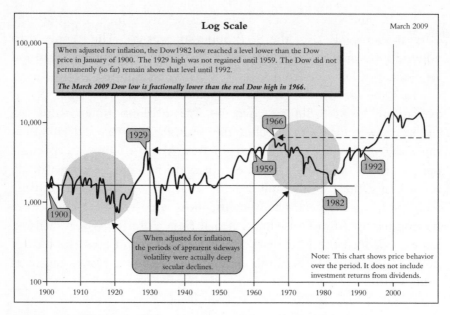

Figure 3.2   Dow Real (Inflation–Adjusted) Price Since 1990
Source: www.dshort.com.

In the early nineties, the way CPI was calculated was changed. There were quality improvements put in. This means that, for example, the price of corn goes up 100 percent in the year, but the government deems that the quality of the corn is also greater than 100 percent over the previous year. This means no price increase! This tweaking was done to lower inflation numbers over the long term.

From the government's point of view, inflation at times can be beneficial. In the seventies and eighties, the demographics of the United States were still those of a young country. Back then, was inflation more beneficial to the government than detrimental? If inflation went up, incomes could go up and more people in the seventies and eighties could pay more into government programs such as Social Security and the like; therefore, if inflation was high in the seventies, the government would obtain more money than it had to pay out. However, in the 1990s and 2000s, the population began to age. More people are going to be recipients of these programs. Under this scenario, you

Figure 3.3 Dow Jones Industrial Average (Inflation Adjusted), Using Shadow Stats Numbers

SOURCE: CyclePro Analysis (www.cycleprooutlook.com), updated October 2008, © Steven J. Williams 2001–2008.

want to keep price increases as low as possible as the government has to pay more and more out.

Figure 3.3 illustrates that if we use the old way of reporting inflation, which was much more accurate and did not underreport inflation, the last two secular bear markets from 1929 to 1949 and 1966 to 1982 took about three-quarters (75 percent) off the markets' value. At the market's bottom in March 2009, the market was off about 66 percent of its 2000 inflation-adjusted high using this method!

This means that most of the bust in terms of inflation-adjusted percentage declines has already occurred as of this writing in early 2010. The combination of the market going down from 2000 to 2009 and inflation eroding value away has caused a major crash in stock prices. Even after the rally of 2009, the S&P and Dow are still about 50 percent below their inflation-adjusted highs of the 2000 secular stock market top. However, while most of the bust in percentage terms is in, we feel there is still a way to go in terms of time.

The Way that Cycles Trade Also Repeat Each Other

We can see that a significant decline has occurred in this cycle from 2000 to 2009. From the decline over those 9 years, we have actually seen the majority of the decline that can be expected (from historical precedents) to occur during this secular decline in stock prices. However, as stated previously, we still have a way to go in terms of time. If we follow the pattern of 1966 to 1982 or 1949 to 1966 or 1901 to 1921, this secular bear market should be about 16 to 20 years in length. But as of 2010 we will be only about 10 years into this secular decline. Therefore, we probably still have another 5 to 10 years left where equities fall in price on an inflation-adjusted basis.

Here is another interesting fact about secular bear markets: Not only are the lengths of the bear markets similar, the makeup of the first and second halves of the secular downtrends is all very similar.

In the first half of a secular bull market, you see the busts. Prior to the bear market, too many people had become positive on the stock market and pushed the markets' valuations too high. People who have no business trading the market are in the market. This is the dumb money. These people are easily shaken out of the market.

In the first half of the 1901 to 1921 secular bear market, there was a huge crash in 1906–1907, known as the "Panic of 1907," that saw the Dow lose nearly 49 percent of its value.

In the first half of the 1929 to 1949 bear markets, there were two major declines: the 89 percent great crash from 1929 to 1932 and the 49 percent smash in 1937–1938.

During the first half of the 1966 to 1982 bear market, there was a 36 percent decline in the market in 1970 and the infamous 1973 to 1974 bear market which took over 45 percent off the market's value.

After all of these bear markets, there were rallies (these are *false rallies* and will be discussed at length in the next chapter). After these rallies, a long trading range followed. In the second half of all of these secular bear markets, the volatility dried up. In the cases of the forties and late seventies, there was not one bear market greater than 35 percent.

What happens is that you experience the busts during the first half of the secular bear market as the easy hands are washed out. Then, over the second half you see a long trading range that is greeted with *high inflation*.

In the late teens, forties, and seventies, we saw extremely high inflation with the market churning sideways. In the seventies, the inflation was the final inflation to catch up with the years of government spending, which included the Korean and Vietnam wars and expansions in government welfare programs. The inflation of the teens and late forties was the result of the government printing money to pay for the costs associated with World Wars I and II.

Figure 3.4 shows the year-to-year inflation rates in the United States in the past 100 years. Note the huge spikes in inflation in the late teens and late forties.

Therefore, if history follows suit, we *will not* see a crash in the 2010s. Rather, what will happen is the market will trade sideways with inflation picking up. Stocks will be losing money in inflation terms but in nominal terms will actually trade sideways. As T.S. Eliot once said, "This is the way the world ends—not with a bang but a whimper." Well, the same could be said for secular bear markets.

Secular bear markets do not end with a panic or crash. They end when the market has done nothing for a period of years and investors are no longer interested. They end with a whimper, not a bang. In addition, the secular trend of bear markets finishing with high inflation confirms the arguments we laid out in Chapters 1 and 2 that the United States will see huge inflation in the coming years.

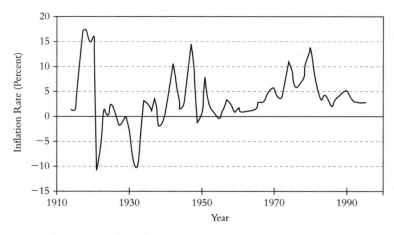

Figure 3.4   Yearly Inflation Rate
SOURCE: Thomas J. Chester, using Federal Reserve numbers.

If we look again at Figure 3.3, we can see these secular trends in terms of years. This chart was compiled by Steven J. Williams at CyclePro. Note that he has divided the up moves and down moves in the stock market into 17.6-year cycles. He shows that if you divide every major move by 17.6 years, you see the start of the next major cycle!

The secular top of the last bull market cycle occurred in January 2000 for the Dow and March 2000 for the S&P 500. If we calculate 17.6 years on top of that, we get the late summer or fall of 2018 as the next time period for when the next major bull market should start.

The Only Chart You'll Ever Have to Use

At nearly every show I speak at, I always use the chart depicted in Figure 3.5 for the simple reason that it illustrates where the market is and does so in an easily comprehensible manner. It shows the long-term trend in one simple picture.

Figure 3.5 is an inflation-adjusted chart of the Dow going back to 1800 (as I mentioned previously, the Dow was invented in 1896, so everything behind that is implied). It shows, in both time and inflation-adjusted decline, that we are still heading for the final inflation-adjusted low in equities. As do Figures 3.1 through 3.4, it predicts that we still have about 5 to 10 years left in this secular bear market.

Note that Figure 3.5 is the up-channel in which the Dow has traded over the past 200-plus years. An *up-channel* is a pattern in which a stock or index trades. When it trades to the bottom part of the channel, the market rallies; when it trades to the top part of the chart, it declines. Whenever, on an inflation-adjusted basis, the Dow has traded to the upper part of the channel, a major secular bear market has begun. These tops occurred in 1906, 1929, 1966, and 2000. The lower end of the channel, 1921, 1949, and 1982, were periods when major moves higher began. This is just more proof that we should experience another 5 to 10 years of decline on an inflation-adjusted basis on the markets.

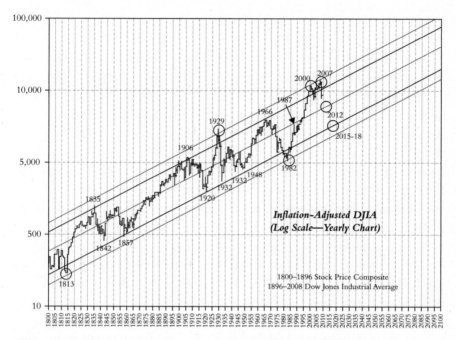

Figure 3.5 The 210-Year Inflation-Adjusted U.S. Stock Chart
SOURCE: CyclePro Analysis (www.cycleprooutlook.com), updated October 2008,
© Steven J. Williams, 2001–2008.

The NASDAQ and the Post-Bubble Decline

As I mentioned previously, the stock market runs in cycles that are usually 15 to 20 years in length. During that period, the stock market goes up in value, followed by 15- to 20-year periods where the market is sideways to down.

However, there is another type of cycle we need to discuss: the bubble boom-and-bust cycle.

In Chapter 2 we discussed the aspects of a bubble. In Chapter 1 we learned that most bubbles end in a parabolic curve where the market trades in a straight-up manner at a near-90-degree angle and then crashes. All bubbles trade in the same way as well. After years of gains, the market blasts off and gets on this unsustainable path and then crashes. This is known as a *financial bubble* or *mania*.

In the late nineties, the NASDAQ experienced such a bubble. At its peak, the Price-to-Earnings Ratio of the NASDAQ was trading north of 100. It was not the first time nor will it be the last time that an economy or market experienced a financial bubble or fell victim to the "madness of crowds." History has seen similar bubbles. The South Sea Scheme and Mississippi Scheme in early eighteenth-century Britain and France, the tulip mania in seventeenth-century Holland, the 1929 Crash, the commodities bubble of the late seventies, and, of course, the Nikkei bubble of the 1980s are all examples of financial bubbles where manias replaced logic and prudence.

However, in this chapter, we are not interested in how these bubbles occurred, but rather in how they trade afterwards. After a bubble blows up, it is not like a normal bear market. As the bubble was based on hot air, so to speak, all of that hot air comes out of the balloon and the balloon deflates. If you have ever seen what a balloon looks like deflated, it is a mere shell of its former inflated self.

When bubbles burst, they do not simply result in a 30 or 40 percent bear market. It is a massive decline of 60, 70, or 80 percent or more. The Mississippi Scheme collapsed to zero, the Dow after 1929 lost 89 percent of its value until 1932, and the Nikkei lost 65 percent from 1990 to 1992 and ultimately fell over 83 percent until its 2008 low. The NASDAQ from 2000 to 2002 lost nearly 78 percent of its value. Bubbles deflate faster than Tiger Woods' sponsors could cancel on him after his scandal broke.

After these bubbles burst, a long trading range ensues. The Nikkei has traded between about 7,000 and 24,000 in the 20 years that followed its peak at near 39,000 in 1989. The Dow spent the most part of the 1932 to 1949 period between 100 and 200 (it had peaked at over 380 in 1929). Gold spent the 1982 to 2000 period between $250 and $550 per ounce after peaking at over $850 in 1980.

Figure 3.6 shows the Nikkei from 1980 to the present. In looking at the figure, you can see the *huge* run-up followed by the crash of 1990 to 1992 and the long sideways-to-downward trading pattern.

Figure 3.7 is the Dow during the 1930s and 1940s. Again, it shows you the huge decline of the 1929 Crash followed by the ups and downs of the 1930s and 1940s.

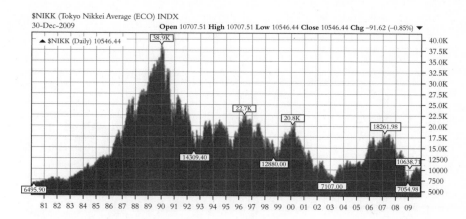

Figure 3.6   Nikkei, 1980–2001
SOURCE: Courtesy of StockCharts.com (http://stockcharts.com).

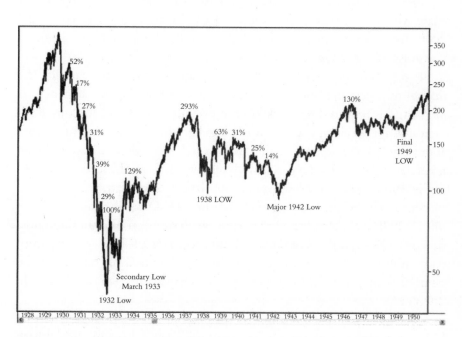

Figure 3.7   Dow Jones Industrials, 1929–1949 Secular Bear Market
SOURCE: David Chapman Union Securities.

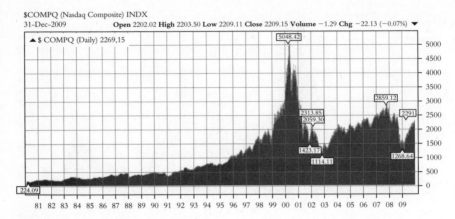

$COMPQ (Nasdaq Composite) INDX
31-Dec-2009   Open 2202.02 High 2203.50 Low 2209.11 Close 2209.15 Volume −1.29 Chg −22.13 (−0.07%) ▼

Figure 3.8   NASDAQ, 1980−2010
SOURCE: Courtesy of StockCharts.com (http://stockcharts.com).

Figure 3.8 is a chart of the NASDAQ since 2000. Looking at that chart, you can see the crash followed by the trading range of 2002–2009. If history holds up, the NASDAQ should have another 10 or so years of trading range.

Figure 3.8 of the NASDAQ shows how it can take years for the market to digest the boom and bust of these extreme market manias. A long time is required to work off the previous excess. From a psychological point of view, it takes nearly a generation for investors to forget about the boom and bust of the prior cycle. The cycle of bust and base takes about 20 years. That is how long it took for gold to base after its top in 1980 and the market to base after the 1929 Crash.

From Figure 3.8 we can see that the NASDAQ is nearly 10 years into its basing cycle. Over that period, we have been in a trading range of 1100–2500 in the NASDAQ. If the NASDAQ follows the trend of past bubbles, it will continue this post-bubble trading range for the next 10 years and then finally be able to start another major uptrend in 2020 or so.

Having examined Figures 3.6 through 3.8, we can conclude that U.S. stocks are in the midst of a long-term secular bear market, which should last another 5 to 10 years. Stocks still need time to digest the bubble of the late nineties and trade down to proper valuations to start a long-term uptrend. The chance of the U.S. stock market starting a 20-year secular bull market at the current moment is probably as about as good as Rush Limbaugh winning the next Democratic primary or any NFL team winning the Super Bowl with Jamarcus Russell quarterbacking the team (although Russell could give Limbaugh a run in the buffet eating contest).

The Commodity Secular Bull Market

Just like the stock market, the commodities' markets also trade in major secular moves. These moves tend to be opposite to the moves of the major stock market. When the market has seen its secular bull markets, commodities usually experience their secular bear markets. It makes sense in logical terms. It is not like money during a secular stock bear market disappears. It just shifts into different sectors—especially since we are in a fiat system where the government can create as much money as it wants.

Good Inflation versus Bad Inflation

Commodities tend to trade opposite to the stock market. During the 1970s, money flowed into commodities as the stock market traded flat. During the 1980s and 1990s, the Dow Jones soared from below 800 to over 11,000, whereas the Commodity Research Board (CRB) Index (an index of 20 commodities including gold, silver, oil, gasoline, etc.) was flat. Many think there was no inflation in the eighties and nineties. However, what the eighties and nineties saw was *asset* inflation. Inflation occurred in financial assets such as bonds, houses, and stocks. However, this is what most people would see as *good inflation*, as most people own an index fund or mutual fund or house and they feel good when these prices go up.

The other sort of inflation is *bad inflation*. This is the sort of inflation we saw in the forties or seventies. This is when oil prices, gas prices, and food prices go up. This is stuff that everybody has to spend money on. Exacerbating people's concerns about these traditional forms of inflation is that these types of prices tend to go up when asset prices are going down, thereby inflicting a double blow on people's perceived spending power.

No one complains about inflation when people make money on stocks or their house. However, plenty of politicians and other individuals complain about manipulation or speculation when oil and gas prices go up. However, this is just the way cycles trade.

Near the top of a certain cycle, there are always speculators and unscrupulous types that trade to take advantage of the bullish sentiment in that cycle or sector. At the top of the commodities market in 1980, we had the Hunt brothers trying to corner the silver market, which pushed the price up to $50 an ounce. At the top of the stock market cycle, we had Sanford and Madoff and their Ponzi schemes, not to mention the secular top in 2000. Cycles break bull markets and bull markets breed greed—there is no way to get around it.

Just because you resent the fact that your gas prices or oil prices go up does not mean you cannot profit from it. Figure 3.9 is the CRB

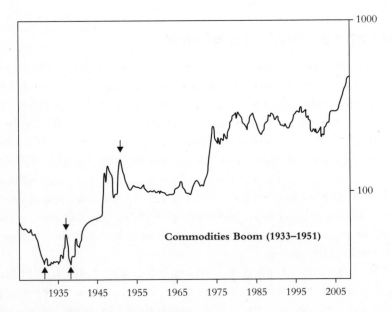

Figure 3.9   CRB Index, 1933–1951
SOURCE: Commodities Research Bureau, courtesy of Steve Saville.

CRB Spot Index (1967=100)
(monthly close) January 1947–January 2009   Index value

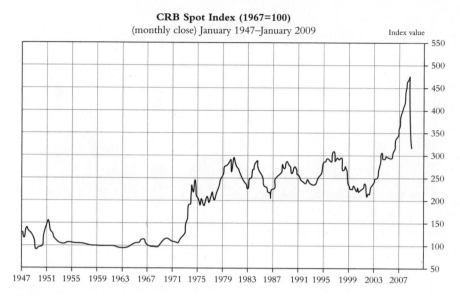

Figure 3.10 CRB Index, 1947–Present
SOURCE: Commodities Research Bureau, courtesy of Steve Saville.

Index going back to 1933–1951, and Figure 3.10 is the CRB Index from 1947 to the present. There have been two major bull markets in commodities (as far as we can trace them) in the past 80 years. The CRB Index advanced from 1933 to 1951. This basically coincides with the 1929–1949 downward cycle in stocks.

The second bull market in commodities saw the CRB Index bottom in 1963, go sideways for about 8 years, and then move higher from 1971 to 1980. In this bull market, the CRB increased over 200 percent. Figures 3.9 and 3.10 show these specific bull markets in graphical form.

Therefore, we can see that during the two major secular bear markets of this past century, commodities had huge bull markets.

The same goes for the secular bull markets for stocks. During these markets, the CRB Index went sideways while the Dow advanced mightily. From the 1951 to 1963–1971 periods, the stock market boomed over 600 percent but the CRB went nowhere. The CRB, from 1971 to 1980, then went into a powerful bull market at the same time as the Dow collapsed in real value. After peaking in 1980, the

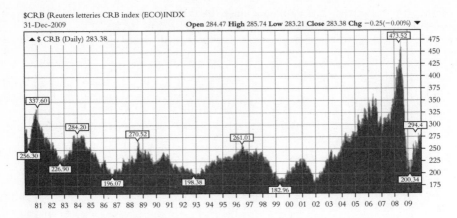

Figure 3.11   CRB Index Since 1980
SOURCE: Courtesy of StockCharts.com (http://stockcharts.com).

CRB crashed into 1982 and then went sideways into the 1982 period.
Figure 3.11 shows the CRB's trading action from 1982.

The CRB's action also dispels an important myth about stocks.
One of the great myths (I like to call it an out-and-out *lie*) we hear
about the economy and markets is that inflation picks up in times
of strong economies and deflation is a threat in weak economies.
However, as we can see by looking at Figure 3.9 through 3.11, in the
past century, whenever there has been a secular bull market in stocks
and a resultant boom in the economy, there has been a secular bear
market in commodities. When there have been longer periods of economic weakness, there have been inflation and higher commodity
prices! Therefore, inflation usually occurs during times of economic
weakness! (Just ask anyone who lived in Argentina or Bolivia in the
1980s, or Weimar Germany in the 1920s, and they will confirm that
economic weakness and high inflation can go together.)

Now let us look at Figure 3.11 in more detail. Note the long sideways pattern from 1980 to 2001. We can see a double bottom at the
1998 and 2001 periods. We then see strengthening in the CRB followed by a breakout of the old highs, followed by a spike into 2008 and
a crash that same year during the deleveraging, which we talked about
in Chapter 2. When funds got their margin calls and had to deleverage,
they had to dump their commodity holdings with everything else.

The Longer the Base, the More the Space

There is an old saying in technical terminology: "The longer the base, the more the space." This simply means that the longer that the market or commodity or stock goes sideways and the larger the base that it builds, the larger the subsequent breakout will become. The CRB built a 25-year base from 1980 to 2005. In 2005, the CRB finally started to break out but then had a setback in 2008.

It is rare for the market to build a 25-year base, break out, go up for a 2- to 3-year period, put in a major top, and then crash and start another major bear market. When the Dow broke through its 16-year base in 1982, it traded higher for the next 18 years. When commodities broke their 20-year trading range in 1971, they traded higher for another 9 years. Therefore, we think that this CRB breakout that began in 2005 should continue to proceed forward and produce higher prices for the next 10 to 15 years. This means that we should see a commodities top take place in the 2015–2020 period.

Does 1987 in Stocks Equal 2008 in Commodities?

In 1982, the Dow and S&P 500 saw the beginnings of huge bull markets. The market rocketed from 777 on the Dow in 1982 to over 2700 in the summer of 1987. It then crashed 35 percent into the autumn of 1987 and fell to under 1700. The market then spent most of the next year basing before taking off during the great bull market of the nineties that eventually saw the Dow climb to over 11,000 in 2000.

The way I see it is that the 2008 smash in commodities equals 1987. Commodities boomed in price from 2001 to 2008. It was a very strong seven-year period in a similar manner that 1982 to 1987 was a strong five-year period in equities. However, like 1987, the rally got too far ahead of itself and there was a sharp, severe correction within the context of the long-term secular trend. We must remember again that Mr. Market is not your friend. The market wants you to lose money. During secular bear markets there are sharp, short rallies designed to have you think that the worst is over; these rallies then sucker people into the market before the bear eats them up. During bull markets there are panics and sharp corrections and declines that scare people out of the market before the bull begins to rumble again. Anyone who sold in 1987 was a fool; if you had sold at the bottom of that market, you missed out on a nearly sevenfold gain into 2000. I feel that anyone who turned negative on commodities or sold out in 2008 will end up feeling foolish in the same way.

The year 2009 in commodities was a lot like 1988 in stocks: a year of basing. We should note that the Dow and S&P 500 did not fully break above their 1987 highs until 1991. Therefore, it might still take another few years for commodities to consolidate their huge gains from the 2008 spike. This makes sense from a fundamental and monetarist point of view. If Friedman is right and it takes a few years for inflation to trickle through the system, we should start to see a big uptick in inflation in the 2011–2012 period. This could be the time when commodities really start to take off.

The long-term secular bull market in commodities merges with our fundamental beliefs that the U.S. dollar is headed much lower and inflation much higher. If that is the case, commodities will rally. This is the great thing about the power of cycles. You don't even have to know anything about the fundamentals! Simply look at the figures. The stock market is currently in a secular bear market. When that happens, commodities go into a secular bull market! If our cycle analysis is right, you still want to hold commodities for basically the next 5 to 10 years and at that time you sell your commodities as that cycle ends and move your money back into traditional stocks.

You can play the commodities' bull market through ETFs that track the commodities themselves. The mainstay commodities to play are gold, silver, oil, and gasoline. Gold and silver will benefit from monetary inflation and the decline of the dollar. Not only are oil and gasoline hedges against a declining dollar but they also benefit from the supply/demand story. Our chapters on gold and other commodities explain the fundamental reasons why you will want to hold these items. Plus we also provide ideas on how to rotate from commodity to commodity in the bull market. For this chapter, we just need to know that commodities will continue to outperform in the coming years and are in a secular uptrend.

Emerging Markets

There is another trend I see going very well in the 2010s: emerging markets. In the 1970s, despite the United States being a huge part of the global economy and struggling during that decade, much of the rest of the world boomed. Even though it was a debt bubble, large parts of South America still grew strongly; the Japanese saw the continuation of their economic boom that started in the 1950s and 1960s. It was not only inflationary plays that boomed in the seventies but some emerging markets as well.

It was during that period that John Templeton made his mark in the world and became one of the world's first international investors. One of the reasons Templeton was able to outperform major U.S. indices in the sixties and seventies was because he had a large part of his funds placed in the booming Japanese stock market of the time.

With the bursting of the Super Bubble, we are going to see more funds flow into emerging markets. In Chapters 8 through 10 we concentrate solely on emerging markets and their fundamentals. However, for this chapter, we just want to see what cycle is operating at the present time.

Right now, China and India are going through their growth revolutions much like the British in the eighteenth century, the United States in its nineteenth-century industrial revolution, and Japan in its twentieth-century economic revolution. What is interesting is that, in the nineteenth century, the United States saw its longest bull stock market. Even with the bust of the 1870s, the United States saw an increase in equity prices for most of the period of 1853 to 1901, a period of 48 years.

Japan, too, saw a bust in the mid-sixties but also saw rising equity prices for most of its secular boom from 1950 to 1989. This was a period of nearly 40 years.

China opened up its economy in 1979 and really started to ramp up reforms large scale in the early nineties. India opened up in 1991 and started to grow en masse in the late nineties. Therefore, if we are about to see a mega-secular boom in each, much like the United States and Japan experienced in the nineteenth and twentieth centuries, we could see higher moves well into the 2020–2030 period.

In addition, as you will read in Chapters 8 and 9, with these markets about to expand their consumer base and still operating at low levels in terms of the nations' standards of living, their stock markets should be early in their booms.

There will be busts in between. The Bombay Stock Exchange (BSE) (Figure 3.12) and Shanghai Exchange (Figure 3.13) both saw nearly 70 percent declines during the financial crisis of 2008. However, in the long run, we will see these indices outperform. As you can see in

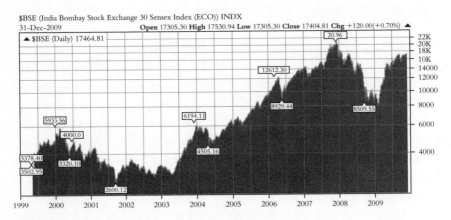

Figure 3.12   Bombay Stock Exchange, 1999–2009
SOURCE: Courtesy of StockCharts.com (http://stockcharts.com).

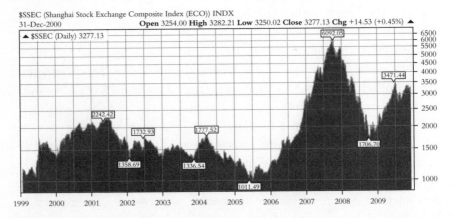

Figure 3.13   Shanghai Stock Exchange
SOURCE: Courtesy of StockCharts.com (http://stockcharts.com).

these two figures, both fell hard during the two bear markets of 2000–2001 and 2008. However, note that despite these large corrections, each market was up by a large amount over the course of the decade.

It should be noted, as well, that in each case, both bottomed before the U.S. markets did. India and China each bottomed in 2001, whereas U.S. markets moved lower into 2002 and both bottomed in October 2008, even though U.S. markets moved lower into the spring of 2009.

Figures 3.14 and 3.15 are the BSE and Shanghai averages divided by the S&P 500 over the past decade. In 2000, the BSE traded at 2.51 times the value of the S&P 500; today it trades at 16 times the value of the S&P 500 (Figure 3.14). This means that, over the past decade, Indian stocks have outperformed U.S. stocks by 600 percent. I expect this outperformance to continue over the course of the next decade.

We can see that the decade of the 2000s began with the Shanghai Exchange trading at roughly the same level as the S&P 500. It now trades at 2.80 times the S&P 500, meaning that Chinese stocks outperformed American stocks by almost 180 percent in the 2000s (Figure 3.15). Again, I think this trend will continue. Chapters 8 and 9 tell us the fundamental reasons behind this anticipated trend staying strongly on the same course in the future.

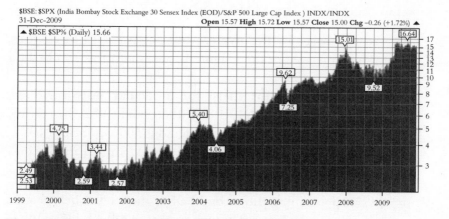

Figure 3.14   Bombay Stock Exchange versus S&P 500
SOURCE: Courtesy of StockCharts.com (http://stockcharts.com).

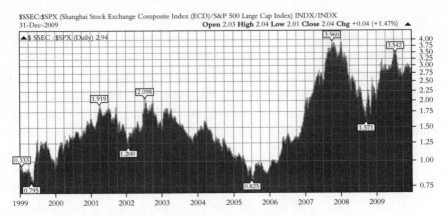

Figure 3.15 Shanghai Stock Exchange versus S&P 500
SOURCE: Courtesy of StockCharts.com (http://stockcharts.com).

Therefore, on top of strong commodities prices, as funds flow all over the world (rather than just into the United States as they did during the Super Bubble era), we will see funds flow into these emerging markets. I expect that this is another major secular trend we will see going forward.

It's Still Too Soon

From this chapter we can see it is still much too early for a secular bull market to begin in the United States. Why?

- **We are too early in the cycle.** Most cycles last 15 to 20 years, and at this time we are only about 10 years into this secular bear market cycle.
- **The valuations are not there for a secular bottom.** Every major secular bottom, 1921, 1949, 1966, and 1982, has started when the 10-year average P/E on the S&P 500 was below 10. At the bottom of the 2009 bear market, we hit 13 times earnings on a 10-year basis but we are still not nearly below 10.

We should be approaching the second half of the secular bear market cycle, which should produce a flat stock market with high inflation.

Commodities run countercyclical to the stock market. Therefore, we should expect that the 2008 commodity correction was a short-term correction and commodities should continue higher into that 2015–2020 period.

Finally, emerging markets such as India and China have outper-formed in the past 10 years. This should continue for the foreseeable future. They will have huge, sharp corrections but those should be used to add positions in those markets.

Chapter 4

The Fake Bull Market

Profiting from Cyclical Moves

I n Chapter 3, we talked about market cycles and how the stock market seems to repeat itself going from one 15- to 20-year cycle to the next 15- to 20-year cycle. We also discussed the nature of these cycles. We noted that early in the cycle we see the big crashes in the market and then, later in the cycle, we see a flat market with higher inflation.

These cycles look easy to discern on the surface. It looks like you buy the market when it is cheap, hold it for 10 to 20 years during the secular trend, and then sell when the stocks become expensive. However, the market has ways of shaking people out. During secular bull markets, there are short, sharp corrections that are very scary. In retrospect, the 1987 crash looks like a blip on the bull market of 1982–2000. However, the crash of 1987 at the time was very frightening. Comparisons to the Great Depression were published in the media and many thought that another depression was about to start.

None of this came to be. The market took a few months to bottom and then moved higher through the late eighties and nineties. In bull markets, corrections are short and sharp. The 1987 crash lasted 55 days; the correction of 1998 was 45 days in length. The bear market of 1990 was a mere 86 days. Corrections in bull markets are short and sharp but somewhat powerful. They shake people out and tend to keep some people out of the entire bull market until they finally give in and buy at the top. As the old adage goes: "Bull markets climb a wall of worry."

Bear markets are just the opposite. The primary trend in a secular bear market is sideways to down. There are huge down moves in a secular bear market. However, the market has short, sharp rallies in a secular downtrend. This acts in exactly the opposite manner as the short, sharp declines in secular bull markets. These increases sucker people in, not out. During these increases, people think that the worst is over. The economic news gets a little better; people are comforted that the market has climbed nearly 40, 50, 60, sometimes 100 percent in a very short period of time.

In this chapter, we will examine the bull markets of the past and examine the reasons why the recent rally of 2009–2010 should not be the start of another secular bull market cycle. We will also isolate the factors that are usually present when a genuine bull market rally takes place. We will illustrate that none of the major factors that are normally present at the beginning of a bull market are currently in place.

History of Bull Markets

Tables 4.1, 4.2, and 4.3 illustrate the history of bull markets during secular bear markets for the Dow Jones Industrial Average, S&P 500, and NASDAQ this century.

The technical definition of a *bull market* is a gain of 20 percent or more and the technical definition of a *bear market* is a decline of 20 percent or greater. So all of the moves in Tables 4.1, 4.2, and 4.3 (except for one in 1947) are at least 20 percent and they ended with a decline of 20 percent or greater.

As we can see, these bull markets contained within secular bear markets are not just little blips higher. From 1901 to the present, these

Table 4.1 Dow Rallies During Secular Bear Markets

Date of Bottom	Date of Top	Duration of Rally (days)	% Gain
1901–1921 Dow Jones Industrial Average Bear Market Rallies			
11/9/1901	1/19/1906	802	144.3
11/15/1907	11/19/1909	735	89.6
9/25/1911	9/30/1912	371	29.1
7/30/1914	11/21/1916	845	110.5
12/19/1917	11/3/1919	684	81.4
1929–1949 Dow Jones Industrial Average Bear Market Rallies			
11/23/1929	4/17/1930	155	48.0
7/8/1932	9/7/1932	61	93.9
2/27/1933	2/5/1934	343	120.8
7/26/1933	3/10/1937	958	127.3
3/31/1938	11/12/1938	226	60.1
4/8/1939	9/12/1939	157	28.4
4/28/1942	5/29/1946	1,492	128.7
5/17/1947	6/15/1948	395	18.4
1966–1982 Dow Jones Industrial Average Bear Market Rallies			
10/7/1966	12/3/1968	788	32.4
5/26/1970	4/28/1971	337	50.6
11/23/1971	1/22/1973	415	31.8
12/6/1974	9/21/1976	655	75.7
2/28/1978	9/8/1978	192	22.8
4/21/1980	4/27/1981	371	34.9
2000–2009 Dow Jones Industrial Average Bear Market Rallies			
9/21/2001	3/19/2002	179	29.1
10/9/2002	10/09/2007	1,826	94.4
3/6/2009	Present time		

SOURCE: Other than the 2002–2007 rally, which I compiled, the rest of the numbers are courtesy of the *Stock Trader's Almanac* with numbers compiled by Ned Davis Research Inc.

cyclical bull markets within the context of bear markets lasted anywhere from 61 to 1,827 days and saw markets move anywhere from 18.4 percent to 157.7 percent in value.

In addition, it appears that if the bear market is long and deep, the ensuing bounce-back rally tends to be more violent. For example, we can see that after the 1932 stock market bottom, where the market fell 89 percent, the S&P rallied over 111 percent in the two months that followed the bottom!

Table 4.2   S&P 500 Rallies During Secular Bear Markets

Date of Bottom	Date of Top	Duration of Rally (days)	% Gain
1929–1949 S&P 500 Bear Market Rallies			
11/13/1929	4/10/1930	148	46.8
6/1/1932	9/7/1932	98	111.6
2/27/1933	2/6/1934	344	113.7
3/14/1935	3/6/1937	723	106.9
3/31/1938	11/9/1938	223	62.2
4/8/1939	10/25/1939	200	29.8
4/28/1942	5/29/1946	1,492	157.7
5/17/1947	6/15/1948	395	24.4
1966–1982 S&P 500 Bear Market Rallies			
10/7/1966	11/29/1968	784	48.0
5/26/1970	4/28/1971	337	51.2
11/23/1971	1/11/1973	415	33.4
10/3/1974	9/21/1976	719	73.1
3/6/1978	9/12/1978	190	23.1
3/27/1980	11/28/1980	246	43.1
2000–2009 S&P 500 Bear Market Rallies			
9/21/2001	1/4/2002	105	21.4
10/9/2002	10/9/2007	1,826	101.5
3/6/2009	Published		

SOURCE: Other than the 2002–2007 rally, which I compiled, the rest of the numbers are courtesy of the *Stock Trader's Almanac* with numbers compiled by Ned Davis Research Inc.

Table 4.3   NASDAQ Rallies During Secular Bear Markets

Date of Bottom	Date of Top	Duration of Rally (days)	% Gain
1966–1982 NASDAQ Bear Market Rallies			
11/23/1971	1/11/1973	415	36.4
10/3/1974	7/15/1975	285	60.4
9/16/1975	9/12/1978	1,093	88.7
11/14/1978	2/8/1980	451	49.0
3/28/1980	5/29/1980	428	80.1
2000–2010 NASDAQ Bear Market Rallies			
9/21/2001	1/4/2002	105	44.7
10/9/2002	10/10/2007	1,827	152.4
3/6/2009	Present time		

SOURCE: Other than the 2002–2007 rally, which I compiled, the rest of the numbers are courtesy of the *Stock Trader's Almanac* with numbers compiled by Ned Davis Research Inc.

We can see also that the 2002–2007 rally was one of the strongest on record with the Dow gaining 92.4 percent, the S&P gaining 101.5 percent, and NASDAQ gaining 152.4 percent.

We can also see that there are a number of these rallies during the course of a long-term bull market. From 1901 to 1921, the Dow had five of these rallies. In the 1929–1949 bull market, the Dow and S&P had seven of these rallies and the 1966–1982 bear market had six of these rallies.

In the current bear market we have seen three such rallies:

1. The 2001–early 2002 rally
2. The 2002–2007 rally
3. The 2009 rally

On average, the three secular bear markets since 1900 have seen six of these rallies. From that simple statement alone, it is reasonable to anticipate about three or more of these rallies before the long-term bear market ends. Of course, if the long-term investor experiences three or more of these rallies, it is likely that the same investor will have to feel the pain inflicted by the long-term secular bear market.

As noted in Chapter 3, during the secular bear markets of 1901–1921, 1929–1949, and 1966–1982, there were major busts about seven years into those bear markets. The numbers reveal the pain: The 49 percent bear market of 1906–1907, the 49 percent decline from 1938 to 1939, and the 48.2 percent bear market of 1973–1974. (Please note that all numbers before 1929 are the Dow, and after that, they reflect the S&P 500. There are two reasons for our using the S&P 500 after 1929: (1) The S&P did not come into existence until 1923. (2) We feel it is a better gauge for the market as it is more diverse. Accordingly, after its emergence, we will use it as the measure for the markets.) Major rallies (e.g., the 89.6 percent rally of 1907–1909, the 1938 rally of 62.2 percent, and the 73.1 percent rally from 1974 to 1976) followed these declines.

This is where I feel we are in this cycle. We are seeing a very strong rally from a very strong decline (the 53 percent decline from 2007 to 2009 was the second worst bear market on record with only 1929–1932 being greater!) in the middle of the current cycle.

If history holds true, then it should mean that the market will top sometime in 2010 and what should ensue is what I call the "trading range of boredom" with the market seeing smaller moves higher and lower and essentially going sideways for the next 10 years.

I should note, too, that if the market peaks in 2010 or 2011 and sees another bear market, it would probably be minor in nature in nominal terms. The 1909–1911 bear market was 27.4 percent, the 1938–1939 bear market was 26.2 percent, and the 1976–1978 bear market saw the market drop 19.4 percent on the S&P 500 (which is not even technically a bear market) and 26.4 percent on the Dow Jones Industrial Average. One of the reasons behind these relatively tiny losses is the obvious fact that people are wiped out in the previous huge decline, so there is not the selling pressure there for the next bear market.

You will observe in the coming years that both the bulls and bears will be wrong. The bulls will declare that this is the start of a major bull market. During this current rally, we have heard many pronouncements that this is now 1982 all over again. The bulls tell us that the market has just blasted off and is about to start a multiyear bull market. In addition, the bears will tell us that the market is about to crash again, and that the Dow is going to 3000 and the S&P 500 will go to 400. However, history tells us that, rather than a crash, we should see multiple moves higher and lower with the market losing its value on an inflation-adjusted basis.

Reasons Why the Rally of 2009–2010 Should Not Be the Start of a Secular Bull Market

With the market having been so strong in 2009, people wonder why we are not starting another secular long-term bull market. The five reasons why this is not a long-term bull market are as follows:

1. **Valuation.** In Chapter 3 we outlined that the underlying purpose of these long-term cycles is a valuation readjustment. Stocks go from overvalued to undervalued in a secular bear market and undervalued to overvalued in a secular bull market. Valuations have gotten a lot better since the secular top in stocks in 2000. However,

they are nowhere near as good as they should be. At the bottom in March 2009, the S&P got to 13 times its 10-year average earnings. It is about 20 times earnings as we go to press. Secular bull markets usually start when stocks are trading under 10 times earnings. Therefore we can see that we still need a valuation contraction before moving on to a long-term bull market.

2. **Psychology.** This may seem strange because there was a near-collapse in 2008 and 2009. However, I do not think that long-term psychology is bearish enough. For example, *Time* magazine's title in December 2009 was a review of the decade. They called it "The Decade from Hell." But the article also stated why things should get better next decade. At a secular bear market bottom in stocks and the economy, you need the ultimate in negative sentiment. An excellent example is the "Death of Equities" article in *Newsweek* in 1979, which occurred just a few years before the launch of a huge secular bull market in stocks and the economy.

   Surely investors are not exuberant like they were in the late nineties, but they still think things will turn the corner. It is only when they lose this hope that we will see a major secular rally. For example, in 1949, virtually no one expected a huge secular UpTurn in the financial markets. Yet, that was the start of a huge bull market. We need more negative long-term sentiment before we can start a long-term secular bear market (see how investors feel about Japan today after 20 years of decline).

3. **Government policy is not allowing the system to cleanse itself.** There are purposes for booms and busts. The main purpose of a bust is for the system to cleanse itself. Recessions are a way of cleaning out the bad. All of the inefficient businesses that cannot survive the downturn are wiped out. All of the investors who cannot handle a downturn in stock prices sell out. Companies go into bankruptcy, sell off assets, and those assets go into strong hands; companies can streamline and come out stronger.

   However, we are not seeing the government letting the system cleanse itself. Part of the reason we are in this mess is because every time we have had a crisis in the past, such as the Long Term Capital Management blowup in 1998, or the Peso Crisis in 1994, the government stepped in to stop the decline from happening rather than letting it play out. This made the dislocations and bubbles bigger and bigger instead of allowing the system to cleanse itself. Everything came to a head in 2008 with the financial crisis, but instead of letting the system restructure itself, the government stepped in and gave money to the banks; the government created zombie banks in Bank of America and Citigroup. The government kept General Motors and Chrysler on life support even though these were two failing institutions. The worst part of bailouts is the obvious fact that taxpayers are going to be left holding the bag.

I think we will have a cleansing moment when we see the government itself go near bankrupt and be forced into major money printing and/or hyperinflation. This development will force government to cleanse itself and cut its size. When this happens, we will be set up for a multiyear secular boom.

For example, in 1933 and 1938, Roosevelt ramped up government spending to get the economy out of the depression of the early thirties and the recession of 1937–1938. Roosevelt's solution was to expand government and spend money to get the economy out of the depression and recession of that time. From 1932 to 1936, federal government spending increased from $4.3 billion to $9.2 billion.

In 1937, it fell back to $8.4 billion. However, when the economy fell back into recession in 1938, Roosevelt ramped up spending and, by 1940, it was back up to $10.1 billion. According to infosource.com, the unemployment rate in 1940 was still 14.6 percent. In addition, by 1942, the Dow was trading back under 100.

It can be argued that the policies of the New Deal caused mini-expansions in the economy from 1933 to 1937 and 1939 to 1940. However, they did not lead to a sustainable economic boom or expansion in employment.

Even Roosevelt's Treasury Secretary, Henry Morgenthau, admitted that the policies of spending to create both economic growth and jobs were failing. He was quoted as follows:

> We have tried spending money. We are spending more than we have ever spent before and it does not work. And I have just

one interest, and if I am wrong . . . somebody else can have my job. I want to see this country prosperous. I want to see people get a job. I want to see people get enough to eat. We have never made good on our promises. . . . I say after eight years of this Administration we have just as much unemployment as when we started . . . and an enormous debt to boot!

—Henry Morgenthau, FDR's Treasury Secretary, May 9, 1939

Government spending, to fight World War II, caused the unemployment rate to drop to 1.2 percent. However, we should note that, by 1944, most jobs created in the war effort were low paying. War is a time of rationing and not exactly a time when prosperity flows. In addition, the postwar economy fell back into recession and the stock market fell back as well.

However, the Obama administration has the exact opposite view. In 2009, the Obama administration announced a $700 billion stimulus program. Later in the year, it was announced that about $200 billion of the TARP program had been paid back. Instead of putting this money toward the deficit, the government announced it would use it to create "jobs." Of course, if government spending to create wealth were the key to prosperity, then Cuba would be the richest nation on earth.

On Tuesday, December 8, 2009, Obama made a statement about the economy at the Brookings Institute. Obama said that the nation must continue to "spend its way out of this recession." This may provide a short-term bounce in the economy in 2010. However, the long-term effects of increasing the national debt will result in increasing rates to attract investors to buy this debt. Increased interest expenses will eat into the government's revenues and will have a much longer detrimental impact.

As we outlined in our chapters on the Super Bubble and the debt bubble, the problem in the United States in the past 30 years has been too much debt and too much spending. You cannot solve this problem with more spending and debt. It is like being an alcoholic; when you are hung over, another shot of jack, sling of beer, and drinking off the hangover will help for another day. But at some time you are going to destroy your liver and your health.

As famed investor Jim Rogers colorfully put it in an interview on CNBC on December 10, 2009:

> The treasury secretary told us that we are going to solve the problem of too much debt and too much consumption with more debt and more consumption; that is like telling Tiger Woods you get another girlfriend and that will solve your problems or five more girlfriends to solve your problems.

The current administration's economic policy is not conducive to starting a long-term sustainable secular bull market in either the economy or stock market.

4. **Secular bear markets end with a whimper, not a bang.** Secular bear markets usually do not end with huge declines and collapses and crashes. Rather they end with a tame bear market accompanied by stocks that have done nothing for years. During the periods of 1921, 1949, and 1982, the stock market had done nothing for 16 to 20 years. It wasn't that people were panicking and everything collapsing but rather investors had just given up on the economy and stock market. It was a sort of quiet desperation and disbelief in the market. That disbelief was why stocks got so cheap at those times; that negative psychology set the tone for huge advances in the stock market and economy.

5. **Interest rates will rise.** Interest rates and stocks tend to be intertwined. When rates go down, it stimulates demand. Consumers and companies can borrow more cheaply. However, with the huge growth in Americans' spending and debt, U.S. rates will soon go higher to attract investors to buy all of the debt being issued. These higher rates will stifle economic growth. This will stifle stock returns over the next 10 years.

How Do We Know When the Real Stock Market Rally Will Start?

If the rally of 2009–2010 and any economic rebound will fizzle out faster than Ryan Leaf's quarterback career, how do we know when a rally will begin? We know about the secular bull and bear market cycles and the valuation cycle. However, the policy of a nation always plays a part. Policy is usually influenced by the part of the cycle you are in. For example, when the cycle was in the early stages in the early thirties, government spent. In contrast, the past few major economic booms and up-cycles in the stock market saw the same policy shifts occur that helped to launch the boom. All these booms and up-cycles saw the following three similar policy shifts:

1. **Interest rates will rise to kill inflation.** In the late teens, inflation roared as a consequence of World War I. In 1920, the Fed raised the discount rate from 4.25 percent to over 6 percent. This caused inflation to decline, and set the stage for the economic boom of the 1920s.

   Inflation was also a problem in the late forties after World War II. The Fed actually started to slowly raise interest rates after World War II. From 1946 to1953, the prime rate slowly went up from half a percent in 1946 to nearly 2 percent in 1953 and 4 percent by 1960.

   It may not sound like much, but you must remember it was the first time since the 1920s that rates had gone higher in a significant fashion.

   In the late seventies, inflation was ravaging the U.S. economy. Paul Volcker, the Fed chair, came in and raised interest rates numerous times from 5 percent on the fed funds rate (where it had been in 1976) to nearly 19 percent in 1980. Inflation fell and it set up the rally and bull market of the next 20 years.

2. **Government spending is cut, not increased.** In 1919, government spending had been soaring because of World War I. Federal government spending, which had been a mere 2.75 percent of GDP in 1914, increased to 24.13 percent of GDP by 1919. However, the government then cut spending as the war ended. By 1922, the federal government was spending only 5.13 percent of GDP, and by 1923, it was spending a mere 4.35 percent of GDP. This reduction in government spending allowed the private sector to expand and set things up for the boom of the twenties.

   In 1946, it was the same scenario. Federal government spending had expanded to 29.93 percent of GDP. The federal government reduced its size after the war, and by 1950 it was spending only 15.25 percent of GDP; by 1951 it was spending 14.42 percent of GDP.

In 1980, when Ronald Reagan came into office, the federal government spent 21.18 percent of GDP; by the year he left office in 1988, federal government spending had decreased to 20.86 percent of GDP. GDP grew in the eighties, so this was not an actual cut; but he did slow down the rate of government spending when compared to the size of the economy. When Lyndon Johnson came to power in 1964, government spending increased from 17.86 percent of GDP in 1964 to 20.86 percent in 1980; Reagan reversed the trend of the growth in the size of government relative to the economy.

3. **Taxes are cut.** In the late 1910s, income taxes on the top rate spiked to pay for World War I. Income tax, which had started in 1913 at a rate of about 1 percent for the lowest bracket and 7 percent for the highest bracket, increased to 6 percent for the lowest bracket and 77 percent for the highest bracket to pay for the war. From 1918 to the mid-1920s, income taxes were cut to 1.5 percent for the lowest bracket and 25 percent for the highest bracket.

Income taxes increased in the thirties to pay for the New Deal programs and World War II. In the forties, income taxes soared to 23 percent for the lowest bracket and 94 percent for the highest bracket. By the mid-fifties, taxes were cut from 23 to 20 percent for the lowest bracket and from 94 to 91 percent for the highest bracket.

When Reagan came into office, he slashed income tax rates. The lowest bracket, which was still 14 percent in the early eighties, was cut to 11 percent by 1988. The top rate, which was still over 70 percent in 1980, was cut to 28 percent by the end of Reagan's second term in 1988.

Accordingly, the three major secular bull market in stocks and booms in the economy of the past 100 years all started the same way:

1. Interest rates increased to kill inflation.
2. Government spending was cut or at the very least slowed in comparison to the size of the total economy.
3. Income taxes were cut.

Today, we have interest rates cut to near zero supposedly to stimulate the economy. Government spending is increasing at a rapid pace to pay for stimulus programs, bailouts, health care, and costs associated with the recession.

Income tax has not been raised. But there is a lot of talk of letting the Bush tax cuts expire; that will raise the top income tax rate. In addition, there is talk of surtaxes to help pay for the new health-care spending (which is really a way of raising taxes) not to mention the possibility of the Value Added Tax, and so forth. So we can see that taxes are nowhere close to rising.

Right now, the policies are totally opposite to what happened during past booms. This is why the rally of 2009 is just that—a rally. It is a false bull market that will turn into a declining bear market sometime in 2010 or 2011.

Prediction—The Ongoing Bear Market

As we have seen from the analysis in this chapter, the current environment is not conducive to the launch of a new major bull market cycle. Valuations are currently too high, the psychology of negativity is not intense enough yet, interest rates cannot go down, and a generally overwhelming despair and disbelief in the markets has not yet arrived. The necessary policies to kill inflation, government spending, and taxes are nowhere on the horizon. Our analysis of historical trends clearly points to an ongoing bear market (complete with bear market rallies) for many years into the future.

Part Three

INVESTMENT STRATEGIES FOR PROFITING FROM INFLATION

Chapter 5

Gold and Silver

Still a Good Investment Opportunity

Investing in gold over the most recent decade—the 2000s—now seems like a no-brainer. We have had the NASDAQ bubble, huge government deficits, housing bubble, two world wars, and so on. However, in 1998, that was not the case.

In my first book, *Stock Market Panic!*, published in 1998, it took a lot of guts to be as bullish on gold as I was. Everyone hated gold. At that time, gold was looked on as a barbarous relic of the past that had *no* purpose or point in the investment world. Gold had done nothing for 18 years. However, in that book, I stated that gold's time had come. It was my opinion that, due to the stock market being near a major secular top (it hit one just over a year after publication) and the coming inflation, we would see a huge uptick in the price of gold. At that time, gold was hovering just around $300 an ounce.

In this chapter, I illustrate why gold should be a major part of your investment strategy. I show you how to buy gold and also tell you why you should invest in gold's sister—silver.

Why Gold?

Many mainstream investors do not understand why gold is the investment of choice in bad times.

Gold has value because of its intrinsic scientific makeup. Gold is the most malleable and ductile of metals. It is estimated that one ounce of gold can be pounded into a thin sheet of 300 square feet.

To see the incredible versatility of gold, all you need to do is watch the History Channel's entertaining series, *Life After People*, which discusses various theories as to what will happen after the end of humankind. This show indicates that roads, buildings, bridges, and monuments will all start to break down within years of people leaving the earth. Some things break down within a few years; most manmade monuments are gone within a hundred years. However, in one episode, the show discusses the fate of the bars of gold that are beneath the Federal Reserve Bank in New York City. Most of what people would build would be gone within a few hundred years if humans left the earth. However, the $200 billion worth of gold that stands under the Federal Reserve would remain intact.

This dramatic illustration emphasizes the unique makeup of gold and why it has value. You cannot print and devalue an ounce of gold like you can a paper dollar. There is no need to try to deflate an asset that would survive for hundreds of millions of years—that fact alone tells you the true worth of gold. This is why it has value. It is virtually impossible for gold to be destroyed.

From the beginning of human monetary activity, people have used gold for transactions. Part of the reason is the malleability discussed. You can use gold in small doses for large transactions. For example, try and trade in oil. Let's say you were buying a used car in 2009. You bought this car for $11,000; let's say you did not want to pay in paper money and wanted to pay in gold. Ten ounces of gold in 2009 were worth about $11,000, whereas it takes about 140 barrels of oil to pay off the $11,000. So which is easier for the individual selling you the car: Give him 10 one-ounce gold coins or import 140 barrels of oil— nearly 600 gallons that weighs nearly 5,000 pounds? Which would the seller take? It would probably be the gold.

This is why gold has been used for centuries as money. It is rare, valuable, and easy to carry and use; most importantly, government cannot print its value away. For example, do we use still use the coins of the Romans or Greeks for transactions? No, but we do still use gold as a means of exchange. Gold is the ultimate exchange instrument and whenever paper currencies fail, then investors and individuals alike will always look to gold as their safe haven. Just imagine if you had lived in Zimbabwe during their hyperinflation or in South America in the 1980s during their hyperinflation. If you had had a few ounces of gold, that gold would have still bought the same amount of food and supplies. However, at the same time, your paper currency would have gone to zero. Gold is the insurance of the financial world.

For example, Figure 5.1 is the value of the U.S. dollar since the Federal Reserve was created in 1913. Note that $1 in 1913 now only

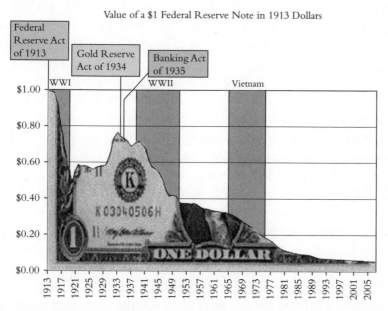

Value of a $1 Federal Reserve Note in 1913 Dollars

Figure 5.1   How the Federal Reserve Has Controlled Inflation
SOURCE: U.S. Bureau of Labor Statistics.

buys $0.05 of goods and/or services. Gold traded at $20 in 1913; it now trades near $1,200 as we go to print. The price of gold has increased 550 percent since 1913 and the value of the dollar has declined by 95 percent!

Reasons for the Gold Bull Market

One thing I do not want to do in this book is to harp on the history of gold or gold mining. What I want to do is to give you a quick overview of why gold is a hedge and then why you will still want to own gold in the coming years. Gold in the long term will hold its value, much like stocks in the long term (e.g., by *long term*, we mean hundreds of years) hold their value. However, gold also, like everything else, trades in cycles. I still think that gold is in its up-cycle and I want you to profit from that.

Let's get one myth about gold out of the way. Gold is one of the few commodities on earth that is not driven purely by supply and demand from jewelry or commercial uses. For example, jewelry demand in India, the largest consumer of gold, saw a recent huge drop-off. In 2009, according to the website bulllionvault.com, India saw its gold demand drop to 336 tonnes for the year, an 18-year low due to the high price of over $1,000 an ounce. Indian demand dropped so much that, in 2009, China overtook India as the number-one consumer of gold. In the 1980s and 1990s, the global economy boomed. Emerging nations started to, well, emerge. Consumer demand for gold increased all around the globe. Yet gold was stuck in a rut. Between 1982 and 2000, gold was stuck in a range between $250 and $550 an ounce. Despite booming global demand, gold did not move up in price Why? Because during that time the global economy was stable and the U.S. dollar was stable for the most part (and strong during the late nineties). There was no fear factor for investors to get into gold. So gold did nothing, despite increased consumer demand.

In addition, due to the weak global economy, jewelry demand all over the world was weak and down in 2009. Yet gold prices have boomed.

So if supply and demand by consumers does not drive the price of gold, what does? The four factors below do:

1. **Monetary policy and inflation.** Aggressive monetary policy or too much printed money will create inflation and cause gold to go up in price. As discussed in Chapters 1 and 2, the U.S. government is printing money and spending money like crazy. This should be inflationary and bullish for gold prices going forward.

2. **Market cycles.** Gold trades countercyclically to the stock market (as I will explain). During the periods of the bear stock market cycles, such as the seventies and the thirties, gold held its value while the stock market declined in value. Gold also has a cycle—but its cycle moves up while the stock market moves down. As we are not finished with the downward cycle in stocks, gold should continue to move higher.

3. **The U.S. dollar decline.** Gold also moves countercyclically toward the U.S. dollar; when the U.S. dollar goes down, gold tends to go up. It is no coincidence that, since 2001, the U.S. Dollar Index has lost nearly 33 percent of its value and gold has gained over 300 percent during that same timeframe. If Chapters 1 and 2 have convinced you that the U.S. government is implementing unsustainable spending policies, the dollar will continue to decline and the U.S. dollar may lose its backing as the world's reserve currency; then gold should do well in that timeframe.

4. **Buying from emerging market central banks.** What makes this gold boom more interesting than booms of the past is that this boom should occur during a time when the U.S. dollar loses its backing as the reserve currency of the world. For example, in November 2009, the Indian Central Bank announced that it was buying 200 tonnes of gold from the IMF. One would assume the Indian Central Bank is doing this as a way to diversify out of dollars and into gold. Table 5.1 illustrates the amount of gold that first-world countries own and the percentage of total reserves it represents. Table 5.2 shows the reserves that emerging countries own and the percentage of the total reserves it represents. Then I took the countries with the 50 largest amounts of foreign gold reserves in the world and separated into these two tables what the western

Table 5.1 Developed Nations Gold and Gold Share of National Forex Reserves

Gold (tonnes)	Gold's Share of National	Forex Reserves (%)
United States	8,133.5	68.7
Germany	3,407.6	64.6
Italy	2,451.8	63.4
France	2,435.4	64.2
Switzerland	1,040.1	28.8
Japan	765.2	2.4
Netherlands	612.5	51.7
European Central Bank	501.4	19.6
Portugal	382.5	83.8
United Kingdom	310.3	15.2
Spain	281.6	34.6
Austria	280.0	52.7
Belgium	227.5	31.8
Greece	112.4	71.5
Australia	79.9	6.0
Finland	49.1	15.1
Sweden	125.7	8.6
Total	21,440.0	36.43* (Average)

*I have weighted the average equally even though those banks have more reserves than others because we want to show the *average* of each separate central bank.
SOURCE: International Monetary Fund.

developed countries own and what is owned by the developing emerging-market countries.

Of the 50 largest foreign reserve countries in the world, 17 are in the west and 33 are in the emerging countries. The developed countries have about four times the amount of total reserves. As we can see from this study, the countries in the west have about 36.43 percent of their reserves in gold bullion. The emerging countries have only about 10.4 percent of their reserves in gold bullion. This means that if developing countries were to up their holdings in gold to developed countries' standards, they would have to more than triple their reserves in gold. In addition, as many of these developing countries are growing rapidly, common sense tells us that their foreign reserves will grow very quickly, which means they will have to buy even more. The recent 200-tonne purchase by the Indian Central Bank tells us that the appetite is there. Central bank buying by developing nations is another reason that gold prices should go up.

Table 5.2 Developing Nations Gold and Gold Share of National Forex Reserves

Gold (tonnes)	Gold's Share of National	Forex Reserves (%)
China	1,054.0	1.5
Russia	607.7	4.7
India	557.7	6.4
Taiwan	423.6	4.1
Venezuela	356.4	35.7
Lebanon	286.8	26.5
Algeria	173.6	3.8
Philippines	154.7	12.1
Libya	143.8	4.6
Saudi Arabia	143.0	10.2
Singapore	127.4	2.3
South Africa	124.8	10.5
Turkey	116.1	5.2
Romania	103.7	7.4
Poland	102.9	4.4
Thailand	84.0	2.1
Kuwait	79.0	11.4
Egypt	75.6	7.4
Kazakhstan	74.5	12.0
Indonesia	73.1	3.9
Pakistan	65.4	15.8
Argentina	54.7	3.7
Bulgaria	39.9	7.1
West African Economic and Monetary Union	36.5	9.9
Malaysia	36.4	1.3
Peru	34.7	3.6
Brazil	33.6	0.5
Slovakia	31.8	60.3
Bolivia	28.3	11.0
Belarus	28.3	23.1
Ukraine	26.9	3.2
Ecuador	26.3	19.1
Total	5305.2	10.4 (Average)

SOURCE: International Monetary Fund.

5. **Gold is a hedge in unstable times.** Similar to the fact that investors buy stocks when times are good, they buy gold when times are bad. It is no coincidence that the gold bull markets occurred during eras such as the 1870s, 1930s, 1970s, and 2000s

as the economy weakened and investors became worried. It should be noted that during these times of economic instability, investment demand picked up to the point where it can often make up for the loss in commercial demand in a secular gold bull market. For example, world gold demand, according to GFMS Inc., has increased from just over 50 tonnes in 2000 to an estimated 1,500 tonnes in 2009!

Now the question is this: With gold near $1,000 an ounce as we write, is it still a worthy investment? The answer is "yes." Gold, like the stock market, also trades in cycles (just like the secular bear stock market cycle). In our opinion, gold is, as we go to print, midway through its current cycle. Accordingly, the gold bull market is only half complete. However, whereas stocks are in a secular bear market, gold currently is in a secular bull market. So if you have missed the gold bull market to date, there still is time for you to prosper from it.

Gold Is Not Dirt-Cheap, but It Is Still Cheap

In 1998, gold was dirt-cheap. When you compared gold to anything— the price of a suit, a loaf of bread, stocks, bonds, and so on—it was cheap. It was trading near historically low levels. Figure 5.2 is the inflation-adjusted price of gold. Note that the 2000 inflation-adjusted low in gold saw gold retract nearly all of its gains garnered during the 1970s bull market. That low put gold back at 1971 levels. Think of anything you buy: corn starch, ice, hamburgers, and cars; was anything trading at 1971 levels in 1998? This told us how cheap gold had become.

As we can see in Figure 5.2, gold has had a nice run off this bottom in inflation-adjusted terms. Gold has increased about threefold since bottoming in the year 2000. However, note that this chart uses CPI numbers and, as we stated in Chapters 2 and 3, the government underreports CPI, which probably means the adjusted all-time high is even higher.

Let's say, for argument's sake, that gold obtains, in the future, the same percentage increase that it had in the seventies when it increased from $35 an ounce to over $850 an ounce or about a 2,300 percent gain. If you take gold from the low of $250 an ounce in 2001 and if it

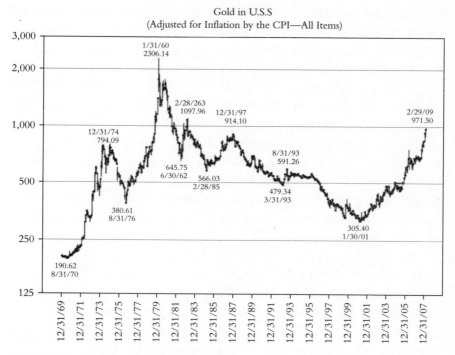

Figure 5.2   Inflation-Adjusted Gold Price
SOURCE: www.thechartstore.com. Copyright 2008.

were to have a similar gain in percentage terms, you would get a gold price of nearly $6,000 an ounce.

Also note that in the 1970s, gold had an inflation-adjusted gain of over 1,000 percent (from $190 in today's dollars in 1970 to over $2,300 in 1980). This means that inflation-adjusted gold could still triple from its current levels. It just matters how much inflation there is. It simply comes down to how much money the government prints. If there is no inflation (highly unlikely), gold could triple from current levels. If massive amounts of inflation are created, gold could go much higher in nominal terms.

The Best Long-Term Gold Indicator

My favorite long-term indicator for gold is the *Dow-to-Gold* indicator. I like it because, in very simple terms, it tells you why you should be willing to wait out the ups and downs in the gold market and ride out

the long-term trend, which is how you really make money in major
trends. Figure 5.3 depicts the Dow-to-Gold ratio. This ratio simply
divides the price of the Dow by an ounce of gold to find out how
many ounces of gold it takes to buy the Dow. It is a reflection of the
cycles we have told you about. During the secular bear market in stocks,
the Dow does poorly and gold does well. (For example, in the thirties, the
Dow went from 380 to 42 and gold jumped from $20 to $35 an ounce.
In the bear market of the seventies, the Dow lost 75 percent adjusted
for inflation, whereas gold gained over 1,200 percent adjusted for inflation.) In secular bull markets for stocks, the Dow does well and gold
poorly. We can see from this chart that the 1920s, 1950s, 1960s, 1980s,
and 1990s were all times when stocks vastly outperformed the price
of gold.

By the late twenties, it took nearly 15 ounces of gold to buy one
share of the Dow, and in the late sixties, it took nearly 30 ounces of
gold to buy a share of the Dow. Things got even more out of control
during the bull market of the nineties and it took nearly 44 ounces of
gold to buy the Dow Jones in 2000! Basically, when it starts to take
more than 15 to 20 ounces of gold to buy the Dow Jones, the Dow
Jones and U.S. stocks are becoming expensive and gold is becoming
cheap. It is at this time that you want to start edging into gold and
edging out of stocks.

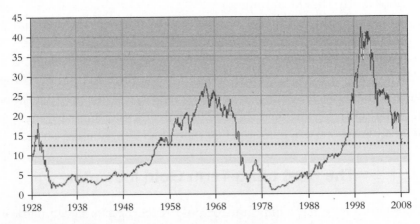

Figure 5.3   Eighty Years of the Dow-to-Gold Ratio
SOURCE: www.bullionvault.com.

This is a very long-term indicator. You just do not jump out of stocks right away but rather you do it over a number of years. However, if you had adopted this type of investing approach, it would have worked out very well over the past hundred years—assuming of course that your health and circumstances permitted you to live that long. By doing this, you would have been selling the Dow Jones at over 300 in 1929 and buying gold at $20 an ounce (until it was made illegal for Americans to own gold when it stood at $35 an ounce in 1932). However, when you sold your gold to the government you would have had a 75 percent gain while the Dow Jones lost over 89 percent of its value.

Americans could not buy gold in the sixties. However, around the world you could. So let's just say you could have purchased gold in the mid-sixties when the Dow-to-Gold ratio got over 15 and 20 to 1 and near 30 to 1 at the top for the Dow. You would have been buying gold at $35 and selling the Dow on average in the 700–800 range. After you made these gold purchases, the Dow kept in the 550–1,000 range from 1966 to 1982, losing 74 percent of its value when adjusted for inflation, whereas gold jumped over 1,200 percent after inflation!

In the late nineties, things again got out of whack. By the mid-nineties, the Dow-to-Gold ratio began to climb to 25 to 1 and higher, eventually peaking at 44 to 1. Again, when the ratio began to get out of whack in the mid-nineties, if you had begun to sell out of the Dow stocks in the 7000 to 8000 range in the mid-nineties all the way to 11,000 in 2000 and had begun to accumulate gold in the $250–$400 range at the same time, you would have made out well. From 2000 to 2010, the Dow Jones was again stuck in a range of 6500–14,000, spending most of its time in the 9,000–12,000 range and losing much of its value inflation adjusted, whereas gold climbed from $250 an ounce to over $1,100 an ounce! The Dow-to-Gold ratio wins again!

On the other side of the coin, you want to start to accumulate Dow Jones stocks and sell gold when the ratio gets under 2 to 1 and especially less than 1.5 to 1.

In 1933, the Dow Jones bottomed at a level of 48; gold stood at $35 an ounce or at a ratio of about 1.3 to 1. Gold was frozen in price and did not move from those levels, whereas the Dow Jones took off, climbing to over 190 by 1937, to 400 by 1955, and 1000 in 1966. Gold did nothing in those 35 years.

In 1980, as inflation blew off, so did gold, with gold hitting a high of over $850 an ounce. At this time the Dow-to-Gold ratio fell to 1.1 to 1. If you had bought the Dow then, you would have seen the Dow increase from under 900 to over 11,000 in the next 20 years, whereas you would have seen gold fall from $850 an ounce to $250 an ounce in the next 20 years.

This is a great long-term method of trading secular bull and bear markets for both gold and equities.

As we write, the Dow-to-Gold ratio is about 9.5 to 1 with the Dow trading at 10,400 and gold at about $1,100. This means that we are no longer at the dirt-cheap levels of 1999 to 2001. However, it also means that we are just midway in the gold bull market and gold is not yet expensive compared to the Dow.

My bottom line is this: In 1992, the Dow Jones Average traded at around 3,500; it was just over four times above its low of 777 reached in 1982 when the bull market began. It still had about 8 years left and another triple left in the bull market. In 2010, gold trades at $1,100, just over four times higher than where it was at its low in 2001 at $250 an ounce. Like the Dow in 1992, I figure that gold has about 8 years left and at least another triple in its bull market. Our Dow-to-Gold ratio confirms this view.

Great Buying Opportunity Coming

I also have some good news. There is a big drop in gold coming sometime in the future and it will present a great buying opportunity. Cycles, as we have previously observed, all follow each other. In the mid-seventies, there was a huge drop in gold prices. From December 1974 to September 1976, gold prices dropped from $195.00 to $103.50 (as per the Comex weekly price) for a drop of 46.9 percent. At that time all the naysayers came out and said that the gold bull market was over. Gold built a base and zoomed to over $800 an ounce by 1980.

From 2000 to 2009, all of the declines in gold have been rather subdued. They have been controlled drops of about 30 percent or so. I am looking for this larger drop to occur, which will launch the final blow-off phase of the gold bull market. It is impossible to predict precisely when it will occur. I don't know if gold will go up to $1,500 and then down to $900 or to $2,000 an ounce and then down to $1,100 in a correction before again taking off. But I do think we will see this correction and this will in turn bring all of the naysayers and gold bears out of hibernation; this dramatic drop will also set the stage for a huge price increase.

However, I do have a final warning. If we get the Dow-to-Gold ratio down to 1.5 to 1 or lower, it will not last long. If I am correct in my cycle analysis and we do not see a huge drop in stock prices but rather a long-term trading range develop, gold and the Dow should meet somewhere around 10,000. However, this will not last long; at this point gold will become a bubble, just like the NASDAQ in 2000 or Japanese stocks in the late eighties. It took just over two years for gold to collapse from $850 an ounce in 1980 to under $300 an ounce in mid-1982. Therefore, you will have to be nimble and not get greedy and be flexible to sell at a gold top. It will be psychologically difficult to sell at that time as all of the economic news will be terrible, unemployment will be sky high, and inflation should be skyrocketing. However, we must stick to the trading disciplines dictated to us by long-term cycles.

Ways to Buy Gold

We can see that everything is in line for gold to move higher in the coming years. So the question arises, If gold is in a long-term bull market, how can one make money in gold?

You can buy the physical metal itself. This is how many gold bugs (a *gold bug* is someone who is always bullish on gold) like to own gold. Many gold bugs see our society breaking down and paper money having no worth whatsoever. They see the financial system breaking down and the only means of exchange being gold and silver. Under this scenario, it is their opinion that you will need gold coins to use as currency. I won't go that far. I see inflation but I do not see this type of Armageddon scenario.

However, I still see gold coins and bullion as an important part of an investor's portfolio. If inflation does get out of control, having these on hand can be of great use. Just think of anyone who had gold coins in the hyperinflations of Argentina, Bolivia, or Zimbabwe. Those citizens would still be able to purchase goods and services with gold coins even as the purchasing power of the currency collapsed.

From an investment point of view you can also buy gold ETFs and funds and gold stocks, all of which will be discussed in this chapter.

Gold Coins

The easiest way to purchase gold is by purchasing gold coins. You can buy gold bars if you want to buy a large amount, but coins are light, can be carried around, and make the most sense.

Many governments issue and mint gold coins. Most of these coins are 99.9 percent pure gold. Most tend to be about an ounce in size. Some coins include the South African Kruggerand, the American Gold Eagle, the Mexican Gold Libertad, the British Britannia, the Canadian Maple Leaf, and the Chinese Panda.

Of those, my favorites are the South African Kruggerand, the Canadian Maple Leaf, and the Brittania. The American Gold Eagle is a top-tier coin in its own right; however, I am a bit more leery of U.S. gold coins because in 1933 Roosevelt made gold illegal to own. On April 5, 1933, Roosevelt signed Executive Order 6102, "forbidding the hoarding of Gold Coins, Gold Bullion, and Gold Certificates" by U.S. citizens. In 1933, approximately 500 tonnes of gold were turned into the U.S. Treasury "voluntarily" at the exchange rate of $20.67 per troy ounce. The government then turned around and increased the official price to $35 an ounce in 1934. It is fantastic the way governments work: forcing people to sell their gold to the government at $20.67 and then revaluing it nearly 75 percent higher just one year later—I wish I could make my portfolio go up like that overnight! I do not think this will occur again, but it is just a bit of a history lesson about the seizure of gold in the United States.

This is why I recommend staying away from U.S. gold coins and that Americans keep some of their gold coins outside of the country. For example, gold coins could be stored in a safety deposit box in a bank in England, Switzerland, or Canada. If you are foreigner living in the United States, a word to the wise: Foreigners who lived in the States in 1933 had their gold seized as well. I don't think the Americans will seize gold this time around; however, as they have done it before, we cannot remove it from the realm of possibilities.

There are numerous gold coin dealers you can buy gold from. A few are listed at the end of this of book if you are interested in purchasing gold using this method.

Gold Bullion ETFs and Closed-End Funds

A *closed-end fund* is a fund that trades on the stock market, as opposed to an *open-end fund*, which holds stocks and actually has to physically give you your funds back from its own portfolio when you sell it. An *exchange-traded fund (ETF)* also holds assets and trades on the stock market.

GLD is a gold ETF that holds gold and trades on the New York Stock Exchange. Other funds include the Central Fund of Canada (CEF NYSE) and Gold Trust Units (GTU to gold NYSE). These funds trade on the NYSE. The Central Fund of Canada, in addition to gold, also holds silver. As these are closed-end funds, they often trade at discounts and premiums to their Net Asset Value (the average per-share value of the fund's holdings).

The Net Asset Value (NAV) of these funds is also a great way to trade the gold bull market. When a closed-end fund trades too much above or at too high a premium above its Net Asset Value, it is a sign that a market is overheated. Investors are chasing that fund and pushing it above its real value. On the opposite side, when the Net Asset Value of a closed-end fund trades at too far a discount to its real value, it can be a sign that investors are too bearish and have pushed the value of the fund too far below its real value. Big premiums tend to happen at tops and discounts at bottoms.

For example, when the Central Fund of Canada trades at a premium of 15 percent or greater above its Net Asset Value, gold often sees a short-term-to-intermediate-term top. When the Gold Trust Units trades at a 15 percent or higher premium, the same result usually occurs. This occurred at the early 2003 and mid-2008 intermediate tops in gold.

However, when both trade at minimal premiums and discounts, it can mark a bottom in gold prices. This occurred at the late 2008 bottom in gold.

The moral of the story is: *Do not* chase these funds if you choose to buy them. If you see the Central Fund of Canada or Gold Trust Units trading at a large premium to their Net Asset Value, be patient and wait for a correction in the funds.

As you can see, there are many ways to purchase gold; you can purchase gold bullion and/or gold ETFs. If you are truly worried about the financial system, you will probably want to own coins as they are the ultimate hedge. However, if you want the liquidity of a stock, you might want to look at the gold-traded ETFs and funds that trade on the New York Stock Exchange.

Gold Stocks

Gold stocks are another great way to play the gold bull market. Gold stocks can actually provide more leverage to the price of gold's potential increases.

Gold stocks possess much more leverage than the price of gold. For example, the Amex Gold and Silver Index (known as the HUI) bottomed in November 2000 at a level of 42; as we go to press, the HUI trades at a level of about 420. This is an increase of 1,000 percent in the past 10 years! Over the same time, gold bullion is up just over 400 percent. Of course, gold stocks have greater risk on the downside. For example, during the financial panic of 2008, gold bullion fell 30 percent in price from its high in March 2008 to its low in November 2008. In contrast, over the same period, the HUI Index fell over 70 percent in price!

We must remember that, for all the positives that we are going to talk about in regard to gold stocks, they are still just that: stocks! When hedge funds had to liquidate during the crash of 2008, they had to sell their gold stocks along with everything else. And even though gold stocks performed marvelously during the 1930s, they crashed with the market on Black Monday in 1929. During a crash in the market, gold stocks will fall with everything else.

Gold stocks possess more leverage for two reasons: (1) profits and (2) reserves. It is simply mathematics: gold stocks are valued on how much money they make and the value of their reserves (or potential future *production* from those reserves) in the ground. When gold goes up in price, it increases both profits and reserves faster than the increase in the gold price. Please note that this is not a book to teach you about the types of gold mining methods, types of mines, and so forth.

Allow me to give you a simple example of how valuations of mining companies work. Let's say that Company ABC produces 1 million ounces of gold at a cost of $500 an ounce and has about 5 million ounces in reserves that are economical. The company has another 5 million of potential reserves, but that is gold that is deeper in the ground; it needs gold prices of $700 or greater for these potential reserves to become economical. At the same time, gold is trading at $501 an ounce; so company ABC makes about $1 per ounce on every ounce of gold it produces. Over the following year, gold increases to $750 an ounce. Inflation is about 10 percent and Company ABC's cost of production increases to $550 per ounce of gold produced. Now, in our example, gold has increased about 50 percent in price from $501 to $750 an ounce. However, ABC's profits increase from $1 an ounce to $250 an ounce—250 times! Plus, all of the reserves that were uneconomical at $500 are now economical at $750. So now the company has nearly 10 million economical ounces in the ground, double what it had when gold was priced at $500 an ounce. Therefore, even though gold goes up merely 50 percent, the company's bottom line and reserves in the ground have both increased much more than 50 percent. Therein lies the leverage of gold stocks.

Types of Gold Stocks

The various kinds of gold stocks are as follows:

- **Large caps.** These are gold stocks that trade on the New York Stock Exchange, AMEX, or Toronto Stock Exchange. They are companies that have numerous properties all over the world and have millions of ounces in gold production.
- **Mid-tiers.** These are smaller gold stocks that have one or two producing properties and have a small amount of production. Most of these types of companies tend to trade on the AMEX, TSX

Exchange, and TSX Venture Exchange. The AMEX trades in the United States and the other two trade in Canada.

- **Junior gold-mining stocks.** These are small exploration companies that are just looking for gold. They are extremely volatile and are often dependent on their ability to raise funds to find gold. These companies usually possess no revenues. Most of these companies trade on the TSX Venture Exchange in Canada.

Large Caps

These are the types of stocks that most investors should invest in. Large caps are liquid and diversified around the world. Large-cap gold stocks include companies such as Agnico Eagle, Newmont Mining, Barrick Gold, Yamana Gold, Eldorado Gold, plus many more. The advantages of these companies are that they are liquid, are easy to trade, and most of them trade on the New York Stock Exchange. These stocks, for the most part, have outperformed the price of gold since gold started its bull market in 2000. The following companies are listed in the Amex Gold Bugs Index (HUI) along with their ticker and weighting in the index:

- Barrick Gold ABX 15.66%
- Goldcorp Inc GG 14.92%
- Newmont Mining NEM 10.11%
- Comp de Minas Buenaventura Ads BVN 5.16%
- Hecla Mining HL 5.15%
- Coeur d'Alene Mines CDE 5.00%
- Gold Fields Ltd Adr GFI 5.00%
- Agnico Eagle Mines AEM 4.98%
- Kinross Gold KGC 4.93%
- Yamana Gold AUY 4.92%
- Harmony Gold Mining Adr HMY 4.92%
- Randgold Resources Ads GOLD 4.90%
- Eldorado Gold Corp EGO 4.87%
- Anglogold Ashanti Ltd Ads AU 4.76%
- Iamgoldcorp IAG 4.72%

Figure 5.4   Barron's Gold Stocks Index Price from 1938 to 2008
SOURCE: www.sharelynx.net

The profit potential for these companies is huge. We noted earlier that the HUI Index is up about 1,000 percent since the gold bull market started in year 2000. Some may think that the bull market is over and done with given those sorts of gains. However, if the gold stock bull market of 1962 to 1980 is any indication, we could just be getting started. Figure 5.4 is the Barron's Gold Stocks Index price from 1938 to 2008.

In the 1960s and 1970s, the Barron's Gold Stock Index was the gauge for gold stocks. It began its 18-year bull market in 1962 and ended it in 1980 (what a surprise—another 18-year cycle!). In 1962, the Barron's Gold Stock Index began its bull market around 30; it then soared to over 1,200 in 1980 for a gain of 4,000 percent! This would tell us that if the HUI were to see a similar increase during this bull market, it could increase to a level of around 1,700; that would still represent a gain of nearly 400 percent from current levels! These gains could be even greater as the fundamentals behind the gold price going higher and weakness of the U.S. dollar are both much greater at the moment than they were in the seventies.

Royalty Gold Companies—My Favorite Model My favorite model for gold companies is the *royalty gold company*. These are companies that, through an investment in another company or direct investment in a mine, receive a percentage of revenues or profits from that mine or company or a direct equity interest in the company.

Mining is a dirty business. And I do not just mean drilling hundreds of feet below the ground. You have to deal with politics and all sorts of natural mishaps, which means dealing with permits, licenses, rock falls, floods, unions, and *yuck*, politicians! The advantage of a royalty company is that it does not have to deal with any of these things. It simply finds quality projects or companies; it they invests in them and receives a percentage of the revenue. The most famous royalty company was Franco Nevada, which was created in 1983. Created by famous investor Pierre Lassonde, Franco Nevada was taken over by Newmont Mining. Ten thousand dollars invested in Franco Nevada in 1983 would be worth over $1.5 million today at Newmont's current price. Current royalty gold companies include a new reincarnation of Franco Nevada, Royal Gold, and Aberdeen International Inc.

Rules for Trading Gold Stocks What I think makes this book different is that I am not just going to tell you that the United States is collapsing and to buy gold and gold stocks and then predict that you are guaranteed to make money. I am going to give you tips on how to trade the gold bull market and how to find companies that will outperform. We must remember that all gold stocks are not created equal!

Rule #1: Look for Companies That Do Not Hedge Hedging is a very common method used in the commodities market to limit (*hedge*) risk. What you do is simply sell your production forward at a fixed price before you sell it or deliver it. This is a way of mitigating the huge up-and-down moves that can be found in the commodities markets and, accordingly, limit risk. For example, let's say you sell 100,000 ounces of gold forward at a specific date for $500 an ounce. That means it doesn't matter if gold is trading at $300 or $700 at the time of sale. You sell the gold for $500.

This method is fine if it is used as a way of securing a percentage of your production against the extreme fluctuations of the commodities markets, say 10 to 20 percent. The problem that happened in the nineties is that many companies used hedging as a form of staying alive. Many companies were hedging up to 50 or 60 percent of their production. We must remember one of the purposes of busts is to eliminate the inefficient companies. However, when gold fell under $300, many companies had sold forward much of their production at $350 or $400 an ounce. This kept inefficient mines that should have been shut down in production; these mines ultimately added to the supply on the market and helped to keep the gold market depressed. Hedging was supposed to be a way of limiting risk; it was not designed as a way for a company to keep itself on life support.

However, the tide turned in the 2000s when gold prices soared. All of a sudden, companies that had hedged found themselves in terrible situations. They had sold production forward at $350, $400, $500 an ounce. Gold started to soar to $600, $700, $800 an ounce and higher and these companies were locked in at the lower price at which they had sold forward. These were gold companies that were not profiting from an increase in the price of gold—how ironic!

This policy showed up in the numbers. Earlier, we mentioned that the Amex Gold Index (HUI) had jumped nearly 1,000 percent since bottoming in 2000. This index has a heavier weighting in companies that do not hedge. The other major gold index—the Philadelphia Gold and Silver Index (XAU)—had a heavier weighting in companies that hedged in its listings; it has climbed merely about 400 percent since 2000!

The good news is this: Most gold companies have now closed out virtually all of their hedges. Barrick Gold and Anglo American, which were two of the largest hedgers in the world, announced in 2009 that they were closing out nearly all of their hedges.

However, I am sure that hedging will not disappear. The first thing you must do when looking at a gold company is look at its hedged position. If it is too large, *stay away!* You want to invest in gold companies that can actually profit from the increase in the price of gold.

Rule #2: Look for Companies That Are Increasing Gold Production and Reserves One of the major problems that large-cap companies such as Barrick Gold and Newmont have had in recent years is that they cannot replace the amount of gold they are producing and depleting from their reserves. Remember, gold companies are also valued on the amount of reserves or future production they have in the ground. Therefore, if gold goes up and a company cannot increase its reserves, its stock will underperform. When you look at a gold company, you cannot just look at the most recent quarterly earnings. You must look and see if a company has mines coming online and if it is increasing its production in reserves. If you have rising gold prices, increasing reserves, and increasing production, that is the golden trifecta!

Rule #3: Be Aware That Gold Stocks Are Volatile! If you are an investor who has been trading the major averages or stock market for a while, gold stocks will shock you with their volatility. History tells us that, in the stock market, you see about a 10 percent correction every year or two and you see a bear market of 20 percent about every 6 years or so. Let me give you a quick example of how other gold stocks perform differently from the general stock market. In my newsletter (*Gold Stock Advisor*), I performed a small study of the volatility of the HUI index from the end of 2006 to the end of 2009. For the purpose of this study, I simply went back and saw how many 10 and 20 percent corrections the HUI index had in that timeframe. What I found was very interesting.

From December 2006 to January 2010, the HUI saw 14 declines of 10 percent or greater; 8 of those declines were of 20 percent or greater. This means that a 10 percent decline occurred roughly once every 2.6 months and a 20 percent decline occurred once every 4.5 months. Therefore, something that happened in the stock market roughly once every 6 years happened in gold stocks two to three times a year! In addition, if you look at Figure 5.3 again, you will see that, during the great gold stock bull market of 1962 to 1980, the Barron's gold index had two declines of 50 percent or greater, despite climbing over 4,000 percent during that time period. We must remember that, in the 110-year history of the Dow Jones Industrial Average, it has had only two declines of 50 percent or greater (1929–1932 and 2007–2009). Therefore, what took the stock market 110 years to accomplish happened in gold stocks in 18 years and that was during a huge bull market in gold stocks!

From 2000 to 2009, the HUI Index has seen 5 declines of 30 percent or more and one huge decline of more than 70 percent in 2008. No securities on earth are as volatile as gold stocks.

Rule #4: Core and Trading Position—Sell Strength and Buy Weakness, and Do Not Chase! So we can see that the long-term trend of gold and gold stocks should be up. This is why I recommend investors have two types of positions: a core and a trading position. Despite the volatility, you should be able to live through the volatility with some of your position. As the long-term trend is up, you should be willing to allocate a certain amount of your capital to gold and/or gold stocks and be willing to wait out the volatility.

However, you should also have a small amount of capital that is committed to the trading of gold stocks to take advantage of this volatility. However, you must be disciplined with this. *Never* chase gold stocks and *never* panic and sell on weakness. Sell into the rally and quietly await the pullbacks. If you get one of those 10 percent pullbacks, put some capital into the gold stocks. If you get a 20 percent pullback, buy a bit more. And if you are lucky enough to see another crash in gold stocks, like 2008, leave some powder dry so you can take advantage of dirt-cheap levels.

Using this two-pronged approach, you should be able to take advantage of the ongoing gold stocks' bull market. Ideally, you will have both of the following:

1. A long-term position so that you do not miss out on the long-term trend
2. A trading position to take advantage of volatility

Rule #5: Be Aware That Gold Stocks Move Faster Compared to Gold on Both the Upside and Downside Gold stocks, as we stated earlier in this chapter, move more than gold to the upside and more than gold to the downside. When trading gold and gold stocks, you can use this volatility to your advantage.

Throughout many years, gold stocks have traded in a direct correlation to the price of gold. When gauging this correlation, we use the

HUI-to-Gold and XAU-to-Gold ratios. The calculation of these ratios is quite simple. You merely divide the price of the indices and then divide them by the price of gold. This gives you a ratio or percentage. For example, if the HUI is trading at 400 and gold is $1,000 an ounce, the ratio is 40 percent.

When gold stocks go up too fast in relation to gold, it is a sign that the gold market is too frothy. At market tops, psychology becomes too bullish and people speculate too much and they go into riskier investments. So, when gold stocks go up too fast in relation to gold, this is a sign of excess speculation. When gold stocks are too high in relation to gold, a correction usually starts. The same goes at a bottom: gold stocks sell off faster, and when they fall too far in correlation to gold, you usually get a bottom in gold and gold stocks.

Figures 5.5 and 5.6 show the HUI and XAU-to-Gold ratios. Historically, whenever the XAU-to-Gold ratio has gone above 26 percent and the HUI ratio above 55 percent, it means that gold stocks are expensive compared to gold; accordingly, gold and gold stocks should correct. If, for example, gold was $1,000 and the XAU was 260 and the HUI 550, that would mean that gold stocks were expensive and due for a correction. This occurred at the 2002, 2003, and 2006

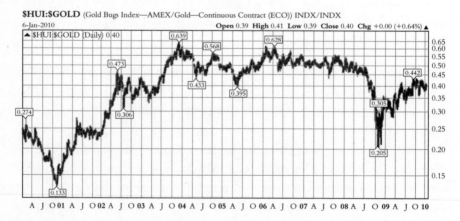

Figure 5.5   HUI–to–Gold Ratio
SOURCE: Courtesy of StockCharts.com (http://stockcharts.com).

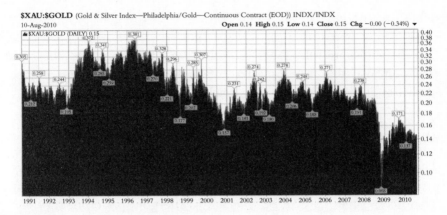

Figure 5.6 XAU-to-Gold Ratio
SOURCE: Courtesy of StockCharts.com (http://stockcharts.com).

intermediate tops in gold and gold stocks, just before gold stocks cor-
rected 35 percent or greater in the months following these tops.

On the flipside, we look for XAU-to-Gold ratios of under 19
percent and HUI-to-Gold ratios of under 45 percent for bottoms in
the gold price. This occurred at the spring 2004, spring 2005, August
2007, and fall 2008 bottoms in gold stocks, all of which were followed
by rallies of 100 percent or greater.

The crash of 2008 led to extreme undervaluations in gold stocks.
The XAU and HUI-to-Gold ratios reached 9 percent and 20.5 percent respectively at the bottom. For the XAU, the 9 percent reading
was an all-time low (and by a large margin, with the previous all-time
low being 15.6 percent at the 2000 bottom), meaning that large-cap
gold stocks had *never* been this cheap compared to gold. For the HUI,
the 20.5 percent figure represented the lowest ratio since early 2001,
when the HUI was under 70! As one would expect, this marked a
huge bottom for gold stocks, with gold stocks roughly tripling within
a year of these extremely cheap valuations.

The good news is that, as we go to press in 2010, gold stocks are
still extremely cheap. The XAU-to-Gold ratio is about 16 percent and
the HUI-to-Gold ratio is about 40 percent. This puts both of these
ratios well within their cheap range. Thus, these ratios are currently

telling us that gold stocks when compared to the gold price are not expensive for investors.

The above are rules for trading the large-cap companies; these are the companies that have large reserves and production. There are also smaller gold companies that are available for investments.

Mid-Tier Companies

These are companies that are developed and usually have one large producing property or a producing property going into production. These companies have more leverage to the gold price but they also have more risk.

Earlier, we discussed how companies are also valued on reserves in the ground. This is one of the major reasons mid-tier companies possess more upside. Let's say Company ABC is a large-cap company and Company XYZ is a mid-tier company. Company ABC has about 20 million ounces in the ground in reserves. Company XYZ has 2 million ounces in the ground. Let's say both find 2 million more ounces. With Company ABC, that increases their reserve base by 10 percent, whereas with Company XYZ, that doubles their reserves! So the stock has more upside because it is starting from a lower resource base. It also has more risk. Large-cap companies usually have numerous resources all over the globe. Let's use the same scenario and let's say company ABC has 2 million ounces in production at 10 different mines around the world with one mine located in Country D. Company XYZ has one property that produces 200,000 ounces. This lone property is in Country D. Accordingly, both have one property in Country D. There is a miner strike at each of the mines in Country D and the production has to be shut down. Company ABC loses only 10 percent of its production, whereas Company XYZ loses all of its production and cash flow. This is the downside of mid-tiers; they are very country specific and property sensitive.

However, the upside is huge. Eldorado Gold (EGO NYSE) is an example of a company that obtained and developed a few properties. It subsequently went up over fortyfold in value (from its bottom in the year 2001) after it developed a few properties into producing mines.

Junior Mining Companies

These are extremely small companies that usually have very small market caps, usually below 50 million and sometimes below 10 million dollars. These companies drill properties in order to build up resources and they hope to produce an economical mine. This is not as easy as it sounds. As only 1 in every 1,000 properties becomes economical, these companies have huge upside. If a company finds and then builds up a huge resource, it can go up hundreds, if not thousands, of percent in value. Many of these companies have, as their ultimate goal, the prospect of being bought out by a larger producing company. An investor should only speculate his or her "play" money in these types of stocks.

Silver—The "Poor Man's Gold"

Silver is the junior precious metal to gold. If gold were a currency, gold would be the dollars and silver, the cents. What is interesting about silver is that, while gold has broken through its 1980 high, silver is still over 60 percent below its 1980 high. However, we should note that the $50 high reached in 1980 was an artificial high that was caused by the Hunt brothers trying to corner the price of silver.

Silver is more volatile than gold. Since the silver bull market began in 2000, silver is up a bit more than gold in percentage terms but its moves higher and lower have been even more volatile than gold.

What I like about silver is quite simply the price. At $17 an ounce, silver has a cheap price. I don't mean cheap as in valuation but rather the nominal price itself. As this bull market matures and more retail investors are drawn to gold, many retail investors are going to look at gold at $1,500 or $2,000 an ounce and will find it too pricey. However, they will look at silver at $20 or $25 and be drawn to it as an affordable way to invest in the precious metals bull market. This is why, near the end of bull markets, silver tends to outperform as the average person pushes the price higher. In terms of percentage gains, silver probably has more upside than gold.

Silver also has equities in the large-cap, mid-sized, and exploration arenas. However, they are few in number. It should be pointed out that the majority of silver is produced as a byproduct of gold. Most of the world's largest silver producers are large-cap gold companies that produce their silver in addition to gold. However, the few pure silver companies that exist are pretty good plays on the current silver price. These companies include Pan American Silver, Silver Standard, and Wheaton Silver.

Precious Metals Will Boom

Gold and gold stocks, along with silver, are in a secular bull market and should move higher in the coming years. Gold stocks are still cheap following the crash of 2008 and will outperform gold as they get back to normal historical valuations compared to gold. Silver is the "poor man's gold" and should outperform gold near the end of the gold bull market as the retail market flows into silver. Gold and silver also trade inversely to the stock market; so as equities continue in their major trading range, gold and silver will boom.

In the coming chapter, you will read why I also like other commodities as an inflation play. Gold has the added feature of being a monetary metal. Gold remains my favorite investment for the coming years, with the other commodities providing secondary ways of playing the continuation of the commodities bull market cycle.

Chapter 6

Commodities

Monetary Inflation and Demand Will
Equal a Commodities Boom

My basic thesis, regarding the continuation of the inflation cycle over the next 10 years, is that the two primary commodities that will preserve and/or increase your wealth are gold and silver. Part of the reason (as outlined in Chapter 5) is because they are monetary commodities that will also act as a hedge against the devaluation of the U.S. dollar and fiat currencies around the world. However, commodities trade in what Jim Dines calls a "wolf pack." This means that, usually, when commodities are strong in price, they are strong together.

It is no coincidence that when gold and silver had a 20-year bear market from 1980 to 2000, so did other commodities such as oil and gas, uranium, nickel, copper, and so on. Not surprisingly, standard stocks also trade together (e.g., unrelated sectors such as technology and banks were also strong from 1982 to 2000 in the secular bull market in stocks). Aspects of similar asset classes trade together even if they are not directly related to each other.

Many have stated that there was no "inflation" during the eighties or nineties as commodity prices were in a major bear market. At the same time, stock prices boomed. This is simply not the truth. As we have noted, in this boom, asset classes trade from under- to overvalued. Once they get overvalued, the market shifts its focus to other classes, which then start their bull markets. There are major turning points in the history of cycles. Such a turning point was the early 1980s when there was a shift from the commodities bull market to the one in equities. The belief that there was "no inflation" in the eighties and nineties is false. As stated earlier, it was asset inflation. However, with the advent of the dot-com and housing bubbles, we have seen another shift— a shift into commodities from financial assets. As governments print more money in the coming years, this money will flow into the commodities markets and they will boom. This chapter tells you how to profit from this boom.

The Easiest Way to Play the Commodity Trend—Own All Commodities

The easiest way to play the commodity bull market is to own all commodities through a commodity index or fund. There are times during the commodity bull market (as will be discussed later) when oil will outperform gold, or wheat will outperform oil, or copper will outperform wheat. The way to diversify and lessen risk is to own all commodities.

The way to do this is to own a variety of commodity indices and ETFs that track the prices of a basket of commodities. The most popular of all of them is the CRB Index or Commodities Research Board Index, which is made up of 20 commodities. Goldman Sachs also has its own commodity index as does the Dow Jones with the Dow Jones AIG Commodity Index. Here is a cautionary note: The problem I find with many of these indices is that they are way overweight in energy-related commodities. For example, the Goldman Sachs Commodity Index has an energy weighting of 78.65 percent and a metals weighting of 6.12 percent; gold makes up only 1.58 percent of the index.

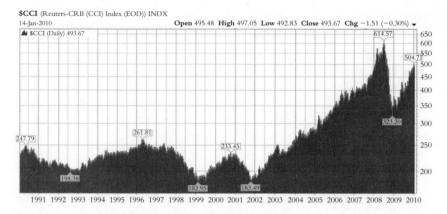

$CCI (Reuters–CRB (CCI) Index (EOD)) INDX
14-Jan-2010   Open 495.48 High 497.05 Low 492.83 Close 493.67 Chg −1.51 (−0.30%) ▾

Figure 6.1 AU CRB CCI Commodities Index
SOURCE: Courtesy of StockCharts.com (http://stockcharts.com).

One of the main indices that I really like is the CRB CCI Index, which has a 17.6 percent weighting in energy, a 17.6 weighting in grains, an 11.8 percent weighting in industrial commodities such as copper, an 11.8 percent weighting in meats, a 23.5 percent weighting in soft commodities such as coffee and cocoa and sugar, and a 17.6 percent weighting in precious metals such as gold and silver. Figure 6.1 is a chart of the CCI going back 20 years.

However, the CRB CCI Index is still not the best index for commodity diversification. The most diversified and best commodity index, in my opinion, is the RICI or Jim Rogers Commodity Index. Table 6.1 shows the makeup of this commodity index with the weightings of each commodity.

Note that there are 35 commodities that make up this index; accordingly, it is very well diversified and covers the entire commodity spectrum as well or better than most commodity indices. An index under the ticker RJI actually trades on the NYSE; so you can buy and trade this index. Rogers also has ETFs that track base metals and agricultural commodities, which we will discuss later in this chapter.

Playing an ETF or fund of commodities is the long way to play it. You can also buy a fund of commodity stocks. However, if you want to trade individual commodities, you cannot just buy and hold. You have to be savvy and be flexible to sell and trade. We discuss some of these strategies and the outlook for some individual commodities in the following sections.

Table 6.1 Rogers Commodity Index Makeup

Crude Oil NYMEX USD	21.00%	Brent ICE1EU USD	14.00%
Wheat CBOT USD	7.00%	Corn CBOT USD	4.75%
Cotton ICE US USD	4.20%	Aluminum LME2 USD	4.00%
Copper LME USD	4.00%	Soybeans CBOT USD	3.35%
Gold COMEX USD	3.00%	Natural Gas NYMEX USD	3.00%
RBOB Gasoline NYMEX USD	3.00%	Soybean Oil CBOT USD	2.17%
Coffee ICE US USD	2.00%	Lead LME USD	2.00%
Live Cattle CME USD	2.00%	Silver COMEX USD	2.00%
Sugar ICE US USD	2.00%	Zinc LME USD	2.00%
Heating Oil NYMEX USD	1.80%	Platinum NYMEX USD	1.80%
Gas Oil ICE EU USD	1.20%	Cocoa ICE US USD	1.00%
Lean Hogs CME USD	1.00%	Lumber CME USD	1.00%
Nickel LME USD	1.00%	Rubber TOCOM JPY	1.00%
Tin LME USD	1.00%	Canola ICE CA CAD	0.77%
Soybean Meal CBOT USD	0.75%	Orange Juice ICE US USD	0.66%
Oats CBOT USD	0.50%	Rice CBOT USD	0.50%
Palladium NYMEX USD	0.30%	Azuki Beans TGE JPY	0.15%
Greasy Wool SFE AUS	0.10%		

The Commodity Trends No One Talks About

Both gold and oil are a lot higher than they were in 1999. However, they went up at different rates at different times. Whereas gold spent most of 1999 to 2001 basing between $250 and $350 an ounce, oil was increasing from under $15 a barrel to over $40 a barrel. Oil also outpaced gold for most of the 2000s until later in the decade when oil topped at $147 a barrel. Oil is still 40 percent below its top as we go to press in 2010, whereas gold blasted through its high of $1,000 an ounce and continues to trade at near-all-time highs.

Different commodities will outperform at different times. For example, during the commodities boom of the 1970s, sugar actually made its high in 1974, whereas the rest of the commodities continued higher into 1980.

As we go to press, many metals such as gold and silver are trading at or near new highs, whereas it may take commodities in the energy complex such as natural gas, oil, and so on years to reach new highs.

However, many commodities were also sold off big-time in the 2008 crash. Some of the hardest hits were commodities that had previously experienced some of the greatest increases from their lows in percentage terms. There will be constant rotation in the commodities' bull market as some commodities outperform others. Rather than just telling you why commodities go up, this chapter shows you how to earn profits by taking advantage of trends using techniques that virtually no one talks about.

Supply/demand will continue to play an important role in the macro commodities bull market. However, I still think that monetary inflation, arising from the devaluation of the U.S. dollar and the printing of massive amounts of money, will play a major role in why commodities head higher in the coming years. We must remember that the global economy saw a huge expansion for most of the eighties and much of the nineties; yet commodities went nowhere in price as the U.S. dollar remained strong.

Historically, commodities trade counter to the U.S. dollar. As the U.S. dollar loses its status as the global reserve currency and is devalued in the coming years, commodities are a great way to play this devaluation. Going the other direction, currencies in nations that primarily produce commodities should see their currencies strengthen vis-a-vis the U.S. dollar.

Commodities for the Coming Years

A quick overview of numerous commodities will now be discussed with a view to discussing the bullish arguments for them longer term and how to trade and profit from these trends.

There are many different commodities to profit from in the coming boom in this sector as well as ways to invest in these commodities. We will look at commodities you should consider investing in and how to invest in these commodities, be it through ETFs, equities, or buying the commodities themselves. The commodities that we will be discussing are:

- Oil
- Natural gas
- Industrial commodities
- Agricultural commodities
- Alternative energies
- Selected important other metals that are rarely talked about

Oil

Oil and gas are, of course, two of the hottest commodities in the world. Everyone needs at least one of these two fuels to power cars, heat homes, and so on. With demand increasing from Asia every day, as Asian economies continue to grow, supply problems loom in the future. Despite any short-term setback (as occurred in 1998), Asia will continue to grow and consume most of the new demand in oil.

Estimates state that the United States will consume just over 21 million barrels per day in 2010 and that this will increase to about 27 million barrels per day by 2040, an increase of just under 30 percent. However, China is estimated to consume 10 million barrels of oil per day in 2010 and will see an increase of 150 percent to nearly 25 million barrels per day by 2040, nearly equaling U.S. demand. At the moment, the world consumes about 87 million barrels of oil per day. The U.S. Energy Information Administration estimates worldwide consumption to increase to 125 million barrels per day by 2040. Most of that increase in demand will come from outside the United States.

The United States consumes about 21 million barrels of the world's demand of 87 million barrels per day. American oil consumption currently uses roughly 23 percent of global demand but the United States represents only 5 percent of global population. China, which possesses nearly 18 percent of global population, represents only 11 percent of global demand. These numbers will become more proportional as China continues to economically outgrow the United States.

In addition, it is estimated that the non–OECD countries are now consuming about the same amount of oil as OECD countries and will pass them shortly for the first time in history.

Also, in 2009, the emerging world saw higher total automobile sales than mature economies for the first time ever. As their demand is coming from a very low level, demand for cars in the third world will continue to increase for some time.

For example, in the United States, per–capita consumption of oil is about 27 barrels per person per year. In South Korea and Japan, it is around 17 barrels per person. In China and India, it is 1.8 and 0.8 barrels per person, respectively. Just imagine what would occur if China and India consumed just 20 percent of what the average American does.

China and India would increase their oil demand by 300 and 400 percent, respectively, per person. And remember, that would be 2.5 billion people increasing their oil consumption by an average of about 4 barrels per day or about 10 billion barrels of oil per year!

This increasing demand story is combined with the theory of *peak oil*. The theory of peak oil is that oil discoveries that peaked in the mid-sixties will continue to decline over time. According to the Peak Association of Oil and Gas, there were over 450 billion barrels of oil found in the 1960s as opposed to about 100 billion barrels in the 2000s. This number is estimated to decline to just over 60 billion barrels in the 2000s. Some experts estimate that world supply could drop to just over 65 billion barrels per year in 2030, whereas demand could be almost twice that total.

My own personal belief is that the estimates on new production are much too low. Increases in technology and drilling methods will result in extraction of oil from tar sands (such as occurs in Alberta's tar sands). As well, an increased ability to drill below the ocean floor will lead to many more oil finds that were formally seen as uneconomical. The BP oil spill will all but put a stop to drilling in many parts of the United States. However, in other nations where there has been much stricter regulation, drilling is progressing as normal. However, these extractions will be expensive. For example, the cost of extracting a barrel of oil in the Alberta tar sands (the Alberta tar sands is one of the fastest growing areas of the world in terms of oil production) is estimated to be north of $70 a barrel. The median price of finding a new barrel is roughly that ($70) around the world. This tells us that oil should not be spending any meaningful time below the $70 level in the coming years and the low prices of 2008 and 2009 were more of an aberration than anything else.

The world will move away from oil as more nuclear plants come online and natural gas becomes increasingly popular, as do alternatives such as solar and wind power. However, oil is still going to be the world's primary source of energy production and consumption for the next 10 to 15 years.

Table 6.2 shows the top 21 countries in the world by the amount of oil reserves they have and the percentage of the world's total that they have.

As you can see, most of the world's oil reserves are in developing countries or in countries that we would consider not to be the most stable in the world. We must remember that two of the countries on the chart, China and India, will probably not be exporting oil as

Table 6.2 Top Countries' Oil Reserves

Country	Reserves (bbl)	Share (%)
Saudi Arabia	266,800,000,000	19.66
Canada	178,600,000,000	13.16
Iran	140,000,000,000	10.20
Iraq	115,000,000,000	8.47
Kuwait	104,000,000,000	7.66
United Arab Emirates	97,800,000,000	7.21
Venezuela	87,040,000,000	6.41
Russia	79,000,000,000	4.45
Libya	41,460,000,000	3.05
Nigeria	36,220,000,000	2.67
Kazakhstan	30,000,000,000	2.21
United States	20,970,000,000	1.54
China	16,000,000,000	1.18
Qatar	15,210,000,000	1.12
Algeria	12,200,000,000	0.90
Brazil	12,180,000,000	0.90
Mexico	11,650,000,000	0.86
Angola	9,035,000,000	0.67
Azerbaijan	7,000,000,000	0.52
Norway	6,865,000,000	0.51
European Union	6,146,000,000	0.45
India	5,625,000,000	0.41
Oman	5,500,000,000	0.41
Sudan	5,000,000,000	0.37
Ecuador	4,517,000,000	0.33
Malaysia	4,000,000,000	0.29

SOURCE: *The World Fact Book*, via Wikipedia.

their own internal demand will use up all of their production. In addition, most of the rest of these nations either are setting up trade deals with China (see Angola or Brazil) or are in nations that the United States is not on the best terms with (see Iran, Venezuela, Azerbaijan, etc.). Accordingly, there is a real possibility for political turmoil and oil embargoes such as occurred in the 1970s.

Trading Oil However, despite the long-term upward projection in demand and price for oil in the coming years, oil is a very spiky trade. It can make moves of 100 percent to the upside and 50 percent or more to the downside in just a matter of months. In addition, oil was the investment commodity of choice during the mid-2000s and I think, because of this popularity, oil might actually lag other commodities in the coming years. For example, Figure 6.2 shows the inflation-adjusted price of oil going back to 1946. What we can see from this chart is that when oil spiked to $147 per barrel back in 2008, it actually went *higher* than its inflation-adjusted top of 1980! By way of contrast, gold is still trading more than 50 percent lower than its inflation-adjusted top of 1980. This simple comparison tells us that oil is not as cheap as gold on a long-term basis. Even with oil's recent price drop and oil around $80 as I write, oil in 2010 is only about 30 percent lower than its 1980 inflation-adjusted high, whereas gold is still 50 percent lower! So on a long-term basis, we can see gold is still cheaper than oil on a relative basis.

In addition, one way I like to value commodities, as you will see from the remainder of this chapter, is by comparing all commodities to the price of gold. In my opinion, gold is the centerpiece of the commodity world; accordingly, I like to divide the price of all other commodities into the price of gold to see how much of that commodity it takes to buy an ounce of gold. This gives me a relative valuation.

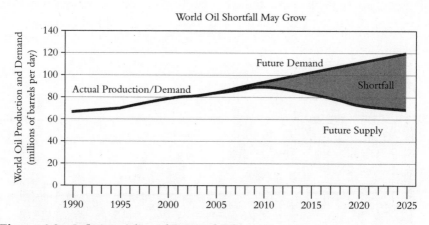

Figure 6.2   Inflation-Adjusted Price of Oil

SOURCE: www.chartoftheday.com. Data on world oil production: U.S. Energy Information Administration; future demand: reference case—International Energy Outlook 2005—U.S. Energy Information Administration; future supply: projections by the Association for the Study of Peak Oil & Gas, April 2006.

Figure 6.3 is the *Oil-to-Gold* ratio. Historically, it takes about 15 to 20 barrels of oil to buy an ounce of gold. However, in the 2000s, this started to dip below 10 and in 2008, at the top in oil, it took only 6.26 barrels of oil to buy an ounce of gold! This was a sign that oil was vastly overvalued and it dropped from $147 per barrel in 2008 to $35 in early 2009! In addition, if you had watched this ratio, you would have been buying gold during most of the 2000s, whereas you would have been avoiding oil. So you would have missed much of the run-up in oil; however, you would have also avoided the collapse in 2008. If instead you had been accumulating gold (as it was cheap compared to oil) in the $300–$500 range, you would have profited handsomely as gold presently is still more than double those $300 to $500 levels!

During the collapse in oil prices, this ratio spiked to 26.43 in early 2009. Whenever it takes more than 20 barrels of oil to buy an ounce of gold, it means that oil is very cheap compared to gold. Whenever oil reaches these levels, as it did in 1989, 1998, and 2009, it is usually followed by a major rally. For example, from its bottom in March 2009 to 2010, oil prices more than doubled, whereas gold prices increased by merely a little over 15 percent!

This indicator can be a great way to trade the oil bull market in the coming years. When it takes less than 10 barrels of oil to buy an ounce of gold, you will want to lighten up on your oil holdings. When it takes more than 20, you will want to increase your oil holdings.

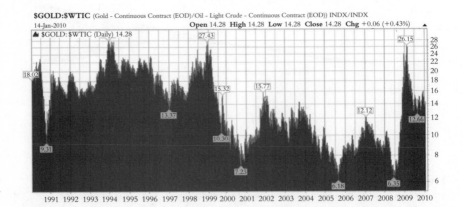

Figure 6.3   Oil-to-Gold Ratio
SOURCE: StockCharts.com (http://stockcharts.com).

There are a lot of different methods to trade oil. There are ETFs, such as the United States Oil Fund (USO), that track the price of oil. You can also purchase large-cap oil companies such as Exxon, Chevron, Suncor, and so on. You can also speculate in smaller oil companies. Fundamentally, there are a lot of advantages to the stocks as they can increase on news of new finds. In addition, the oil stock universe is a lot larger and less volatile than the precious metals universe.

Natural Gas

Natural gas will also see long-term upward demand. Since 1970, global natural gas demand has gone from 300 billion cubic meters to over 800 billion cubic meters at the moment. In addition, unlike oil, we are actually seeing large increases in natural gas production in North America. Natural gas is also much cleaner than oil. The Boone Pickens (Pickens is an energy investor who has gained fame for his political campaigns on how to reduce American reliance on imported oil) plan consists of using natural gas as a substitute for gasoline in cars. I think the easiest shift to cleaner energy is to convert dirty gasoline engines and oil power plants over to the use of natural gas. Numbers as of 2005 show that about 23 percent of U.S. energy production comes from natural gas.

Trading Gas Natural gas is a very difficult market to trade. Since the commodities bull market began in the late nineties, natural gas prices have increased from $1.80 a cubic meter to over $5.75 a cubic meter as I write for a gain of over 330 percent. However, the gains and losses in between have been enormous. From 1998 to 2001, natural gas increased from $1.80 a cubic meter to over $9 before collapsing to $1.91 in late 2001. It then increased to over $15.48 in 2005 before falling to $4.38 in 2006. Natural gas increased to $13.58 in 2008 before falling to $2.70 in 2009! These figures reflect huge fluctuations of 500 to 600 percent followed by declines of 800 percent.

In addition, at the 2008 low of $2.70, natural gas had actually fallen below its 1999 low in inflation-adjusted terms! Therefore, we can see that, while the long-term trade is up, the volatility in natural gas is gut wrenching. Holding natural gas longer term is just not going to work if you are trying to make money from it.

Profiting from Natural Gas There are two major ways to make money in natural gas and both are simple.

1. You can own a quality natural gas company. A stock like EnCana, for example, has increased from just over $5 a share in 2000 to $30 a share as we go to press. Chesapeake has increased from under $1.00 in 1994 to $27.67 as we go to press (although CHK has seen three huge decreases of over 80 percent in that 16-year timeframe; so it is a big-time volatile company).
2. You could choose the XNG (natural gas index), which tracks natural gas stocks; this index has increased from 101 in 1999 to over 500 as we go to press. FCG, the First Trust Natural Gas ETF, is an ETF of the natural gas index. I think top-tier quality natural gas companies are the easiest way to play natural gas price increases.

However, I do not think you should chase returns. You should wait patiently to purchase natural gas when it gets cheap.

How Do We Know When Natural Gas Is Cheap? The ratios I use to trade natural gas are the Natural Gas-to-Oil and Natural Gas-to-Gold ratios. Again, these ratios compare natural gas to these other commodities and we determine how many units of natural gas it takes to buy a barrel of oil or an ounce of gold.

- **Natural Gas-to-Oil ratio.** When it takes fewer than 6 units of natural gas to buy a barrel of oil, natural gas is expensive and you will want to sell your natural gas. This occurred in late 2000, most of 2003, and late 2008; all those dates were good times to sell natural gas. In each case, natural gas dropped 50 percent or more in the months following this extreme reading.

    On the other hand, when it takes more than 13 units of natural gas to buy one barrel of oil, you will want to purchase natural gas. This occurred in October 2001, July and October 2006, summer 2007, mid-2006, and August 2009. In every case, it led to a great buying opportunity. The exception is 2008, when both oil and natural gas topped together (the ratio just got high because oil was going up faster than natural gas). On the other hand, it should be noted that the ratio of 25.70 to 1 in mid-2009 was the highest ratio ever.

This meant that in terms of the price of oil, natural gas was *never* as cheap as it was that summer. Not surprisingly, natural gas rallied from $2.70 to near $6.00 in just a few months.

This brings us to an important point when trading using these ratios. Do not use them to trade blindly. Be aware of the situation in all of the commodities. For example, in mid-2008, you could see both natural gas and oil spiking, and from the nosebleed levels they traded up to there was not a whole lot of upside. Accordingly, you would not buy natural gas even though it was trading at a cheap valuation compared to oil. A check on the Gold-to-Natural Gas ratio (discussed next) would confirm that natural gas was expensive. However, in summer 2009, you can see the ratio was out of whack because natural gas was trading at low valuations compared to oil (and also gold). That was the time to make the trade.

- **Gold-to–Natural Gas ratio.** Like oil, you can also trade natural gas against gold. Whenever it takes fewer than 75 units of natural gas to buy one ounce of gold, that is when natural gas is expensive. This occurred in late 2000, early 2003, and late 2005 and mid-2008; these were all major tops for natural gas. When it takes over 150 units of natural gas to buy one unit of gold, natural gas is very cheap. This occurred in 1995, 1999, late 2001, and mid-2009; these were all great buying opportunities for natural gas. At the 2009 bottom for natural gas, it took over 367 units of natural gas to buy one ounce of gold! I think, in retrospect, the August 2009 period will be looked on as a great buying opportunity for natural gas.

Industrial Commodities

Industrial commodities include commodities such as iron ore, copper, and nickel. The easiest commodity for trading purposes is copper. The arguments for these commodities are the same as for oil. Simply, the emerging world will continue to grow and continue its demand for these metals. For example, U.S. Global Investors estimates that in the next 25 years, the global demand for copper will be equal to all the copper that has ever been produced in all of human history. We do not need to beat this demand story to death. There are a million articles written regarding this amazing phenomenon. These articles back up my argument that we are in a long-term bull market for commodities. What I want to do in this book, like no other, is to show you how to make money from this commodities bull market.

One aspect you have to understand about most of these commodities is that they are not long-term holds. As we discussed in the natural gas section, most of these commodities are very volatile; you have to trade them unless you are holding a basket of different commodities, which diversifies you. But on an individual basis, you must trade them.

For example, copper bottomed in 2001 at $0.65 cents; it then rocketed to $4.08 in 2008 before collapsing to $1.25 in late 2008 during the financial crisis. Afterwards, copper promptly rallied back to $3.54. Again, I trade copper by the Gold-to-Copper ratio and determine how many pounds of copper it takes to buy one ounce of gold. Typically, it takes about 300 or 400 pounds of copper to purchase one ounce of gold. Whenever it takes more than 400 pounds, copper is cheap and you want to buy copper; when it takes less than 300 pounds, copper is expensive and you want to sell your copper. In 2003, it took over 500 pounds of copper to buy one ounce of gold. From that point on, copper increased from well under $1 a pound to over $4 a pound in just three years! Then, in 2006, copper got very expensive and it took only 165 pounds of copper to buy one ounce of gold. While gold advanced from 2006 to 2008, copper remained flat in the $4 range. Then copper collapsed in 2008. However, by early 2009, copper got ridiculously cheap in terms of gold, as cheap as it had ever been. By early 2009, it took over 700 pounds of copper to buy 1 ounce of gold. In March 2009, while speaking at the Prospectors and Development Conference in Toronto, I made the comment that, with gold trading near $1,000 and copper around $1.60, I would want to melt down my gold and turn it into copper. Subsequent to my comments, gold had a nice run until the end of 2009, gaining about 20 percent. However, copper did even better, gaining over 100 percent to $3.50 a pound!

Figure 6.4 is the Gold-to-Copper ratio.

You can trade large-cap copper stocks such as Freeport McMoran or ETFs such as the Dow Jones AIG Copper fund (JJC) or the Rogers Metals Fund as ways to play and trade industrial metals. However, again, I would say these are trading vehicles and you should trade them based on when copper is cheap rather than holding them longer term.

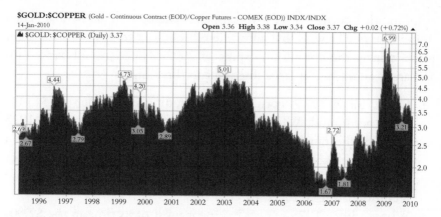

Figure 6.4   Gold-to-Copper Ratio
SOURCE: StockCharts.com (http://stockcharts.com).

Agricultural Commodities

Some of the best deals in the world right now are in agricultural commodities. The basic math is as follows: In the sixties, there were 3 billion people in the world; now there are 6 billion. Plus, with the economic growth in Asia and other developing nations, there is going to be more demand for food. More grains will be needed to feed livestock and other animals as these nations consume more. Yes, technological development means that more food can be mass-produced at cheaper prices. However, at some point in time, expanding demand for food caused by increased standards of living will cause increases in food prices. We already saw the impact of this development in 2008 when spikes in the prices of wheat, rice, and soybeans caused rioting in many nations.

Food stocks are at very low levels. For example, the numbers, in recent years, indicate that there is about 50 days' supply of grains worldwide. This is about 30 percent lower than the traditional average of 75 days of supply and is the lowest level in over 40 years. Therefore, a bad drought, in a major producing area, could cause spikes in food prices. In 2008, we saw such spikes.

This is already reflected in the long-term prices of agricultural commodities. What is really interesting is how these commodities have traded as of late. We will look at the prices of five major agricultural commodities: corn, wheat, soybeans, rice, and oats. What has happened in the case of all five is that all of them broke out to new all-time-high prices during the commodity spike of 2008. They have all backed off and are now trading at large discounts to these highs.

- **Corn.** Since 1975, corn has been trading in a range of $1.00–$4.25 per pound. What is interesting is that, from the period 1975 to 2008, the range was mostly $1.00–$2.50 with the high end in the $2.00–$2.50 range. In 2008, the price spiked to $4.25 per pound and has since come back to $2.20 per pound as I write and is consolidating in that area.
- **Wheat.** Since 1975, wheat has spent most of its time in the $2.00- to $6.00-per-bushel trading range with $5–$6 representing the high end of the range. In 2008, there was a huge spike to over $12 a bushel! Wheat has since come down from this spike. It trades around $5 a bushel as we write and has been trading in that area for most of 2009 and 2010, consolidating in that area.
- **Soybeans.** Since 1975, soybeans have traded in a range of $5–$9 with $8–$9 representing the top end of the range. In 2008, soybeans broke out to $17 per bushel! They have pulled back to about $9.50 per bushel as we write. Soybeans have spent most of 2009 and 2010 at around $10 per bushel.
- **Rice.** Since 1975, rice spent most of its time trading between $6 and $10. In 2008, there was a huge spike to over $21. Rice has spent most of 2009 and 2010 trading in the $12–$14 range.
- **Oats.** Since 1975, oats have traded between $1.00 and $2.50 per bushel with the high end in the $2.00–$2.50 range. Like all of the agricultural commodities, oats had a huge breakout in 2008, climbing to over $4.25 per bushel! They have come back and are trading in the $2.00–$2.50 range as I write in 2010.

I mentioned these examples of all five of these agricultural commodities for a reason. Note that all of them have traded the same way. For nearly 30 years, from the mid-1970s to the mid-2000s, these commodities all traded in certain trading ranges. In 2008, all of these agricultural commodities broke *above* these ranges and traded to new all-time highs. Then, in 2009, they came back to earth. However, the new ranges are at much higher levels. Basically, the old resistance levels that had acted as resistance for nearly 30 years are now the *support* levels. Resistance has become support. We have a higher base. It might take a few years for this basing to play out, but once it does, you will see these commodities yet again move to new all-time highs.

Profiting from Agricultural Commodities There are also ETFs that track agricultural commodities. They buy the futures for agricultural commodities and hold them in a basket. Such ETFs are the Power Shares Agricultural Fund (DBA) and Rogers Agricultural ETF (RJA).

Another way to play agricultural commodities is through potash and fertilizer companies. *Potash* is the name given to potassium carbonate. *Potash fertilizer* is the name given to potassium oxide, which is used for fertilizers all over the world. Of course, if we see more demand for food, people will need more fertilizers to better cultivate their land and grow food. If the prices of food move higher, there will be more farmland planted as it becomes more economical to do so and, therefore, this in turn will create more demand for potash.

The largest potash-producing nation in the world is Canada, which accounts for about 30 percent of global production and has over 60 percent of global reserves. The large-cap potash company of choice is Potash Inc., which trades under the symbol POT. (Note: As this book is going to press POT has a takeover offer for $40 billion from BHP.) In 2008, before the crash, there was a mini-mania in potash stocks, with many smaller-cap stocks rising hundreds of percent in price in just a few months. This brings us to an important point: Even though the long-term fundamentals are strong for a sector, this does not mean that the stocks will participate. To put potash property into production requires a very high capital investment and most of these smaller companies will never see it to fruition. Therefore, you are better off buying just the large-cap companies.

Another ETF that tracks agriculture is MOO, which is a collection of agricultural commodity companies such as Potash, Archer Daniels, and Monsanto. As these companies are not victims of contango (*contango* is when a futures contract is rolled over to a higher price—for example, say corn is trading at $3.00 on the March contract; if you roll it over to the April contract that is trading at $3.50, you do not experience that

$0.50 gain in price), a group of the large-cap companies might very well be the best way to play the coming agricultural commodity boom.

You could also look at farm property in places such as Saskatchewan, Brazil, Chile, the midwestern United States, or the countryside in India, Thailand, and Vietnam, and so on. These are places where there is farming property that could be purchased—this is another way to directly participate in the boom in agriculture.

Alternative Energies—Uranium and Geothermal Energy

We are all familiar with the talk of clean energy. Clean energy alternatives are part of a definite trend. Two of my favorite ways to play the clean energy craze are through uranium and geothermal. Right now in China, for the five years ending 2010, they have built 22 nuclear reactors. They plan on building between 60 and 130 more depending on which estimates you listen to. This, of course, means a huge demand for uranium. The positive about nuclear power is that, if produced correctly, it is very clean. France, for example, has over 80 percent of its power produced by nuclear plants. And once a plant is set up, uranium costs only about 6 percent of the cost of production (this means, if uranium doubles in price, the cost of energy will increase by only about 6 percent) as compared to 20 to 30 percent cost of production for the natural gas required for natural gas plants.

Uranium In December 2009, India announced that Russia was going to help it build 12 to 16 nuclear plants in India. In addition, at some point, North America will catch up to this trend, especially with the politically correct demand for cleaner power. This will, therefore, create a huge demand for uranium. Uranium had a boom in the mid-2000s, trading from under $8 per ounce in the nineties to over $140 per pound in 2007. Uranium trades at around $45 per pound as I write and seems to be basing in this area. The stocks had a mania in the mid-2000s as well. Many junior stocks went from gold to uranium during this mini-bubble and spiked and collapsed. This is what I am talking about when I say that, in spite of the fact that the commodity is in a bull market, the stocks may not be. Most of these junior stocks were nothing more than moose pasture and some uranium properties that could never be developed; accordingly, many of them crashed. Unfortunately, however, many of the quality companies crashed with them. When investing, look for uranium companies that produce the metal. Most uranium companies can make money at $45 uranium and if it goes back toward $100 (it should attain that level once all of those plants in India, China, and other emerging markets come online), they could really go up more in price.

Geothermal Energy *Geothermal* is energy using heat from the earth's core and converting it to electricity. Worldwide geothermal plants have the capacity to produce about 0.3 percent of the world's power; so you can see there is a huge potential of growth.

Geothermal is likely the most environmental friendly of energies. The visible plumes seen rising from some geothermal power plants are actually water vapor emissions (steam), not smoke. Geothermal power plants do not burn fuel. Unlike fossil fuel plants, they release virtually no air emissions. A case study of a coal plant, updated with scrubbers and other emissions-control technologies, revealed emissions of 24 times more carbon dioxide, 10,837 times more sulfur dioxide, and 3,865 times more nitrous oxides per megawatt hour than a geothermal steam plant. Geothermal also uses 1/70 of the fresh water that the typical coal plant does. The most famous instance of geothermal success is the case of the tiny island state of Iceland. Iceland produces all of its energy from geothermal plants.

The interesting aspect about geothermal, from an investment point of view, is that there are virtually no pure geothermal companies. Most geothermal production is in large conglomerates such as General Electric, which has a geothermal division. There about 6 pure geothermal companies, only one of which—U.S. Geothermal—trades on the U.S. exchanges. The rest, which include Nevada Geothermal and Polaris Geothermal, trade on the Canadian Venture Exchange in Canada. However, these companies are very top-tier. They are not just little pump-and-dump micro-caps looking to take advantage of a fad. All of these companies possess properties that are going into production. However, geothermal is quite capital intensive. The reason that most small-cap companies do not venture into the geothermal arena and large companies do, is the fact that the typical geothermal plant takes about $100 million or so in capital expenditures to put into production.

Most of the world does not lie in the right geological zones in order to tap into the world's core for geothermal production. However, it is estimated that in the United States, geothermal could produce enough power for people who live in Arizona, Nevada, and much of southern California, or about 15 million people. If that were to occur, it would go from 0.3 percent of power production to 5 percent, which is a 17-fold increase. So, even if geothermal just produced 5 to 10 percent of the world's power (which potentially it could), there is a huge amount of growth potential for that industry. In addition, small nation-states such as those in Central America or Iceland can provide power for their entire populations' needs with geothermal, thereby reducing dependence on oil. So, for smaller nations in the right geological environment, the benefits provided by geothermal energy are very attractive. If you are interested in learning more about these geothermal companies, please take a look at my publication *Addicted to Profits* (www.addictedtoprofits.net).

Other Metals

There are many other metals in addition to the usual suspects. Many of these are less well known but are very important to the global economy and can be just as profitable as the better-known metals. Platinum and palladium are key elements in catalytic converters; hybrid cars need rare earths to run. There will be increasing demand for these metals in the coming years and it is important to add them as a part of a commodities portfolio.

Platinum and Palladium These are the two poor orphans of precious metals. Platinum is similar to gold in that it is very ductile and not easily corroded. Palladium is the main component of catalytic converters, which are used to keep cars running cleanly.

Like gold, platinum saw a huge spike to over $1,000 an ounce in 1980. It collapsed to under $300 in the early eighties. During the spike in commodities in 2008, platinum spiked to over $2,000 an ounce. Platinum declined to under $1,000 in 2008 after the crash and trades around $1,500 as I write in 2010. Palladium spiked to over $300 an ounce during the commodities bubble of 1980 and then fell to about $50 an ounce in the mid-eighties. There was then a *huge* spike in palladium prices in the early 2000s as palladium climbed to over $1,000 an ounce as Russia cut exports. It fell back to $160 an ounce in 2003, rose back to over $500 in 2008 before falling to $170 an ounce in late 2008. It trades around $450 an ounce as we go to press.

The platinum market has over 90 percent of its supply coming from Russia and South Africa, not exactly two stable places; so platinum should increase in price if anything unstable happens in these two nations.

Palladium is also produced mainly in the same two unstable countries. According to the CPM ground and PGM yearbook, over 82 percent of supply comes from Russia and South Africa, and 14 percent from North America.

There are a few major companies that produce platinum and palladium. Two of the larger companies are Anglo Platinum and North American Palladium. In addition, there are ETFs that will be launched for these metals in 2010.

As these metals are mostly produced in Russia and South Africa, their prices are subject to the caprices of politics in those countries. For example, in the early 2000s, the Russians all but stopped exports and that caused a huge spike in the price. In addition, if the move toward clean cars picks up, demand for catalytic converters and platinum will spike up.

Rare Earth Metals Lesser-known but important metals are the rare earth metals. Rare earth metals are a collection of 17 chemical elements in the periodic table. Basically, in lay terms, rare earths are mostly the *ums*, which include lanthunman, cerium, promethium, rhodium, and so forth. The most interesting aspect of rare earth metals is that many of them are used in a lot of clean energy technologies. According to the American Geological Survey, rare earth elements are incorporated into many modern technological devices, including superconductors, refining catalysts, and hybrid car components (primarily batteries and magnets). Until 1948, most rare earth metals were produced from placer sand deposits in India and Brazil; these deposits still account for a small part of global production. The United States produces about 2 percent of world production. However, the largest producer of rare earths is China, which produces over 95 percent of them.

As rare earths are needed for hybrid cars and other energy-saving technologies and 95 percent of them are produced in China (which has warned it may export less rare earths in the future), more discoveries of rare earths are required if politically correct politicians are to fulfill their goal of clean technologies.

As I write in 2010, rare earths are the newest fad in the resource market. Many rare earth stocks are going up a lot on any sort of good news. However, (similar to uranium and potash), just because the long-term fundamentals are very good for rare earths (especially if hybrid cars hit the market en masse), this does not mean that all of these stocks will survive.

I think rare earths have a very strong future, but be very selective when you buy them. They could be in another mini-bubble and investors are advised to not chase stocks in these industries.

Monetary Inflation and Demand Will Lead to a Commodities Boom

In this chapter, we have given you a quick overview of the commodities market. We have looked at everything from oil to natural gas to agricultural commodities to rare earths. There are very positive long-term fundamentals for these markets as emerging markets grow. However, we have directed the reader to note and beware of the various mini-bubbles in the micro-cap stocks in sectors such as potash and uranium in recent years. Accordingly, be careful when speculating in these specialty sectors.

In addition, do not chase commodities themselves. We have outlined techniques in this chapter that you can use to buy commodities when they are cheap and to lessen your risk overall.

For someone who has a longer-term point of view and is more conservative, you may just want to buy a commodity ETF and enjoy the ride! If we are correct, 2008 was very similar to 1987 in stocks; 2008 was a short, sharp correction in the longer-term commodity bull market. However, we must remember that stocks did not fully pass the 1987 high until 1991, four years later. So it might take a few more years before the commodities bull market revs up again. However, it should catch fire even without supply and demand factors. Future printing of money by the United States should continue to cause future inflation and devaluation in the U.S. dollar. These two economic evils should continue to drive the prices of commodities upward over the longer term.

Chapter 7

Value and Contrarian Investing

Investing at a Point of Maximum Pessimism

As the bull market of the eighties and early nineties turned into the stock mania of the late nineties, people forgot about value. Everyone wanted to become the next dot-com millionaire. People were willing to bid every no-name tech company up to any ridiculous price. The NASDAQ, at its peak in the year 2000, was trading at a P/E of well over 100. This is in the stratosphere by any valuation method.

History is replete with accounts of mad manias such as the Tulip Mania and Mississippi Scheme where people bought into wild stories and investments based on little to no fundamentals. We now laugh at these stories. We wonder how people could have been so stupid as to buy into these obviously ridiculous bubbles. In retrospect, are we any smarter? I mean stocks like pets.com; were they really any different?

In the mania of the late nineties, which stretched into the housing bubble of the 2000s, what was lost was value investing. As stated in our chapter on cycles, the purpose of these long-term cycles is for stocks to get back to median valuations. In a bear market cycle, stocks go from overvalued to undervalued, and in a bull market cycle, from undervalued to overvalued.

However, what was lost in the go-go years of the late nineties was the thought of income from investing. Dividend yields on U.S. stocks went to all-time lows because no one was interested in income from investing. I mean, who cared about making 5 percent a year in a dividend when you were getting a 100 to 200 percent capital gain per year from an Internet stock!

It should be noted that the greatest investors of our generation (e.g., Buffett, Templeton) were all value investors. They were investors who bought stocks cheap, held, and often looked for income. There are only so many George Soros's or John Paulsons who can speculate and make huge bets and profits from shorter-to-intermediate trends. The rest of us, as mere investing mortals, have to live with finding undervalued assets and then holding them for the long term.

In this chapter, I illustrate why it is so important to be a contrarian, to go against the crowd, to buy value, and to use the power of undervalued assets, mass pessimism, and dividend yields as allies on your side.

Buying at the Point of Maximum Pessimism

Buying at maximum pessimism is a lot more difficult than it may seem. It is not just as easy as reading a bunch of negative articles about the economy in the *New York Times* and then deciding the news is bad and you want to buy.

John Templeton had a simple belief in regard to how bull markets are born and how markets trade in a long-term trend. Most markets, be it gold, stocks, or widgets, all trade the same way. If you trade based on psychological principles, you will nearly always make money in the long term. Templeton was quoted as follows:

> Bull Markets are born on pessimism, grow on skepticism, mature on optimism and die on euphoria. The time of maximum pessimism is

the best time to buy and the time of maximum optimism is the best time to sell.

www.thekirkreport.com/2004/02/sir_john_temple.html

The first great trade that John Templeton ever made was in 1939. At that time, the United States was still reeling from 10 years of the Great Depression. Unemployment was still in the high teens and the economy seemed like it would never pick up from its 10-year malaise.

However, the rumblings of war were in the air. The Nazis were feverishly spreading their evil empire throughout Europe. Templeton knew that the U.S. industrial complex would have to be ramped up again to supply weapons to Europe and that the United States might even need to build up its own army to fight in the war itself.

He knew that this could cause a big pickup in the economy. However, where to profit from this pickup? Templeton realized that it would be perversely the worst companies that would profit most from an economic turnaround. As explained in the great book, *Investing the Templeton Way*, he figured that many of the worst companies were the best leveraged to this economic rebound. Basically, they were terribly run and the only way they could turn around was if there were an improvement in the macro economy. As the economy had been in a depression for most of the previous 10 years (other than a slight artifi- cial government-induced blip from 1935 to 1937), there was no reason for people to think there would be a macro pickup and all of these stocks were priced for a depressed economic environment.

Templeton went to his former boss and asked for a loan of $10,000 so he could buy 100 stocks that were trading at under $1.00 per share. The reason for the selection of the $1.00-per-share price was the fact that most of the companies that were weak and more leveraged to a turnaround in the macro economy were trading at under $1.00 a share. In all, he bought 104 companies, 36 of which were in bankruptcy. Within the next five years, as U.S. industrial production boomed due to the war, this $10,000 turned into $40,000. During the same time period, the Dow gained only about 80 percent.

Templeton was able to think outside the box. He saw value in near-bankrupt companies because he could see that the war effort would lead to an increase in industrial production and economic activity.

If he had told anyone that he was buying bankrupt companies 10 years into a depression and actually wanted to find the worst companies because they had more leverage to a potential economic turnaround, people would have said he was crazy. However, in contrarian investing, it is not unusual that although at first most people think you are crazy, you usually end up being correct.

It Ain't Easy

During times of maximum pessimism, a stock market or even economy can be imploding and collapsing. In late 2008 and early 2009, we saw the financial system in the United States, and in much of the western world, almost collapse. Many thought it could be the end of the markets as we know them. This is why it is so tough to buy at a bottom. At a bottom all the news is bad; everyone makes excuses as to why the market will never turn around. People are losing their jobs and companies; even heretofore-solid ones are going broke.

Ironically, when you feel totally confident about your investments and everything looks good, that is usually the time to sell. When everything appears hopeless, that is usually the best time to buy.

Let me give you an example. During the first quarter of 2009, I became extremely bullish on the financial markets. Yes, I know we were experiencing the financial crisis; Obama had been elected and he was not seen as friendly to markets. The economy was in a shambles. Bank of America and Citigroup had been all but nationalized. All of this put together equals maximum pessimism.

However, I was scouring the equity world for stocks. In my study, what I found were all sorts of low-priced stocks, just like John Templeton had found in 1939. I saw Ford, Citigroup, Bank of America, and MGM plus many others trading at under $10 a share. I thought back to the dot-com boom of 1999. At that time, any company with a dot-com at the end, no matter how bad the fundamentals, was trading in the hundreds-of-dollars range. I simply came to the conclusion that in a 10-year span we had gone from one extreme to another. We had gone from every piece-of-garbage company trading at hundreds of dollars to some of the top companies in the world trading in the single digits.

In addition, I became really bullish on emerging markets. I thought that emerging markets would emerge much stronger from the crisis than the United States. Countries like India, China, South Korea, and Taiwan had none of the toxic assets that U.S. and European banks had. However, because emerging markets are much more volatile, they had been hit harder as funds pulled out. While the S&P 500 fell 53 percent to its bottom in 2009, the Bombay Stock Exchange fell over 65 percent!

I also liked the casino stocks; many of these stocks, such as Las Vegas Sands, Wynn, and MGM, had huge amounts of debt and had fallen over 90 percent in value! As the wealthy consumer disappeared, many of these stocks had fallen off the face of the earth.

Profitable Trades in Maximum Pessimism—2008 and 2009

In March 2009, I put out a report called "Eleven Investment Trends for 2009 and Beyond." In that report, I outlined 11 sectors I was really bullish on; they included gold, oil, gas, casino stocks, emerging markets, and even the banks! At that time, the banks were down about 80 percent on average from their highs. Everyone hated them because of the TARP bailout plan and because they had helped to bring the economy to its knees.

Casinos, banks, and emerging markets were three of the hardest-hit sectors. However, I remembered John Templeton's words: "Buy at the point of maximum pessimism."

One of my favorite companies was Tata Motors, the Indian automaker that I still own a bit of. This is the classic example of a maximum pessimism/value trade. As you will read in Chapter 9, I am extremely positive on the future of India. When the Indian market tanked in late 2008, I began to research it more and more. I had seen a news piece on the Nano. The Nano is the cheapest car in the world; Tata produces it. Tata Motors had collapsed from $20 per share to $3. They had a huge debt load from a takeover of Jaguar in an attempt to expand into foreign markets.

Even after the Jaguar takeover, Tata remains primarily an Indian carmaker. Indians have huge savings; they save at a rate of 35 percent of GNP per year. Car sales had fallen in India like everywhere else during the bust of 2008. However, I suspected that much of these savings and pent-up demand was good for the Nano.

The Nano was a concept created by Ratan Tata, one of the great Indian industrialists. Ratan saw an Indian family all riding on one scooter. He realized that this must be changed and he wanted to bring out a car for the people. So he started on a journey to making a car that a lower- or middle-class Indian could afford. The result was the Nano; it could retail for $2,000–$2,500. With the combination of (1) the stock being so depressed, (2) high Indian savings, and (3) mass pessimism in the markets, I put Tata Motors on my list at $3.50 a share.

The performance of the stock exceeded even my wildest expectations. Indians had to pay $6 each just to apply to get on a draw list to buy the first generation of the Nano! For the average Indian, this is a large amount of money. There were 203,000 applications just to be considered to be put on a list. To 100,000 of those applicants, Tata allotted cars that would be delivered by the end of 2010!

The stock began to soar as the market bottomed. Tata (which trades under the symbol TTM) hit over $10 per share by the summer and by early 2010 was trading at over $17 per share! I recommended taking profits at around $10 but holding a small core position to take advantage of huge future growth potential in Tata. Selling Tata Motors in 2010 is like selling Toyota in 1980!

This is the classic maximum pessimism trade. Think above and beyond the crowd. No one wanted to hear about an Indian carmaker at the depths of the financial crisis. However, you could see the potential market and value in the stock.

I also liked casino stocks such as Las Vegas Sands and MGM at under $3 a share. Again, in the financial crisis, who wanted to hear about heavily indebted casino stocks? Again, it was the ultimate trade in maximum pessimism. MGM climbed to over $14 a share and Las Vegas Sands climbed to over $20 a share!

In January 2009, in a cover article in *Investor's Digest of Canada*, I talked about junior mining stocks and how they had collapsed during the crash of 2008, when the average junior miner fell over 80 percent in value. With tight credit markets, juniors are totally dependent on financings. However, I bet that all of the stimulus measures would be inflationary down the line and that the juniors would come back.

Many of the juniors I talked about it in this article doubled and tripled in value, with one climbing over 600 percent. Again, it's maximum pessimism. Sometimes, ironically, it pays to buy the *worst* companies in the hardest-hit sectors because they are the ones that will rally the strongest!

After outperforming for years, emerging markets also fell hard during the financial crisis of 2008. As hedge funds were forced to liquidate, they had to sell their positions in emerging markets. As these markets are smaller than and not as liquid as major markets, they fell hard. The Shanghai Index fell from a high, in 2008, of over 6,200 to 1,664.92; the Bombay Stock Exchange fell from 21,200 to just over 8,000; Taiwan's exchange fell from 9,859 to 3,955; South Korea fell from 2,085 to 892.

There was an argument before the financial crisis called *decoupling*. The idea behind decoupling was that foreign markets could be insulated from a drop in the U.S. market. However, after all of these markets tanked during the financial crisis and the U.S. dollar roared upward, people threw out this idea. Actually, they went to an opposite belief. Because the U.S. dollar was the reserve currency and the United States was the largest economy in the world, it had the easiest access to capital. Its market actually fell less and its currency was strong. Right near the bottom of the crisis, many so-called experts started to argue *against* investing in emerging markets, stating that they could be hit even harder than the United States because their exports would be hit hard and they did not have easy access to capital.

However, anyone who looked inside the situation could see that reality was different from the generally held perceptions. Emerging markets were much cheaper than the United States at the March bottom; many stocks listed on emerging markets were reaching multiyear lows, trading at single-digit P/Es and yielding north of 7 or 8 percent. Also, emerging markets had their financial crisis in 1998. At that time, many of the countries did not have foreign reserves, were running huge current account balances, and were dependent on foreign borrowing to grow. However, this time around, they had streamlined their financial systems and had huge reserves that they could sit on as the storm passed. In addition, as the U.S. dollar had rallied strongly from July 2008 to March 2009, you could also buy these stocks in undervalued currencies.

It was at this dreary time, in March 2009, with the MSCI Global Index having fallen nearly 70 percent off its highs, that I wrote an article in *Addicted to Profits* explaining why emerging markets were great buys and why they would outperform the U.S. market in the coming bull market. Over the next nine months, whereas the United States saw a strong rally of about 70 percent, the MSCI Global Index climbed over 120 percent in value.

Technical Ways to Profit from Maximum Pessimism

Now it was just not the tone of the times or valuations that told us that 2008–2009 was a period of extreme fear and panic. In my newsletter, I watch dozens of technical indicators to gauge fear and greed in order to decipher whether to buy or sell. Bottoms are a lot easier to spot than tops, believe it or not. Tops can take months or years to play out, whereas bottoms tend to form a lot quicker. Part of the reason is that at tops you do not have so much greed but rather complacency. People become complacent and this can last for a long time. For example, there was a great deal of complacency in the market from 2005 to 2007. It took the market more than two years to top. However, the emotion of fear is much more intense and easier to spot. This intensity leads to extremes in technical indicators. For the purposes of this book, I will concentrate on three of the many technical indicators I watch to determine and trade at maximum pessimism.

Indicator #1: The VIX

The VIX is a measure of implied volatility on the Chicago Board of Options. The VIX is basically a gauge of fear and greed. When the VIX is low, it is a sign that complacency is high. When the VIX is high, it is a sign of fear. The VIX usually spikes during large market declines. A VIX reading around 20 represents complacency; a VIX rating of 30 and higher and especially 40 and higher represents fear.

Like complacency and fear in general, the VIX is a lot easier to use to predict market bottoms than market tops. The VIX can often trade below 20 for months and months as a market tops. However, it has a very good track record predicting bottoms. The great thing about

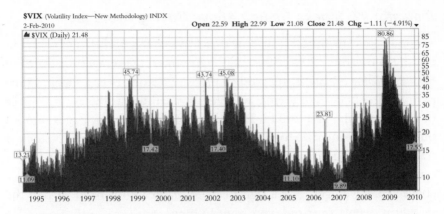

Figure 7.1 Chicago Board of Options Volatility Index
SOURCE: Courtesy of StockCharts.com (http://stockcharts.com).

using the VIX is that if you think that markets are going through a
period of pessimism, you can use the VIX to confirm this. Figure 7.1
is a 15-year chart of the VIX. Note the big spikes in 1998, 2001, 2002,
and 2008. All of these spikes over 40 led to intermediate or long-term
lows in the market. The year 1998 was the bottom of the Asian crisis
and the LTCM blowup, 2001 was a key bottom after the attacks of
9/11 when many global markets bottomed, and 2002 was the bottom
of the dot-com bust.

The year 2008 was of course the financial crisis. The VIX for the
2008–2009 period reflects the extreme fear we had in the markets.
Usually when the VIX goes over 40, it trades there for a few days or
maybe a few weeks; the market sees an extreme amount of fear and
then rallies. Because of this, I refer to the late 2008–early 2009 period
as the fear bubble. The VIX traded above 35 for the entire period from
the fall of 2008 to March 2009. And it spiked as high as 80; the only
other time it got this high was the 1987 stock market crash. The VIX
spent nearly six months at extreme fear readings. This was the time to
buy. Of course, this fear was followed by a huge rally in the markets
into 2010. The VIX does not tell you what markets or stocks to buy
but it is a good indicator to use to confirm your beliefs. If you believe
the market is at maximum pessimism and stocks are cheap, check the
VIX; if it is spiking higher, odds are you are seeing a market panic and
a great buying opportunity.

Indicator #2: Stocks Trading Above Moving Averages

Another great technical indicator that I like is the percentage of stocks trading above their 200-, 50-, and 20-day moving averages for the S&P 500. A *moving average* is the average price of a stock over a specific time period. The 200-day moving average, for example, is the average price of a stock for the past 200 trading days. These moving averages smooth out the direction of a stock price. In technical terms, when a stock is trading above these averages, it is considered bullish action; when it trades below, it is bearish action. However, when too few stocks trade above these averages, it is a sign that the market is oversold. When the market is deeply oversold, you want to buy.

When you see less than 20 percent of stocks trading above their 200-day moving averages, less than 10 percent above their 50-day moving averages, and less than 10 percent above their 20-day moving averages, it is a sign that the market is deeply oversold and will rally strongly.

Over the past 10 years, this has happened only four times:

1. September 2001, during the post-9/11 selloff
2. The latter part of 2002 and early 2003, as the bear market bottomed
3. Early 2008
4. The late 2008–March 2009 period.

September 2001 was followed by a strong six-month rally that took the S&P 500 up over 30 percent from its lows. The 2002–2003 period was the *low* of the bear market; March 2008 was followed by a very strong bear market rally into July 2008 and the November 2008–March 2009 period was, of course, the low of its bear market.

When you see these oversold levels:

- Less than 1 in 5 stocks trading above their 200-day moving averages
- Less than 1 in 10 above their 50-day moving averages
- Less than 1 in 10 above their 20-day moving averages

it is usually a sign of a significant bottom or at least a good trading bottom.

During bull markets, more stocks are going to stay above their 200-day moving averages as this is a longer-term moving average and the longer-term trend is higher. However, in sharp corrections during bull markets, you can see readings below 20 percent for the 50- and 20-day moving averages. If you believe the market is in an uptrend and you see these sorts of oversold levels on the short-term moving averages, that usually marks a short-term bottom. And the market moves higher.

Indicator #3: Investor's Intelligence

Investor's Intelligence (www.investorsintelligence.com) is a poll of advisors and newsletters on their opinions about the market. These "experts" get placed into three indicators: bulls, bears, and neutral. For our purpose, we throw the neutrals out and just use the bulls to the bears. I like to use it as a ratio. When this ratio is 3 to 1 or higher, meaning there are three times as many bulls as bears, it is a sign that there is too much positive sentiment and the market tops. When you get more bears than bulls or the ratio goes under 1 to 1, that is a sign there are too many bears and the market bottoms.

Like all of these indicators, Investor's Intelligence has a hard time calling tops. It can stay overbought for months until the market tops, or sometimes too much bullishness is just a sign of a short-term top. However, like all of the other indicators, it is a great indicator at a major market bottom.

In October 2007, at the top of the market, the number of bulls to bears skyrocketed to over 3 to 1. However, in 2003 as the market *began* its rally, the number of bulls to bears stayed at a 3-to-1 ratio for months and months as the market climbed. This is why we say it is tough to call tops with this indicator. However, at bottoms it is fantastic: 1994, 1998, 2002, and 2008–2009 were all periods where there were more bears than bulls; this indicator at those times predicted important bottoms for the stock market. In addition, the bearish reading in late 2008 (when many global markets bottomed) was 55 percent; the only other times in the past 20 years we saw such high bearish readings were at the bottom of the 1991 recession and in late 1994, just before the market began a huge five-year move from 1995 to 2000.

As we can see from all of these indicators, they are *very good* at predicting market panics and bottoms. Therefore, in addition to determining whether stocks are cheap, you can use these indicators to confirm that there is maximum pessimism and that you are buying at the point of this maximum pessimism.

You can find the Investor's Intelligence numbers in *Barron's* every week and on www.investorsintelligence.com.

When Investing, Ask Yourself One Key Question

If you want to buy at maximum pessimism, you must ask yourself one simple question that the great Jim Rogers says you should always ask when you buy something. The question is: "How much can the stock go down?" Theoretically, anything can go to zero, but realistically, will it? I mean at $3.50, Tata had fallen over 80 percent from its high of over $20 a share. How much further was it really going to go? Sometimes it is not *what* you buy but *when* and *how much* you buy it for. If you had waited six months, you would have bought Tata for over $10, which is a big difference from buying at $4.

Another case in point was Apple Computers at the depths of the 2002–2003 tech bust. Apple was trading at just over $6 a share, which is over 80 percent below its 2000 high of $37 a share. A few failed lines of Macintosh computers and the tech bust had brought the company down. However, Steve Jobs was back on board after spending time at Pixar. The company was about to aggressively market its new product, the iPod. It was going to become a media company, which would give it a niche, rather than going head-to-head with Microsoft. Then it came out with a new line of upper-end laptops, the iPhone, and so on. Their stores were full; Apple was back. The stock soared from $6 to over $200 in the four years that followed. Again:

- Buying at maximum pessimism
- Knowing that Apple had new product lines
- Realizing that the company had a top-tier CEO

would have brought anyone great profits.

Emerging markets, as previously discussed, were another recent example of a trade at maximum pessimism.

You must fight the emotion of fear when you buy at maximum pessimism. You must ignore the emotion and the negative sentiment that is all around you and buy. This why I feel I am different from most pundits out there. Rather than constantly spouting doom and gloom, I am always looking for bargains. Shrewd investors always look for ways to take advantage of the gloom.

The few examples I have given you illustrate the wisdom of this approach. The years 2009 and 1939 were 70 years apart and worlds apart in cultural terms. However, both years were placed during times of struggling economies and cheap stocks. Both gave great buying opportunities. In each case, if you had selected the worst-run, most heavily indebted and beaten-up stocks, you would have made huge amounts of money over the months that followed.

Incorporate Dividend-Paying Stocks with Maximum Pessimism Buying

There is an additional advantage in selecting dividend-paying stocks and buying them at beaten-down levels.

Again, you must be on the lookout for bargains. Every once in a while, for whatever reason, a great company goes on sale. Maybe it is a bear market where all stocks are hit; maybe it is a legal problem; maybe it is a onetime hit, and so on. However, if there are still strong fundamentals at the company and you feel that the company will rebound and perform in the coming years, you should go and buy it. There is an unwritten rule that whenever a strong blue-chip company falls 65 percent from its all-time high you should buy it, no questions asked. Some of these companies may go the way of GM or Enron and go bust. However, more often than not, when a brand-name company goes on sale, it will soar afterwards. In addition, if the company rebounds and has a history of paying a stable dividend, the potential dividend yield will be great.

By way of yet another example, let's take the case of McDonald's, the world's top-tier fast-food company. In the early 2000s, a bear market and the low-carb craze devastated McDonald's stock price. The movie *Super-Size Me* helped to sink McDonald's persona; a strong U.S. dollar in the early 2000s also took a bite out of profits. McDonald's fell from a high of $43 per share in late 1999 to just over $10 per share in 2003. That is a decline of over 77 percent. However, the signs of a turnaround were all there.

McDonald's was expanding in foreign markets. As countries develop, they tend to consume more meat and especially more red meat. The cheapest way to do this is by eating at McDonald's; so it only makes sense that they would benefit first from this trend. Also, with the U.S. dollar weakening and McDonald's selling more abroad, that would help the bottom line. Also, let's face it—for most people in the United States, healthful eating is a fad. Much of the population lives on fast food. After the fad effects of *Super-Size Me*, McDonald's adjusted its menu and started to take the trans fat out of French fries and the like.

The stock bottomed and then soared. From $10.69, it went to nearly $65 as I write, a gain of sixfold in seven years. In addition, McDonald's pays a dividend of $2.20 a share or 3.5 percent. However, on that $10.69 price, that $2.20 represents a dividend of over 20 percent per year! Let's remember the *rule of 72*, which states that you calculate your yield into the number 72 to find out how long it will take you to double your money. This means that if you had purchased McDonald's at just over $10, the current dividend would be doubling your money almost every three years! This is the power of buying good, solid dividend-paying stocks when they are depressed.

Look again at my Tata Motors trade. As I write in 2010, Tata pays only a $0.10 dividend. That is still about 3 percent at my $3.50 price. However, let's say Tata returns to profitability and ups its dividend to $0.50 at a $20 stock price, which is just a 2.5 percent dividend. However, at my $3.50-per-share price, that is 14 percent per year!

Another example of a stock that had a short-term smash was Altira. This stock was one of the spinoffs from Philip Morris. This stock tanked from 1998 to 2000 from over $10 a share to $3.15 on news of class action lawsuits from its cigarette division. However, this was a legal payout that would be finished at some future time. We must remember that people are always going to smoke. I don't care if they *know* it can kill them; smoking will always continue. After this payout, there was a good chance that this business would return to profitability. The stock has since rallied to over $20 per share. The dividend is $1.38 per share. Let's say you had purchased it at $4 a share back in 2000. You would be making nearly 35 percent per year just in dividends!

The advantage of high dividends is that they cushion you against a decline in the stock. If you are making 35 percent a year on your Altria stock in dividends, the stock can fall 35 percent and you come out flat. In addition, you can then *reinvest* dividends to own more of the stock going forward. You can *live off* these dividends if you wish to do so. In today's world, where governments pay nothing in short-term interest, dividends such as these are going to become even more important.

Value, Contrarian, and Distressed Investing

Buying distressed assets when they are out of vogue and cheap is just another strategy I recommend for the coming years. On top of investing in the macro trends such as gold, oil, and other resources, we recommend being patient and waiting for solid large-cap companies that pay dividends. If a company such as this falls either due to a short-term problem or market decline, take advantage of such a company's decline. This is so especially if it has a history of long-term dividend payouts. *When* you buy is important; it is much better to buy a great business when it is cheap rather than when it is fairly priced or overvalued!

Buy pessimism. When emerging markets or casino stocks or banks had collapsed in early 2009, they were the best sectors to buy. The most hated and most beat-up sectors often give you the most upside going forward. Being a contrarian and buying beat-up companies takes a lot of guts, but as we have seen from this chapter, you can make a lot of money doing so!

Templeton's Point of Maximum Pessimism

John Templeton passed away in 2008, ironically, during the financial crisis, just when panic, fear, and maximum pessimism took hold of the markets. This chapter is somewhat of an ode to him. Whereas it was not the beginning of a new secular bear market, the late 2008–2009 period was a great trading opportunity partially due to all of the fear that forced the markets lower. Many stocks in the hardest-hit sectors, such as banks, casinos, and automobiles, in the year that followed the March 2009 bottom rose 200, 300, and even over 1,000 percent. While stocks may be in a trading range for the next 5 to 10 years, spurts of fear and panic will bring overvalued sectors and great investing and trading opportunities for those who are willing to be contrarians and use fear to profit from gobbling up undervalued assets.

Part Four

INVESTING IN EMERGING ECONOMIES

Chapter 8

China

How and Why You Should Invest in
an Economic Superpower

O ne must remember, when looking at China, that the back–
ward, communist agrarian society that we often associate with
China is not really reflective of that country's past. Going back
to ancient times, the Chinese were for thousands of years one of the
most progressive, advanced societies in the world. If you go back "just"
several hundred years, to the Middle Ages, you would see a China that
was miles ahead of the European continent.

China is the largest country in East Asia and the most populous
in the world, with over 1.3 billion people. It seems obvious, if not
inevitable, to many that China is on its way to becoming the world's
foremost economic superpower. For most of the past two millennia,
China was home to the world's largest economy. Though it missed the
Industrial Revolution, the economic reforms, enacted in the 1970s,

transformed the country and made it one of the world's major economic powers once again. The shift from a centrally planned, closed system to a more market-oriented economy with a rapidly growing private sector has made the People's Republic of China a key player in the global economy. These reforms, formally known as "Socialism with Chinese Characteristics," began with the phasing out of collectivized agriculture. There were major increases in the pricing of agricultural products, and eventually there was a dismantling of the "collective system," which was replaced by the "contract responsibility system." This promoted an egalitarian standard in which private citizens were held responsible for the profits and losses of the enterprise. Later, the Chinese implemented the gradual liberalization of costs in other sectors of the economy along with fiscal decentralization, increased autonomy for state enterprises, the foundation of a diversified banking system, the development of stock markets, rapid growth of the non-state sector, and the opening to foreign trade and investment. All of this has led to one of the most rapid industrializations in world history.

My theory of cycles and movement is not merely one of commodities versus U.S. equities, but that there is a major secular shift in economic power from west to east, with China being the largest of the emerging economies. Your investment philosophy should not only lean to inflation-orientated plays such as gold and commodities but should also move to these nations. As Dr. Marc Faber, editor of the *GloomBoomDoom* report, has stated in many recent articles, nearly 25 percent of your invested capital should be in emerging economies. In this chapter I show you why China should be part of this investment portfolio and how to invest in this economic superpower.

Basic Overview Since 1940

The Chinese government presently operates as a communist state, run by the Communist Party of China (CPC). Although there are about eight non-communist parties, the CPC maintains overall control. For the most part, China has enjoyed a politically stable environment since the end of its civil war in 1949. Legal reform became a government priority in the 1990s, and legislation was enacted to modernize and professionalize the nation's lawyers, judges, and prisons. Additionally, criminal law and criminal procedures have been amended to introduce cogent reforms. The criminal law amendments abolished the crime of "counterrevolutionary" activity, while criminal procedure reforms encouraged the establishment of a more transparent, adversarial trial process.

Diplomatic relations with most major countries are good and, with increasing free trade, friendly relations with most countries are expected to continue. China's focus is on maintaining its "peaceful rise," with gross domestic product (GDP) growing around 10 percent annually, compared to 3 percent or so in the United States. To offset the effects of the global economic crisis, the government announced a financial stimulus of around ¥4 trillion spread over two years. However, new spending by the government was actually only about ¥1 trillion; the rest was spending that was already allocated as part of the government's budget. As of 2009, China has surpassed Germany as the world's leading exporter. Despite the current economic downturn, its share of world exports jumped to almost 10 percent, up from 3 percent in 1999. China currently garners 19 percent of the U.S. export market. China has now also become the world's second-largest economy with the economy growing to $4.91 trillion in size. Chinese GDP per capita is also about one-hundredth in the world.

China's economy, despite the market reforms and foreign investment from major firms all across the world, is still somewhat centrally run. China is actually building up infrastructure and other needs for its economy in anticipation of further future growth. For example, many malls and airports in China are famously half empty as they were originally constructed with future demand in mind. China, in addition, possesses an empty city that was built in Inner Mongolia in 2009 as a part of the stimulus spending designed to drive China out of the worldwide economic crisis of 2009.

The World's New Creditor and the Power it Breeds

In the twentieth century, the United States became a major creditor as gold from the vaults of London was slowly transferred to New York. The Americans even gave the British an emergency loan during World War II so they could meet their financial obligations during the war. Back then, the United States was the creditor and the U.K. was the debtor. As late as the 1980s, even with a significant debt load, the United States was still somewhat of a self-sufficient nation as only about 20 percent of the country's debt was owned by foreigners. With the advent of the Super Bubble (which we previously discussed) in the 1980s, foreign debt obligations began to grow. As China expanded its economy and opened up, its main export market was the United States. Accordingly, the United States and China began a mutually beneficial relationship where the Americans would buy "stuff" from China and China would buy Treasury bills from the United States. This arrangement contributed to the amount of U.S. debt owned by foreigners, rising to nearly 50 percent of GDP by 2009.

The Consequences of Being the Creditor—Geopolitical Power

So, *big deal*, you may think. The United States used to own a lot of British debt and now the Chinese own a lot of American debt. Well, debt can become the ultimate weapon. In the mid-1950s, the British were due to hand over the Suez Canal to Egypt. However, Nasser, then president of Egypt, wanted to nationalize the canal. The British thought the canal had strategic importance and wanted to keep ownership over it. In 1956, Britain and France with the support of Israel decided to attack the Egyptians.

The Americans disagreed with this military venture. Eisenhower threatened that he would dump a portion of the British debt that the Americans had loaned to the U.K. during World War II if the British did not cease this adventure immediately. This was essentially war by finance. If the Americans had followed through on this threat, British interest rates would have skyrocketed and the British economy, still recovering from World War II, would have screeched to a standstill. The Brits pulled out and the Suez Canal went over to the Egyptians.

Now China owns a huge chunk of U.S. debt. The current total is closing in on $1 trillion worth. This is only about 8 percent of U.S. debt outstanding, but, if the Chinese were to jettison their entire holdings, that would have an enormous impact on the U.S. economy. In the short run, this is unlikely, as by holding U.S. debt, the Chinese can help keep their own interest rates low and assist their own economy. However, it is our opinion that China will become less dependent on the United States going forward. As we go to press, China has a huge savings rate of about 35 percent of Gross National Product. The Chinese save anywhere from 30 to 60 percent of their income. While Americans have lived beyond their means, the Chinese have lived beneath theirs.

The Chinese are going to rebuild their purchasing power. For example, consumer spending as a percentage of the Chinese economy fell from 52 percent of GDP in 1982 to 33 percent in 2008! During that same time, savings went from 33 percent of GDP to 52 percent. The investment rate as a percentage of GDP has increased to 45 percent of GDP. The Chinese are now in the process of trying to create consumer demand by instituting spending credits. China is a nation of 1.3 billon people; so, if they can just create one-quarter of the demand that they get from the United States on a per-capita basis, they will replace all of the exports they send to the United States. In addition, we must remember that there are 3.6 billion people in Asia. This is 12 times the population of the United States. Accordingly, if Asia as a whole can create one-twelfth of the demand for products on a per-capita basis that the United States gets from China, you are going to see Asia replace the demand from the United States.

It is noteworthy to remember that for the first time ever, in 2009, car sales in the emerging world surpassed car sales in the first world. That statistic will eventually trickle down to sales of refrigerators, televisions, DVDs, clothes, and other consumer goods. Therefore, in the long term, China will be able to find other markets to replace the United States. Therefore, the Chinese should become less dependent on the United States at some point in the future.

A number of consequences will flow from this export evolution to alternative markets. First, this means that China will eventually buy less U.S. debt. However, it also means that the U.S. debt that China currently possesses can be used as leverage in a wide variety of economic-warfare scenarios. I predict that sometime in the relatively near future the United States will go into a venture that the Chinese will not agree with. Maybe it will be Iran, as China has good relations with Iran. I remember, when traveling to China in 2004, seeing ads for Iran as a great place to travel to. If the Americans do plan a strike against Iran and the Chinese don't like it, the Chinese will warn the Americans that if they continue with this military venture, they will dump their U.S. debt. At that point, just as the Suez crisis represented a shift from British world dominance to American, this type of potential conflict could represent a shift from American dominance to Chinese dominance. Right now, people see conflicts as unlikely because these two have an economic bond. But, remember that at the turn of the twentieth century, many saw war in Europe as unlikely because there was mass trade and economic inter-dependence among European nations. Fifty years later, there had been two major world wars in Europe. However, the Chinese might not have to use guns or air power over the Americans, but rather the most powerful force of all—economics.

Chinese Growth—Miracle or Bubble?

We have all seen the Chinese "miracle" of the past 30-plus years. China has averaged nearly 9 percent growth per year during that time period. Millionaire business owners have evolved in China and we are not merely talking about owners (like those in Russia) who may have risen to power due to political connections. We are talking about *entrepreneurs* who have started businesses in exporting or in local hotels or selling to the local population.

As stated earlier, the main component of Chinese economic growth has come in the form of export selling to the United States and the rest of the western world. Figure 8.1 shows this in graphical form. Exports from China, which were just over $5 billion a month in early 1990, skyrocketed to over $135 billion a month in 2008. However, in early 2009, these plummeted due to the downturn of the global economy. Figure 8.1 shows this boom and then bust in exports of the Chinese economy.

To fight this drop in exports, China initiated a huge stimulus plan. China brought down a ¥4 trillion stimulus plan. That is approximately $583 billion, making this stimulus plan not much smaller than the U.S. stimulus of $700 billion. However, the Chinese economy is only about

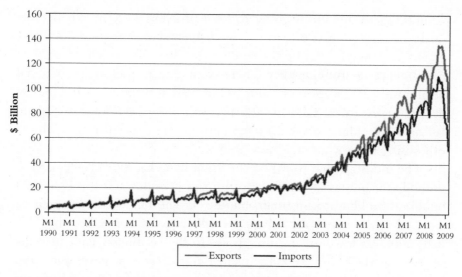

Figure 8.1 China: Monthly Exports and Imports
SOURCE: www.japanfocus.org/-Brad-Setser/3016

$4.33 trillion in size. Therefore, while the U.S. stimulus was about 6 percent of GDP, the Chinese stimulus was over 13 percent of GDP or nearly twice that of the U.S. plan based on the relative sizes of their respective economies. The breakdown of the Chinese GDP was ¥1.5 trillion infrastructure, ¥1.0 trillion in post-earthquake reconstruction, ¥370 billion in technology advancement, ¥210 billion in sustainable development, ¥150 billion in educational development, ¥400 billion in social welfare, and ¥370 billion in rural development.

Amazingly enough, the deficit in 2009 from all of this spending was only 2.2 percent of GDP, as compared to over 11 percent for the United States in the same fiscal year. China also, because of its huge surpluses and savings, is nowhere near a government debt crisis with a government debt of only 22.2 percent of GDP, one-fifth of the total government debt, as compared to GDP, that the United States has. At the G7 meeting in Inuvik, Northwest Territories, Canada, one of the G7 talking points was the bubble going on in China. The most notable concern was the bubble in the Chinese property market. We sometimes think that western governments need to stop looking at things with rose-colored glasses or they should look in the mirror. Yes, the

Chinese credit bubble is going to be a problem early in this decade. Loans in 2009 increased to well over 100 percent over their 2008 levels. Money supply was up 30 percent in China for much of 2009 to help finance its stimulus plan. There were empty cities built; there has been some misallocation of capital. However, as we just stated, Chinese debt as a percent of GDP is 22.2 percent. They have huge savings to fall back on. The average Chinese person is not speculating in stocks or housing like the average American was.

The industrialized world on the other hand has *huge* problems with unfunded liabilities in the form of unpaid pensions and the U.S. debt bubble is building to unsustainable levels. The bubble they should be worried about is not the Chinese credit bubble, but rather the U.S. debt bubble. However, this just speaks to the continued arrogance the western world has in looking at emerging nations as developing and not realizing that they, themselves, have much in the way of serious economic problems.

As stated in Chapter 2, the United States has a total debt bubble of 350 percent of GDP including private-sector debt. Getting a handle on Chinese debt as a proportion of GDP is tough, but we would think that it is somewhere significantly south of 100 percent. So if the debt bubble in China explodes, it will be a negative; however, it is nowhere near the size in relation to the economy that the American debt bubble is to the U.S. economy. Accordingly, we do not expect it to have a dramatic effect on the Chinese economy.

We are reminded of two bubbles in the eighteenth century. These are the South Sea bubble in England and the Mississippi Scheme in France. Both blew up around the same time. The Mississippi Scheme sent France into a depression, near bankruptcy, and eventually helped to lead to the French revolution as it forced the nation into financial ruin. The South Sea bubble in England, however, blew up and did no serious damage to the English economy. The subprime and housing bubble in the U.S. nearly destroyed the U.S. economy. However the Chinese bubble is nowhere that large. We are willing to bet that, while this lending bubble will burst and the Chinese stock market might decline, any implosion of any Chinese bubbles will not have the ruinous effect that the implosion of the U.S. debt bubble will have on the U.S. economy.

The Effect of China's Surplus—Worldwide Investment

There is an argument in the west that there is an ongoing worldwide struggle involving a great clash between U.S. freedom interests versus evil Chinese capitalist/fascist initiatives. The supreme irony of this propaganda is that the Chinese are the ones who are acting as global capitalists at the moment. Whereas the United States uses its resources for bankrupt government programs and wasteful wars in Afghanistan and Iraq, the Chinese use their cash to invest in resource-rich nations of Africa in order to secure a supply of natural resources. Africa is starved for capital to develop these resources and China is providing that link. According to United Nations Conference on Trade and Development, or UNCtad (www.unctad.org), China has invested over $50 million in 8 African nations and has investments in 19 African nations. I reside in the small country of the Bahamas and the Chinese are investing $2.5 billion for new resorts, building a $30 million sports stadium here and have provided the Bahamian government $150 million worth of loans at minimal interest.

There could be many reasons for their doing this: to secure votes at United Nations meetings, to garner first-right building contracts, and so on. The bottom line is that the Chinese are investing all over the world at a time when the United States is hurtling toward bankruptcy. A long journey is said to start with a just few steps and China's imperial footprint is beginning to appear all over the planet.

Will China Rule the World?

Will China dominate the planet as the next great empire? It is obvious that China will continue to grow. I do believe that it will become an economic power. However, I am not as bullish about China as some of my colleagues are, for one simple reason: It is my opinion that in the end the most prosperous societies are the freest. It would be hypocritical for me to bash the United States for continuing to take away economic and social freedoms and then argue that China will dominate the world with an economic model that is still much less free than that of the United States. History tells us that many of the great superpowers of the world—ancient Greece, the Roman Empire, the British

Empire, with its form of parliamentary democracy, and the United States—were some of the freest nations of their time. They were not perfect. However, it is no coincidence that on top of economic power, the British and Americans have also led the globe in terms of literature, music, and film.

Writers such as Upton Sinclair in the United States and Charles Dickens in the United Kingdom have been able, through literature, to expose the social horrors of their time. Sinclair's classic, *The Jungle*, exposed the filth and exploitation of the U.S. meat-packing industry, and Dickens, through classics such as *Oliver Twist*, detailed the horrors of child labor and the like. Many Chinese filmmakers criticized their own government after the success of *Slumdog Millionaire*, stating that such an open film about the underbelly of Chinese society would not be tolerated by the Chinese government. If this book makes its way to China but must be edited to delete out these rather mild musings, or if I am placed on some sort of Chinese blacklist afterwards, it will show that China is still a repressive society and needs to open up in order to realize its full economic potential.

We have recently seen Google threaten to close down operations in China after many of its Gmail accounts belonging to human rights activists were cyber-attacked. Google has about 31 percent of the Chinese search engine market, which is worth an estimated $600 million. However, problems such as these illustrate the problem of combining economic freedom with social restrictions. In the long run, it will not work. China should work on some sort of plan to democratize, much like Pinochet of Chile did in 1980, when he announced a 10-year transition to democracy and then gave up power. Just like Pinochet, the Chinese leaders are no saints, but at some point you have to read the writing on the wall. India is much more backwards in some ways. However, the power to oust the government via elections also will keep India from blowing up even in times of economic downturns.

An illustration of the problems that China's centrally planned economy will experience is revealed in China's population demographics. In recent years, the Chinese developed their one-child-per-family doctrine. Ignoring for a moment the human rights implications, let us just look at China's population distribution from a purely demographic viewpoint. Demographics play a role in the secular trends that we talk about in this book. For example, the great boom of the 1980s and 1990s in the United States and the 1960s, 1970s, and 1980s in Japan occurred in part due to favorable demographics. During these respective timeframes, both the United States and Japan saw a large portion of their populations hit their peak earnings years. This large group of workers and earners had money to invest and it helped to expand their economies, stimulate consumer demand, and drive up asset prices. However, in the 2000s and beyond, the United States is seeing the retirement of the Baby Boomers, who will in turn become net sellers of equities and in addition will burden the system in the form of payouts from a number of entitlement programs.

The one-child-per-family policy in China has damaged its demographic makeup. For example, in China nearly 50 percent of the population is between 15 and 44 years old. And nearly 44 percent of the population is between 30 and 59. Let's examine more closely that 44 percent of the population that is between 30 and 59. In one generation, or in about 30 years, they will be between 60 and 89. Instead of contributing to the economy, they will become dependents. In addition, because the one-child-per-family model favored males, the ratio of males to females under 15 years of age at the moment is 1.13 to 1. The fertility rate among women in childbearing years is 1.75 children per woman. In a nutshell, this means that China could become "old" in 30 to 40 years when it should be becoming rich. This is important as the last two great global empires both had growing populations within them. The United States had mass immigration and the United Kingdom had huge population growth as it vastly expanded its empire around the world, taking in people from the colonies.

If China cannot grow (it seems odd that a nation of 1.3 billion people could experience population as a problem!) and becomes saddled with a large, dependent and aged society, that contingency would hinder its growth growing forward. We must remember that, in the 1990s, one of the main hindrances that plagued Japan was demographics. One of the main reasons that Japan did not overtake the United States as a dominant global power, like some thought it would, was because population stagnated and Japan got old. All of a sudden it had a huge segment of its population on the receiving end of entitlements and this was a burden on Japan's financial system. If China does not reverse course, it could be in danger of repeating these same mistakes. For China, I think the fear will be more of productivity problems than cost concerns. I believe that, as western entitlement programs eventually go up in the coming years, the eastern world will not make the same mistakes. The eastern world learned from its credit bubble of the 1990s. It will institute private pensions, and in Asia, many more people take care of their parents. Eventually, the western world will have to end its entitlement welfare-state mentality and nations in the east, seeing the problems in the west, will not make the same mistakes.

In the end, I think that *demographics* and *democracy*, the two big *D's*, represent big problems for China. China, despite its large population, must ironically start having babies again, and it must make the transition to democracy. Severe economic downturns are inevitable in any large economy and they will happen in China. Even as the United States built itself into a great power, it had huge downturns in 1907, 1929, and 1937. However, in China, any huge downturn that results in mass unemployment could in turn force a democratic revolution.

How to Invest in China

Despite these problems, China should produce an unprecedented number of investment opportunities. The problems of demographics or a potential revolt into democracy probably will not occur for at least another 10 to 20 years. The Chinese investment case is complicated by the fact that Class A shares are restricted to foreigners. However, there are many ways to get around this restriction. Investments in China can be made as follows:

- **Commodities.** If you are scared of directly investing in China, you can invest in commodities or other plays that will indirectly do well because of the secular boom trend in China. China's economy will continue to demand more and more commodities due to the requirements of a large economy with 1.3 billion people growing at 9 percent. Part of the commodities argument is not just the U.S. dollar devaluation or monetary money printing but demand coming from China and India. China already ranks first or second in demand for most industrial commodities such as gold, nickel, copper, oil, and gas. Therefore, you might look at commodities (as pointed out in Chapter 6), as an indirect way to play the China boom without having a direct risk in China. As you will read in Chapter 10, commodity-producing countries that export to China may be another way to play this boom.

- **China ETFs.** There are a few ETFs that trade on the New York Stock Exchange that reflect Chinese stocks. Also many large-cap companies in China (see below) trade on the New York Stock exchange. The largest, most liquid ETF is the FXI, which holds large-cap Chinese banks, infrastructure, technology, and insurance companies. This is the simplest and broadest way to play China.

- **Chinese ADRs.** In addition, many large-cap companies such as China Telecom, China Southern Airlines, Baidu, and Jlin Chemical Industrial Company also trade on the New York Stock Exchange. Buying a large bank or telecom company can sometimes be the simplest and smartest way to play the growth of an economy. For example, imagine if you had owned Bell or AT&T from the 1930s to the 1990s; you would have made a killing in both stock price and received a huge amount of dividends to boot. For example, the China Telecom ADR has already more than doubled since going public on the NYSE in 2003 and pays a nice dividend of near 3 percent.

- **Hong Kong listings.** Many Chinese companies have listings in the Hong Kong stock market. These are mostly mid- to larger-tier companies. These are the types of companies that could be much leveraged to the Chinese economy. In addition, you have the advantage of buying them on an advanced and liquid exchange such as Hong Kong.

- **Small-cap Chinese stocks trading on OTC and U.S. exchanges.** These investments can bring great rewards. After all, the largest capital gains are usually in small to mid-sized companies that expand and grow into mega-conglomerates. Of course, this is what companies such as Dell Computers, Apple Computers, and Microsoft did in the eighties and nineties. A few of these will list on the OTC or AMEX and grow tremendously. However, there is also a lot of risk in this type of investing. China's accounting standards are still dubious by western standards and these are the types of companies that are most likely to fudge numbers and the like. Many of these companies will take advantage of rolling their businesses into a *shell company* (a company that has no business and is just an empty shell) to take advantage of exposure to the American investor. You should be careful, because many of these companies will inflate their stories or just not be able to pull off their business plans.

In the past, I invested in and followed a power company that could not get a final approval from the Chinese government. I went to China and saw the power plants, the company's connections, and so on, but that was still no help when the final approvals came down. More recently, a few contacts that I have recently provided me with information regarding a Chinese company that did a shell takeover and graduated to the AMEX exchange. However, when looking at its earnings numbers closely, you can see that it is very suspect and the company looks like some sort of big promotion with little behind it (how U.S. regulators can let a thing like this list on a major exchange is beyond me). This type of investment was very hot in 2009 because there was little or no action in the North American IPO markets after the credit crunch of 2010. While these types of investments can bring great rewards, they also contain great risk.

China's Role in Your Investment Portfolio

I have my reservations regarding China. However, for the next 5 to 10 years, China will continue to grow at a rapid rate and expand its economy, especially on the commodity and infrastructure side. Therefore, I think that prudent investors should look to a Chinese investment as a small part of their portfolio, either indirectly through commodity plays or countries that sell commodities to China or directly through the Chinese stock market and Chinese companies.

Chapter 9

India

A Long-Term Investment Strategy

A s shown in Chapter 3, the Great Super Cycle investment strategy should also include major global, emerging economic super-powers. Although China is perhaps the most obvious choice, the other rising giant of the twenty-first century is India. Many have even referred to India and China as *Chindia*, a sort of combination of two great giants with a population of nearly 2.5 billion opening up their economies to the free market.

From 2000 to 2010, the S&P 500 fell 24.1 percent while the Indian market actually rose 248.9 percent. This is a secular trend that is just starting and should continue. As you will read later in this chapter, India actually opened up its economy later than China and there-fore is earlier in its upward expansion and this expansion is occurring from the ground up. In addition, India has one of the youngest popu-lations in the world, leading to very strong demographic trends that should also drive consumer demand and the stock market higher. In this chapter, I will show you how India became an emerging economic superpower and how you can profit from its dominance.

India's Rise to Prominence

Most investors seem to think that the rise of Chindia is a recent phenomenon.

However, what these investors fail to realize is that the rise of China and India is more of resurgence rather than a new development. According to the books *The World Economy: A Millennial Perspective* and *Historical Statistics in the Sixteenth Century*, Mughal India was the second largest economy in the world, representing about 24.5 percent of the global economy. The largest economy at that time was Ming's China, which represented nearly 25 percent of the global economy. Therefore, India and China in the sixteenth century were actually global leaders that represented nearly 50 percent of the global economy! In a way, we are just tracing back to those roots.

According to the same books, Indian Emperor Akbar's treasury in 1600 was 17.5 million pounds compared to the empire treasury of Britain, which was about 16 million pounds at that time. By 1700, India had instituted common levies and duties around the Mughal Empire and the Aurangzeb's exchequer was over 100 million pounds, twice the size of Europe at the time, thus making India the world's largest economy.

Then, in the eighteenth century, the Mughals were replaced by the Nawabs in the north, Marathas in the Central, and Nixams in the south of India, somewhat fracturing the country.

This allowed the British to take over and stake India as a new continent. While the British did build the infrastructure of India's great railway system, institute common law, and bring some stability, Britain's main purpose was to exploit resources from the Indian economy. We must remember that it was India, not the Caribbean, Africa, nor even the United States or Canada, that was considered to be the jewel of the British Empire. This is the main reason the British tried to hang on to it for so long.

However, the British legacy had devastating long-term impacts on the Indian economy. The economy was deindustrialized with much of the manufacturing moving to Great Britain. India, which at one time in the seventeenth century had represented nearly 25 percent of the world's economy, had dropped to a mere 3.8 percent of the global economy by 1952. Now, much of this diminution was due to the huge growth of North America and Europe cutting into India's share, but also much of the loss was due to stagnant growth over that timeframe.

In addition, in a reaction to overbearing foreign influences, such as the Dutch and British East India Companies, which were not normal companies (they possessed their own armies, etc.), India went into an isolationist/socialist mood post-independence, fearing that foreigners could again exploit the country. Many of the banks were nationalized in the mid-seventies and the economy remained stagnant, going from one crisis to the next. Jokingly, the stagnant economy was referred to as the "Hindu rate of growth," as growth only averaged 3.5 percent and per-capita incomes rose 1.3 percent per year from the 1950s to the 1980s. In addition, in 1950 it took 4.70 rupees to buy one U.S. dollar; by 1990 it took 17.50 rupees to do so. During this time period, India was a basket case with heavy state involvement in the economy complete with five-year plans.

Not surprisingly, in 1991, the country entered into an economic crisis. The government debt, which had been 35 percent of GDP in 1980, had increased to 53 percent of GDP by 1991. The country had to devalue its currency and put in economic reforms pursued by Manmohan Singh (current Prime Minister). The rupee fell to 45 rupees per dollar by 1992 but has been relatively stable since (trading around 46 rupees per dollar as I write in 2010). The country secured a $2.2 billion loan from the IMF and began the reforms. Duties, which were as high as 355 percent in 1991, were cut to 12.5 percent in 2009.

Corruption and Poverty—India's Achilles Heel

India still has its fair share of problems. Corruption and red tape are endemic in the government. One statistic indicates that, in 2008, over 100 people running for parliament were under criminal investigation;

these criminal investigations include incidents involving rape and other forms of violent crime. According to Arabianbusiness.com, 63 candidates in the 2009 elections had some sort of criminal record, with 39 having serious charges against them!

In addition, India has huge problems with infrastructure. Old roads and small airports are holding the country back, not to mention huge amounts of red tape. For example, neighboring Pakistan ranks much higher in terms of freedom from government interference in business practices and procedures. India also has water shortages and imports 85 percent of its oil. However, the latter problems will bring great opportunities for those who can find solutions for them. In the case of oil, India has discovered huge offshore natural gas reserves in the Indian Ocean; they just need to extract them. By some estimates, India's offshore reserves could get them to be energy self-sufficient.

Many critics also point to the fact that there are 22 languages in India, and the Mumbai terrorist attacks do show some fear of Islamic fundamentalism. After all, there are over 150 million Muslims in the nation. However, it should be noted that considering the mixture of Muslims, Buddhists, Hindus, and Christians, this nation of over 1.1 billion people has actually seen relatively little in terms of religious fighting.

The country also has high illiteracy rates (nearly 35 percent) and the pollution in major cities is terrible. India must also try to implement some sort of universal public education system; this is no small task in a nation of over a billion people.

India also is much more socialistic than China in many ways. It is more difficult to build plants or expand some industries because of its democratic rule. This slows down growth. For example, Tata Motors was to build its plant for the Nano in West Bengal in Singur, but had to move to the plant to Gujarat (another province in India) because of protests. Until the 2009 election, leftists and communists played a large role in the Indian parliament and, accordingly, reforms were held back. India's debt-to-GDP is much higher than China's. According to the CIA's *2009 World Fact Book*, as of 2008, Indian debt is hovering around 58 percent of GDP, a percentage that is more than double China's rate of debt, which is 22 percent of GDP. However, these are normal problems in a developing third-world economy. In the long run, India should be able to overcome them. In the past 20 years, India has already overcome many of these obstacles and has become one of the fastest growing economies in the world.

India—More Opportunity than China in the Long Run?

I am actually in a minority but I am much more bullish on India than China in the long run. As you just read, India has its fair share of problems. Indian democracy often translates into myriad procedures and obstacles that result in long delays when one tries to get things done. However, it also ensures that people are not "run over" in the name of economic growth and so-called progress. In the longer run, I believe this will result in much more sustainable long-term growth. My own personal view is that I would rather grow at 7 percent this way than 9 percent in a totalitarian, centrally controlled manner.

In addition, as stated in Chapter 8 on China, I truly believe that in the long run the most economically successful nations are also the nations that possess the greatest number of general freedoms. India is a parliamentary democracy and has adopted aspects of the British common law system, which features strong property rights. In a recent interview with the *Economic Times*, Professor Niall Ferguson summed up the potential of India as follows:

> And one reason that I'm long on India rather than China is that India has a better institutional basis of development than China does. I think that representative government, rule of law, meaningful private property—these are keys to success. They were keys to western success.
>
> China doesn't have these things. In the end, if you don't have these things, you are just a planned economy with a market wrapped around that.
>
> Look at what the Soviet Union was in the 1930s. If you went there in 1936, you would be very impressed—they were building huge canals, buildings, highways, large cities and what not. But it became clear by the 1970s that the negative externalities of industrialization were huge and the impact of population control and central planning were negative. And sure enough, Russia fell apart. Now, I'm not

saying that it's going to happen in China any time soon. But if you take a 20-year development, it's huge.

So, I think at some point in the growth of India and China, there will come a time when China's strategic policies will produce unintended consequences.

Interview with Niall Ferguson, Economic Times of India,
January 10, 2010

You must remember that, when building an economy and nation, it is not just free market policies, regulation, and taxation that are important. You must also build a culture. India has shown more openness than China. India has its Bollywood movie industry, a world-famous book fair in Jaipur, and has even produced bestselling books such as *The White Tiger, Behind the Assassins, Maximum City: Bombay Lost and Found*, and *Q and A* (the book that the movie *Slumdog Millionaire* was based on). Much of this literature does not depict the country in the greatest light. Actually, when reading these books, you get a sense of the rawness of much of Indian society. They remind you of Dickens exploring the dark underbelly of British society in the nineteenth century. This type of openness will help India in the long run. We must not forget that the last two great superpowers, the United States and Britain, possessed this type of openness and that is *no* fluke.

India's demographics are also much better than China's. Actually, they are as good as any country in the world: 31.1 percent of the Indian population is under 14 years of age. There are 700 million Indians under the age of 35. The median age is 24.4 years. The fertility rate in India at the moment is 2.75 children for every childbearing woman. This means that they are replacing the population with a youth movement that should provide benefits to the country in the future.

When you have a population this young, two things can happen. Either you have to provide people with a growing economy or meaningful jobs, or you will see social and civil unrest. In addition, as India grows into its potential, it is better to have more young people take responsible roles in its society as opposed to being forced to provide for an aging population. Also young people tend to be more progressive. Young people will not be so interested in the tradition of the caste system or traditional marriage but will be more interested in opening up the economy and moving forward. They will be more open to foreign investment, foreign peoples, socially mixing with foreigners, and so forth.

In addition, Indians, like the Chinese, save huge amounts of capital. According to the Macro Economic Data for Emerging and Developed Nations, or CEIC (www.ceicdata.com), data, it is estimated that the Indian savings rate increased from 20 percent to nearly 31 percent from 1990 to 2008.

In addition, India's export of choice seems to be more sustainable than China's. China grew on cheap exports to the United States; we noted how that has dropped off in the past year. India, on the other hand, has mainly become a tech-oriented country. It has developed call centers that have worldwide reach. In addition to this, many companies, worldwide, option out work to Indian engineers as the wages are lower. India has somewhat made its intellectual capacity one of its main exports. Roughly one-third of all of the engineers in the world emanate from India. Yes, India must continue to build a manufacturing sector to move its economy forward. However, India is unlike China. China's growth is based on exporting to foreigners, much of it going to the United States. India can build a manufacturing sector based on selling to Indians and the rest of Asia.

India lags behind China a great deal in terms of its infrastructure. China has spent billions building roads, canals, malls, and airports. By way of contrast, the Indian infrastructure is old and archaic. For example, most of the railroads in India are still descended from the British Empire. China expects its economy to grow into the new infrastructure. The infrastructure in India has done the opposite—it has lagged behind the growth in private industry. According to the *India Times*, Infosys, the tech giant of India, spends $5 million a year in transporting its employees to its offices as there is no major transportation in the city of Bangalore.

The bad news, obviously, is that the lack of infrastructure hinders India's economic growth. Time spent sitting in traffic sucking in bad air or waiting for flights at airports all damage the efficiency of a nation. According to Jagwish Bhagwati, an economist at Columbia University, this deficiency in infrastructure could take as much as two points off GDP. The good news is that India is starting to deal with its infrastructure problems. From an investing viewpoint, this deficiency will lead to infrastructure plays and opportunities. The government has announced a plan to spend nearly $500 billion in infrastructure. Infrastructure spending as a percentage of GDP is estimated to be about 11 percent by 2011, up from about 4 percent of GDP in 2000.

Again, I tend to look at this lack of infrastructure as a positive thing. People in India are building from the floor up. There are all sorts of small entrepreneurs who own spice and fruit shacks and other forms of small businesses. There are also many top-tier companies in India. The government is lagging behind the private initiatives. Therefore, the government can build infrastructure and not worry about the country growing into the infrastructure. This buildup will increase productivity and economic growth even more.

It is a positive that, even though there is some planning in the Indian economy, it is not as centrally planned as it could be. Due to a fractured political system, the average entrepreneur has been growing and is leading the way into the future while the government is behind. An economy has a way of building itself if it is free. Just look at the United States in the nineteenth century. There was virtually no economic plan. Everything was built from the ground up; yet during that time the United States boomed with huge growth in industry, railways, and numerous commercial enterprises. The 1950s highway expansion in the United States was built for the movement of military goods when first planned, but this infrastructure ended up creating a vast multitude of roads that enhanced travel and transport; this in turn increased productivity.

India is also behind China, which could mean more upside. China began reforms in 1978 and really expanded them in the early nineties. India began reforms in 1991 and really expanded them in the late nineties. India is therefore about 10 years behind China and earlier in its growth phase. In addition, GDP per capita in India is $2,900. This means it would have to more than double just to get to Chinese levels! This means more upside. The average Indian needs to *double* his or her wealth just to catch up to China.

In China most of the economic decisions are made by a few leaders in Beijing. India's decisions tend to arise from a mishmash of ideas flowing from both private and public institutions. As India is not as centrally planned, it should not experience the excesses China has endured.

As discussed in Chapter 9, in reaction to the recent global economic crisis, China initiated a dramatic stimulus plan that included a huge increase in the amount of debt loaned out privately. Many critics are worried that this will create a bubble. However, India, while engaging in its own stimulus plan, saw nowhere near this type of lending. Most Indian banks are still under some form of government control as a result of the nationalizations of the 1970s. They are very conservative and did not get caught up in the subprime mania. India did not go crazy during the recent downturn to try to stir demand. Therefore, if China does see a downturn, yes, India would be hit by this and its markets would fall and its economy would slow, but the Indian economy is nowhere near as vulnerable as China is in on this front.

The monetary policy of India is very strong. As you can glean from this book, I am not a big fan of money printing and central bankers. I feel their endless ability to constantly inflate has damaged the global economy a great deal. However, India has one of the few visionary central banks in the world. Their recent purchase of 200 tonnes of gold illustrates this. They don't own a lot of U.S. Treasuries that would be vulnerable to a variety of inflationary scenarios. In addition, unlike the Federal Reserve, the Indian central bank admits that asset bubbles play a huge role in the growth and contraction of an economy. They will use monetary policy to slow asset bubbles rather than just looking at inflation. If the Central Bank of India can steer India away from the serious asset bubbles that have plagued other countries, that would be very positive for the long-term future of the Indian economy.

Under the Radar—A Good Thing!

This lack of central planning may actually help India in the long run.

Let me give you an analogy. If this were the early twentieth century, the United States would be Britain, an empire near its top and on its way down, with wars, public debts, and a general spending over-expansion stressing the public pocketbook. China could be Germany. Few remember that, in the early twentieth century, most would have predicted that Germany, not the United States, would challenge and surpass the United Kingdom as the world's next superpower. Germany was in Europe, which was still the center of global economic activity, notwithstanding the growing economic power of the United States. Germany was slowly building its empire. In 1900, Germany's empire included German East Africa, Cameroons, and German South-West Africa on the African continent and German New Guinea in Asia. It was building a huge manufacturing base.

The United States, while increasingly viewed as a growing giant, was not taken quite as seriously. Throughout the nineteenth century, it experienced massive economic growth; however, it was also marked by bank runs, panics, and a civil war. From the viewpoint of the rest of the globe, no one really thought that a country that was at war with itself just 40 years previously would be the world's superpower within a generation. Germany looked like the more reasonable choice. Of course, two world wars later, with the hyperinflation in Germany squeezed in between, the United States stood alone as the world's superpower.

India seems chaotic and unorganized in its growth. The current choice for the next world superpower is almost unanimously for China given its obvious and growing economic clout. However, this does not mean that China's ascent as the next superpower is guaranteed. While it is impossible to predict the geopolitical future, it would seem to us that China has many more ambitions in the way of imperial goals than does India. If China chases these, it could lead to instability, whereas India is focused on growing its own economy.

Being a contrarian, I feel that all of the hype surrounding China has left India in the background. For example, as pointed out by Dr. Marc Faber, in the 2010 *Barron's* roundtable (the roundtable participants discuss the outlook for the U.S. and global economies for the coming year), none of the participants made any mention of India whatsoever. This is a country of 1.1 billion people that possesses one of the fastest growing economies in the world. Yet the so-called experts aren't paying attention, at least for 2010! Remember, if no one is buying, it means there is considerable pent-up demand that will drive the market higher once people realize what is going on and dive into the Indian market!

The World Needs India

The world also needs India for future growth. India is in a very dangerous area of the world. Pakistan, Burma, Bangladesh, Nepal, Bhutan, Afghanistan, Turkmenistan, Bangladesh, and Sri Lanka surround it. Most of these are nations that contain no legacy of democracy; they are unstable or at war within. If India can develop into a stable democracy within the midst of this instability, it could really help the region.

In addition, if the United States falls from grace into bankruptcy and drops from its current status of world superpower, a democratic nation needs to replace the role played by the United States. After World War II and the rise of communism and the decline of the British Empire, the Americans were right there to pick up the slack. The United States almost seamlessly filled the void left behind by the collapse of the British Empire. While I do not think that India can fill this void entirely, it would be a plus for the world for India to at least pick up some of the slack and fill the void as a mega-democracy to balance out China's authoritarian rule.

Therefore, not only is it a must that India succeed for itself, but it may be essential for the rest of the world as well. The good news is that history is on India's side. For all of the problems and stumbles India has had and will continue to have, it is encouraging for India to realize that the world's last two superpowers were nations that possessed the rule of law, property rights, and large, educated, English-speaking populations. India has all of these advantages and China has none of them. A strong India can offset the growing power of China. Whether you are a fan of China or not, this balancing of power should have positive effects on the world's economies.

Part of the problem with the United States is that, since the decline and fall of the Soviet Union, the United States is virtually the world's lone superpower. This has allowed it to make many terrible foreign policy and economic mistakes without any real repercussions. For example, after mistakes in ventures in Afghanistan and Iraq, who was really there to keep the Americans accountable? By way of contrast, in the eighties, the Americans were there to keep the Russians accountable for their folly in Afghanistan. The British and Americans were there to keep the German and Japanese imperial powers in check during World War II. A superpower unchecked, regardless of what country it is, is usually not a good thing. Power corrupts and absolute power corrupts absolutely.

If the United States, like the British Empire, eventually goes into bankruptcy, it could leave the Chinese as the world's only superpower. The world needs a counterbalance to this.

How to Invest in India

Investing in India is a bit easier than China. Like China, you can buy foreign ADRs or ETFs. However, unlike China, after going through a bit of formality, such as setting up an account with an Indian broker and providing the proper information (e.g., proof of residence, passport photo, etc.) and paying a small fee, you can set up an account and trade stocks directly on the Bombay exchange.

Indian stocks have actually outperformed Chinese and global equities for a while now. Figures 9.1 and 9.2 compare the Bombay Stock Exchange to the Shanghai Stock Exchange and MSCI Emerging Markets Index since 1999. As we can see from Figure 9.1, in 1999, it took 3 shares of the Shanghai Stock Exchange to buy the Bombay Stock Exchange; it now takes 5.5 shares. As India is now rising from a

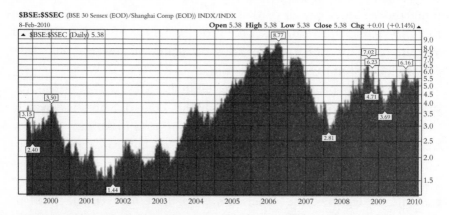

Figure 9.1   Bombay Stock Exchange versus Shanghai Exchange
SOURCE: StockCharts.com (http://stockcharts.com).

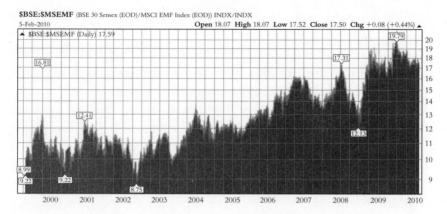

Figure 9.2   Bombay Stock Exchange versus MSCI World Index
SOURCE: StockCharts.com (http://stockcharts.com).

lower level economically, the stock market could continue to outperform in the future.

Outperformance in the past does not guarantee that India will outperform in the future. But, with the Indian economy having much
more leverage and upside than most other economies and with the government finally catching up with infrastructure investments, the time
seems ripe for India to continue to outperform. Not that there aren't
risks—the recent accounting fraud of Satyam dramatically illustrates
that India, like everywhere else, possesses criminals and crooks that will
abuse the system and take advantage of investors. However, the fraud
was found, charges were filed, and the company was taken over by
stronger hands.

Another positive for Indian stocks going ahead longer term is
that most Indians do not yet invest in equities. As the average person's standard of living increases, he or she will have more disposable
earnings and money to invest in equities. This will add to demand for
Indian equities.

There are numerous ways to invest in the coming growth in the
Indian economy and stock market:

• **Natural resources and commodities.** An indirect investment
  in India, like China, can be done by buying natural resources. As
  India booms in the long term, it means more demand for copper,

steel, concrete, and so on. So you can buy commodities and/or companies that produce commodities.

- **Indian ETFs.** Like China, there are many Indian ETFs that trade on U.S. exchanges. These ETFs, for the most part, track the large-cap Indian companies. Many Indian companies are leaders in automobiles, steel, and technology. These funds include the Indian Ishares Trust, the India Fund, and the Morgan Stanley Indian Investment Fund. These will give you exposure to the largest companies and large parts of the Indian economy. This is the easiest and safest way to play the Indian economy given the diversification involved with these investments.

  We must note that the Indian market is very volatile. In the 2000–2002 bear market, the Bombay Stock Exchange fell nearly 60 percent. In 2004, on news that parliamentary elections put a left-of-center party into power, the market fell over 30 percent in a few months. In 2006, the Indian market quickly fell nearly 35 percent in a just a few months. During the 2008 bear market, the Bombay Stock Exchange fell over 65 percent. In every case, the market rallied 50 percent within a year and gave investors great profits. Therefore, I would patiently await such corrections in the Indian market and add to your positions in Indian ETFs if/when corrections happen.

- **Indian ADRs.** Even though the country is in the initial stages of economic growth, the Indian economy and stock market have some of the most well-established top-tier companies in the world. These companies include Tata Steel and Tata Motors (steel and automobiles), Infosys (technology), Hindalco (aluminum), and Sterlite Industries (metals and mining). Just like the Indian stock market, these companies are very volatile because they trade with the volatility of the Indian market. Similar to the approach we suggest for the general Indian market, you should wait patiently for these companies to decline and get cheap. If I may use an analogy, it could be like buying Standard Oil, General Electric, Ford, and so on in the early twentieth century. Of course, these stocks all went a lot higher over a 20- to 40-year timeframe.

- **Indian large and smaller stocks on the Bombay Stock Exchange.** There are over 4,700 listed companies on the Bombay

Stock Exchange (BSE). The Exchange has a market cap of $1.1 trillion. By comparison, there are over 2,700 companies listed on the New York Stock Exchange and the market cap of the New York Stock Exchange is about $28 trillion. You can buy medium- and large-sized companies on the BSE. However, the greatest opportunities are in the smaller companies. Because the number of both native Indians and foreigners trading Indian stocks is rather small, there are a lot of smaller unknown deals that trade at very cheap valuations. There are literally dozens of companies on the BSE that trade at single-digit P/Es and double-digit dividend yields. These are the types of companies where you will need to know someone on the ground in order to determine whether they are good investments. You need to either go to India yourself to confirm whether these companies are great bargains or have some-one who does the groundwork for you. I plan on a few trips to India over the course of 2011 and 2012 in the hope of discovering some of these companies.

Overall, it is actually much easier to invest directly in India than in China, especially, because as we go to press the Indian government is in the midst of easing restrictions for foreign investors.

India—Organized Chaos That Will Continue to Grow

India is the *ying* to China's *yang*. While China is a well-organized, cen-trally planned, and emerging economy, India is the messy little brother who seems to get a lot done, despite not having quite the level of organization. Yes, there will be setbacks with interfering politicians and revolts against foreign investment from time to time. However, I feel that India's democracy and rule of law might make it a better long-term investment than China.

Chapter 10

Investing in Other Emerging Global Markets

I t is common knowledge that India and China are the big daddies of the global markets. However, there are many small emerging nations that present great, if not greater, opportunities. I have researched dozens of nations and am suggesting a few that I think are the best to invest in.

Many of these nations are flying under the radar with most analysts in the investment industry totally ignoring them. Some of them are beaten up due to the financial crisis and some have depressed stock prices despite years of growth in their economies. Others will benefit from the continuation of the global commodity boom.

I have gone global in this research, reaching into Asia, South America, North America, and Africa. I have probably left out a few nations, but we only have so much room in this book. So, let's get started investing.

Australia and Canada

The safest way to invest globally at the moment is through Australia and Canada. We have argued that the growth of money supply and the continued expansion of the economies of China and India will cause a long-term uptrend in commodity prices. Canada and Australia both possess markets and currencies that are commodity based. If you believe that oil, gold, and other resources will continue to be in vogue (as we outlined earlier in this book), Australia and Canada will be great markets to be in.

Both are very mining friendly; they have two of the largest junior mining industries in the world. The Canadian oil sands have the largest unproven oil resources in the world; they are estimated to be larger than the Saudi oil fields. With smaller populations, these two nations will be the sellers of resources to the larger developing nations of Asia. Another advantage is, despite overheated real estate markets, that both countries possess very stable, well-run banking sectors, unlike much of Europe and the United States.

Australia

Australia, from the rest of the world's point of view, has almost a comedic aspect to it. The country possesses a unique, local English dialect; its cities have strange names; the use of the word *mate* and the classic comedy movie *Crocodile Dundee* have added to the humorous element of world opinion. For years, Australians were regarded as socialist surfers with bad tempers. However, Australia currently has one of the more dynamic economies in the world. It flirted with socialism in the seventies and had the typical results: high unemployment, low productivity, and high inflation. The Australians did not even float their currency until 1983.

There are problems; the current account deficit is over 4 percent of GDP; taxation is still high. However, for the most part, Australia is well run at the moment and held up well in the global economic crisis. It has an overheated property market but the banks are very well run and there were no bailouts or anything of the like. The Australian unemployment rate is 5.5 percent, something the United States would do somersaults to obtain.

In addition, if you are looking at a fixed-income investment, Australia is about the only nation in the world at the moment that has real nominal interest rates. Short-term interest rates are over 3 percent and long-term rates are over 5 percent! So, if you are interested in a fixed-income investment, Australian bonds, especially on the short end, are more enticing than most.

Australia's economy has boomed in recent years by taking advantage of its natural resource sector and proximity to Asia. The Australian dollar, which nearly went down to $0.50 to the U.S. dollar in the late nineties, has ridden the back of increasingly strong commodity prices to nearly $0.88 as I write in 2010.

Australia has seen huge growth in exports to China. For fiscal 2008–2009, Australian exported over $39 billion worth of goods to China. This represented over 17 percent of Australian exports and China is Australia's second largest export market. Of these exports, sales were over $22 billion from iron ore, over $3 billion from coal, $1.3 billion from wool, and over $1 billion from copper.

The resulting good news is that Australia has been somewhat more insulated from the U.S. downturn due to Australia's economic growth arising from increasing exports to China and the rest of Asia. The bad news is that if China does see a serious slowdown in its economy, this will adversely affect Australia. However, as the longer-term economic prospects are very bright for China and Asia, this should benefit Australia over the next 5 to 10 years.

Some of the largest companies in the world (such as News Corp) are Australian companies.

The Australian market tends to trade with commodity prices. As commodities are a play on growth in Asia and the emerging world, Australia is a good, conservative way to play this. If you are averse to investing in lesser-known emerging economies, Australia is a great, safe way to play foreign markets.

A major problem in Australia is that recently Australia proposed to increase taxes on resource companies. This caused the Aussie dollar and many resource companies to drop in price. The government is now backing off this proposal. However, this is something worth looking at going forward.

How to Invest In Australia There are literally dozens of Australian ADRs that trade in the United States. They range from media companies like the aforementioned News Corp to gold companies such as Lihir Gold to banks such as National Bank of Australia to another mining company, Newcrest Mining.

You can also play the Australian market by buying the Australian Ishares (ticker: TWA). If you wish to play the Australian currency, you can buy the Australian Currency ETF (ticker: FXA).

You can also get a broker who can trade Australian shares. I have an excellent broker in Australia who specializes in smaller mining stocks. This will give you direct access to the Australian resource market.

Australia is going to see a slowdown in its housing market and could be hit by some short-term weakness in China. However, if Asia continues to boom, the Australian economy and stock market should be a direct beneficiary.

Canada

This is the country of my origin. Canada seems to be a colder version of Australia. They are both large, resource-based economies that were victims of socialism in the sixties and seventies. Canada's stumble was due to the failed experiment of Trudeau-style socialism. (Pierre Trudeau, the prime minister of Canada in the late sixties to early eighties, was very flamboyant, but he rapidly expanded the size of government and either nationalized or tried to nationalize numerous industries, which turned into a disaster).

Despite a worldwide resource boom in the seventies, Canada did not benefit despite the fact that the economy has a large resource base. The deficit, due to the expansion of social programs, bloated to over 7 percent of GDP in 1983. Unemployment hit double digits and the Canadian dollar, which spent much of the fifties and sixties above the U.S. dollar, sank below 70 cents.

However, Canada began to reform in the eighties. It entered NAFTA, which opened trade borders; then, in the nineties, Canada slowed down the rate of government spending and this resulted in balanced budgets and surpluses during the 1990s and 2000s booms. Canada, while still having a reputation of being a socialistic country with its universal health-care system and high personal income taxes, is actually quite business friendly. It has a very competitive corporate tax rate that is much lower than that of the United States. Its universal health-care system also somewhat subsidizes business; many U.S. companies, especially automakers, moved operations to Canada so they could escape excessive health insurance costs prevalent in the United States.

Canada also has not converted to xenophobia like the United States has in the wake of 9/11. In the early eighties, Canada had its own terrorist attack as Sikh terrorists blew up Air India flight 182 from Montreal en route to London; 270 Canadians died in the attack. The investigation of the case was later bungled as well. However, the country did not go paranoid over airport security; they did not restrict immigration from India or the rest of Asia. Canada still has very liberal immigration laws. These laws will help Canada alleviate the financial strain of retiring Baby Boomers.

The most noteworthy aspect of the Canadian financial system is the stability of its banks. There is an overheated housing market in many Canadian cities, especially in Vancouver. However, the Canadian banks just simply do not have the leverage that their U.S. counterparts had during the housing bubble in the United States. More importantly, the Canadian banks do not have the securitization of debt. There are no subprime mortgage-backed securities leveraged 30 to 1. In addition, the Canadian government in the 2010 budget took measures to try to slow down home lending. This action alone makes the Canadian government more active than governments in Europe and the United States during their housing bubbles.

Of course, Canada has been hit by the U.S. economic downturn. Being a neighboring nation, Canada is dependent on the United States for exports; 75 percent of its exports are sent to the United States. As Canadians often say, if the United States coughs, Canada catches a cold. And right now the U.S. economy is puking a lung and a kidney.

Canada is easily the largest exporter of oil to the United States, exporting over 1.9 million barrels of oil per day to the United States. This is nearly double the Saudi exports to the United States, which total about 1 million barrels of oil per day.

However, Canada is increasingly expanding its exports to the emerging countries of Asia. From 2002 to 2006, exports increased from $4 billion to $8 billion to China. Much of this increase was in the form of raw commodities.

Recently, Whole Foods in the United States announced that it would not purchase oil from the oil sands in Alberta because it sees it as dirty and not carbon friendly. Obama has made comments against "dirty oil" and while not pointing to Canadian oil directly, he is hinting at the oil sands type of oil. (Oil sands oil is heavy because it is not purely drilled as is the case with an offshore rig; it is a process of separation of oil from the tar of the oil sand fields.) However, I can tell you that China and the rest of Asia will happily take this oil. (The recent catastrophic Gulf of Mexico spill seems to have given U.S. politicians a different perspective on what "dirty oil" really looks like.)

Vancouver has also become somewhat of a gateway to Asia with many Asians residing in the city. This can only help Canadian trade and economic relations with Asia going forward.

In addition, Canada is the fifth largest country in the amount of gold production and is a leader in many other types of metal production.

As we mentioned earlier, we are very bullish on agriculture. To maximize agricultural yields, you need fertilizer. Fertilizer is made from potash. Potash is produced in only 12 countries around the world, and 75 percent of this production comes from two nations. One of those nations is Russia, which produces 22 percent of the world's potash. The other is Canada, which produces over 53 percent of the globe's potash. If you believe there will be a boom in agriculture, Canada is set to boom.

A very interesting part of Canada is the province of Saskatchewan. Saskatchewan is located in the Canadian prairies. Until recently, Saskatchewan was known for three things: (1) being the birthplace of Canadian socialism; (2) people packing their bags, and subsequently (3) leaving the province permanently.

Because of the province's harsh environment, rural-based depressed economy, and anti-business tendencies, the province exported people for years. The population of Saskatchewan in 1900 was about 1 million; today it is still about 1 million!

However, recently, the province has announced itself open for business, especially in mining. The province is rich in coal, diamonds, potash, and uranium. Not only that, but much of the same geology that makes up the world-famous Alberta oil sands reaches into Saskatchewan.

I was lucky enough to be the first keynote speaker at Saskrocks, a mining conference in Saskatoon. Saskatoon is the business capital of Saskatchewan; it is a small city with a population of just over 200,000 people. You could see that this was a place on the rise when I was there in 2008. It had the feeling of a trend in its very early stages. It was still relatively unknown but starting to murmur.

If you can handle the winters (it can get down to 30 degrees below zero), Saskatchewan should be a place where real estate, business, and farming boom in the coming years.

How to Invest in Canada Investing in Canada is very easy. The TSX exchange is very liquid and possesses many major companies from the frequently bankrupt Nortel to the resource giant Barrick Gold (ticker: ABX) to communication giant Rogers Communications (ticker: RCI) to oil giant Suncor (ticker: SU). All of the major companies trade on the New York Stock Exchange.

However, I suggest that, if you are bullish on commodities and want access to the mid-tier and junior mining industries (both of which should boom in the coming years), you obtain a broker that can trade Canadian listings. The CDNX, an exchange made up of mostly junior listings, is the premier exchange in the world for junior mining venture capitalism. Now, these stocks are extremely risky, but for some of your risk capital, it will probably be the place to be for the next 5 or 10 years. In my own investment newsletters, I specialize in covering many Canadian resource companies.

If you just want to play the Canadian market or currency as a whole, you can buy the Canadian Ishares (ticker: EWC), or the Canadian Dollar Trust (ticker: FXC).

Canada, like Australia, is a safe first-world way to play a commodities bull market if you do not have risk tolerance.

Asia

Another way to invest globally at the moment is through the Asian markets, particularly Japan, Taiwan, South Korea, Indonesia, and Vietnam.

Japan

Many people see Japan as the black hole of investing. This can happen when, in a 20-year period, you are down over 70 percent from
your highs. However, as stated in Chapter 3 on cycles and psychology,
when a market is out of favor and has done nothing for a long period
of time, then *that* is the time to buy.

A lot of it has to do with *valuation contraction*. The Japanese market
is down 70 percent in 20 years, but earnings have not fallen as fast and
many stocks in the market tend to be very cheap fundamentally. Plus,
remember markets move on buying power and psychology. When no
one is in the market, there is a lot of pent-up buying on the sidelines
that can drive the market higher. You just need a trigger.

For example, in 1949, the trigger was the postwar expansion. The
United States boomed as the middle-class rose. People bought cars
and houses and made more money than ever as there was very little
competition around the world. In the early eighties, multiple triggers
were unleashed when Volcker raised interest rates and killed inflation
and then Reagan cut income taxes and unleashed buying that had been
pent up on the sidelines (the savings rate of the United States by the
early eighties was into the double digits).

The winning of World War II also caused a positive psychological
spirit that helped people forget the bust of the thirties and reinstituted
their belief in their nation and companies (these things are important as
you need a trigger). In the early eighties, after the defeat in Vietnam,
Americans again needed a trigger. Multiple triggers appeared to revive
American self-confidence and optimism. These included such dispa-
rate events as the "Miracle on Ice" hockey game of the 1980 Olympic
Games and the releasing of U.S. hostages in Iran. However, the major
catalyst, which launched the bull market of the nineties (and made it
stronger than the bull market of the eighties), was the arms buildup
and subsequent bankruptcy of the Soviet Empire. These political
events unleashed hundreds of millions of people into the global free
market and produced a positive reflection of the United States itself.

Japan needs such a trigger. Right now, the population is depressed.
Its export-based economy was a disaster in the 2009 bust. There was
a decline of over 10 percent in GDP in the first quarter of 2009 as

the global economy imploded. The government debt is 170 percent of GDP (Japan, however, can support higher debt levels than the United States. Its people have high savings rates and its debt is all domestically owned, not foreign-owned like that of the United States, which helps keep interest rates low.). Even if Japanese interest rates rise, the economy is so unleveraged at the moment (with little investing and high savings rates) that rising interest rates won't make much of an impact.

Japan has a huge problem with demographics; it is a very old nation. The average age is 42 years old. It has had to increase pension contributions and decrease payouts in recent years. They are not replacing population fast enough. They still have a restrictive immigration policy, so they are not replacing population with mass immigration. According to World Bank numbers, Japanese population has remained roughly flat over the past decade.

However, with that said, there are still signs of change. Recently, the Democratic party of Japan defeated the Liberal Democrats in the 2009 election. This is the first change in the Japanese government in over 60 years. This has not led to a huge change in Japanese policy but new governments can always be open to more change, especially if it is forced upon them in *having* to adapt to it.

What is the trigger for Japan? It will probably come from abroad. Despite its demographic problem, Japan is still a nation that takes pride in its goods and has some of the top-tier companies in the world. Toyota (despite its recent problems), Honda, Nintendo, Sony, and so on are all world leaders in their fields that produce top-tier products.

We must remember that what helped Japan in the seventies and eighties was its superior industrial production. Japan began to surpass the United States in terms of quality in the sixties. It then increased exports to the United States in the seventies and eighties. During the bubble of the eighties, there was a worry that Japan would overtake the United States as the global superpower and end up owning the United States.

Japan, despite its real estate bubble bursting and declining demographics, is still a leader in many industries. It will now become the high-end exporter to Asia. Yes, we know that much of Asia has built up large manufacturing bases. However, when it comes to top-end electronics, cars, and other merchandise, China and others just cannot compete with Japan.

There are 3.6 billion people in Asia. There are about 300 million in the United States. Therefore, if Asia can build up just one-twelfth of the demand that the United States has for Japanese products, on a per-capita basis, it can replace this demand. For example, in January 2010, Japan announced that exports to China alone surpassed exports to the United States. This is the first time in a generation that exports to any country had surpassed those to the United States. Japan now exports about 920 billion yen per month to China (about US$1.1 billion) and about 720 billion yen per month to the United States (about US$800).

As Asia recovered faster in early 2010 than North America and Europe, you could see a positive impact on Japan as exports increased due to exporting more to Asia.

In addition, on the housing front, the burst in the bubble has led to declining home construction. In 2009, an estimated 788,410 homes were built, the lowest number since 1964. Housing prices, on average, were estimated to be down 40 percent from their 1989 top. Even with a shrinking and flattening population, new apartments and homes must be built to replace older structures. At some point this should rekindle Japanese real estate. The Japanese banks have also cleared out the bad debts from the eighties and they were not too badly hit by the financial crisis of 2009. Many of these sectors look cheap.

How to Invest in Japan As I am bullish on Japan from a secular point of view, the easiest way to invest in Japan is through an ETF that represents the entire market. The Japan Ishares (ticker: EWJ) looks like a great way to play the market.

You can also buy some of the Japanese companies. Toyota (ticker: TM) looks like a good bet after its recent problems with recalls and the like. Any further weakness that comes from that scenario would make TM a very good buy. Honda (ticker: HMC) will be in a position to benefit from the Toyota weakness. On the electronics front, Sony (ticker: SNE), Hitachi (ticker: HIT), and Nintendo (ticker: NTOY) are some Japanese large-caps that trade on the NYSE.

Japanese banks also would be good value bets. Banks that trade on the NYSE include Mitsubishi UFG Financial Group (ticker: MTU). I think the banks are long-term plays, so you buy them and hold on.

I also like many of the Japanese small–caps. The small–caps in many cases have fallen more than large–cap companies and pay some nice dividends. The Japan Smaller Capitalization Fund (JOF) should advance as Japanese companies advance.

We should note that a stronger Asian economy is more important to Japan than a weaker yen. When Asia began to recover in late 2009, Japanese exports exploded! Therefore, if Asia booms, they will be willing to pay Japan for its superior goods no matter what the yen is doing.

Japan looks to be at a secular low. One of the major factors that will drive it out of this secular low will be the long-term rise of Asia. Japan reminds me of the United States in 1949 or 1982, a stock market ending a long-term downtrend that is cheap. I would look to buy Japanese stocks on any dips in the coming years.

Taiwan

Though it has been sovereign since the end of its civil war, Taiwan is a country often overshadowed by its relationship with mainland China. To date, only 24 countries acknowledge its existence as a separate state, in part because China continues to claim ascendancy over it. In truth, the island nation stands as another one of East Asia's "Economic Tigers."

Boasting the seventeenth largest economy in the world, Taiwan has a dynamic capitalist economy. Despite continued tensions, attempts to frustrate Taiwanese investment and foreign trade by the mainland Chinese government are gradually receding. Taiwan, as an independent economy, acceded to the World Trade Organization (WTO), and became the Separate Customs Territory of Taiwan in January 2002. Many large government-owned banks and industrial firms have been privatized and GDP growth has averaged about 8 percent during the past three decades. As with the other Asian trade and industry powers, Taiwan's success was initially fueled by land and agricultural reforms. These reforms allowed for the development of a class of landowners who would invest their capital in other economic endeavors and start the engine of foreign trade that has propelled Taiwan's rapid growth in the past 30 to 40 years.

Export composition changed from predominantly agricultural commodities to industrial goods, which now stand at 98 percent. Currently, Taiwan's most substantial industrial export sector lies in the stratum of electronics. The world's largest supplier of contract computer chip manufacturing, Taiwan leads the way in LCD panel manufacture, DRAM computer memory, networking equipment, and consumer electronics design and manufacture.

With the onset of the 2009 recession, Taiwan has faced some economic issues. Heavy dependence on exports makes the economy vulnerable to downturns in world demand. However, the economy is beginning to recover and most forecasts project 3 to 4 percent growth for 2010. Taiwan's dependence on the U.S. market should continue to decrease as its exports to Southeast Asia and China grow and its efforts to develop European markets produce results (WFB, 2010).

The main reason to like Taiwan is the valuation of its stock market. The country has seen huge growth in its economy since the eighties; yet its stock market has done very little. This has made the market very cheap. Figure 10.1 is the Taipei stock market going back to 2007. According to the International Monetary Fund, Taiwan's GDP per capita on a purchasing power basis has increased from just over $8,800 per person in 1989 to $29,828 in 2009. Yet the Taipei Index, which peaked at over 13,000 in 1989, fell to just under 4,000 in early 2009!

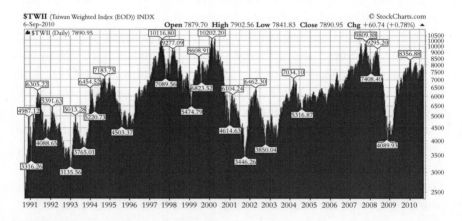

Figure 10.1 Taipei Index
SOURCE: Courtesy of StockCharts.com (http://stockcharts.com).

This tells us that Taiwanese stocks compared to the growth in the economy are extremely cheap.

Taiwan is a huge supplier of computer chips and other technology-related hardware; this sector makes up over one-quarter of its exports.

Many may be worried about disputes between Taiwan and China. However, with the two countries increasingly becoming dependent on each other for economic trade, relations have actually improved on this front in recent years.

How to Invest in Taiwan Taiwan has a few ADRs, which include Taiwan Semiconductor Company (ticker: TSM), which trades on the NYSE. Taiwan is more interdependent with Asia as well, with over 44 percent of exports going to China, Hong Kong, and Japan as compared to over 16.22 percent to the United States. The country is also dependent on the imports of natural resources, so it keeps foreign exchange reserves high.

However, as I think this is a macro play on the country, you will probably want to own the entire country and market, as it is so cheap at the moment. The Taiwan Fund (ticker: TWN) trades on the NYSE. Coming out of a 20-year bear market, the Taiwanese market is very cheap. Standards of living and the economy have seen huge advances in the past 20 years, but the stock market has not reflected this. Like Japan, I would look at Taiwan on nearly every dip.

South Korea

Since the 1960s, South Korea has become a major trading partner to the world's largest economies. In 2009, the country surpassed the United Kingdom, Russia, and Canada as the world's ninth largest exporter and became the world's thirteenth largest economy, a feat unimaginable in the destitution that was left postwar.

Following the "Korean War" (1950–1953), South Korea embarked on a transformation that has come to be known as the "Miracle on the Han River." During this time the country underwent rapid acceleration in export and industrial growth, technological development, and educational advancement. The Park Chung Hee government, which strengthened financial institutions and introduced flexible economic planning, introduced a currency reform. The government promoted importing of raw materials and technology at the expense of consumer goods and encouraged savings and investment over consumption.

Manufacturing continued to grow rapidly in the 1980s and early 1990s. However, the government became increasingly restrictive with its citizens. The assassination of Major General Park in 1979 saw the emergence of a vocal civil society that led to strong protests against authoritarian rule.

> The 1992 election of a long-time pro-democracy activist Kim Young-Sam marked the first civilian elected president in 32 years. They have had democratic elections ever since. South Koreans voted for a new president in December 2007. Former business executive and mayor of Seoul Lee Myung-bak's 5-year term began with his inauguration on February 25, 2008.
>
> www.state.gov, 2009

Since the 1960s, South Korea has seen a spectacular GNP expansion that averaged more than 8 percent a year, growing from US$3.3 billion in 1962 to US$204 billion in 1989, and eventually breaking the trillion-dollar mark in 2004. Today the country continues to exhibit financially strong stability. The country learned from its mistakes of the 1997 crisis. At that time, South Korea had become dependent on foreign credit and when the crisis hit, it did not have the proper reserves to fall back on. The country had to go to the IMF for a bailout and liberalize much of its economy. Thereafter, the leverage was sucked out of the economy and the country could embark on a more stable financial future.

As with Taiwan, per-capita GDP in South Korea has increased rapidly in the past 20 years without a corresponding increase in the stock market. GDP per capita has increased from $7,272.79 in 1989 to $27,790.60 but the South Korean stock market, like the Taiwanese market, is still below its 1989 high!

How to Invest in South Korea The easiest way to invest in South Korea is via the South Korean Ishares ETF (ticker: EWY). Only a few

South Korean ADRs trade in the United States; we suggest that if you are interested in investing in South Korean securities, you get an international broker who has access to this market.

Indonesia

Indonesia seems to escape under the radar at this time. It is strange that a country of over 240 million people seems to find little to no investment interest in the west. It may be an aversion to Muslim nations or the fact that Indonesia was extremely corrupt under the Suharto regime in the eighties and nineties.

However, Indonesia has freed up its economy in recent years. The recent election in 2009 reinstituted a pro-growth government. Yet, despite the problems Indonesia has seen, it's GDP per capita increased from over $1,100 dollars in the late eighties to over $4,100 in 2009. Indonesia's economy is still deficient in terms of infrastructure and education.

The country is early in the stage of economic liberalization. It just began major reforms in the mid-2000s, so it is also in the earlier stage of its boom.

The Dow Jones Indonesia Index has seen a huge boom since its inception in 2004. We would wait for dips in it before buying this market. There are a few ADRs that trade on the Indonesian market, which include the Indonesia Fund (ticker: IF) and Telecomm Indonesia (ticker: PTK).

I like Indonesia going forward, but I see more current value in places like Taiwan and South Korea.

Vietnam and Other Asian Nations

The gem of the region at the moment might well be Vietnam. This could be where Taiwan or South Korea was 20 to 30 years ago. The ironic thing about the "better-dead-than-red" wars of Asia 40 years ago is that all that was needed to defeat communism was patience. By the mid-eighties, it was apparent that the communist system in these nations was failing and they began to slowly liberalize their economies.

Historically a collective agricultural economy, in recent times there has been a recommitment by Vietnamese Authority to economic liberalization and international integration. The "Doi Moi" plans for structural reforms, which will help to modernize Vietnam's economy, are being implemented and there have been talks of promoting more competitive export-driven industries.

After nearly a decade of negotiations, Vietnam finally joined the WTO in January 2007. WTO membership has provided Vietnam an anchor to the global market and reinforced the domestic economic reform process. In fact, Hanoi is targeting an economic growth rate of 7.5 to 8 percent during the next four years. The country has also seen enormous growth in GDP per capita and has grown from $300 per capita in 1980 to nearly $2,900 per capita at the moment!

The country is running quite large deficits at the moment in wake of the financial crisis and must make sure that it does not make the same mistakes that Taiwan, South Korea, and others made in the mid-nineties, which led to financial crisis and severe economic downturns. However, if such a downturn would occur, it could perversely bring a great buying opportunity.

Investment opportunities are still limited for North American investors in Vietnam at the moment. The only U.S. listing is the Market Vectors Vietnam Fund (ticker: VNM), which is a good way to play the country. Otherwise, you had best get a broker who can trade Vietnamese-listed companies.

There are obviously other huge investment opportunities in Asia.

Sri Lanka just ended a 28-year civil war. Whenever a country emerges from a war (like Vietnam 25 years ago, or Chile 35 years ago, or Korea 50 years ago), it presents great opportunities. Prices are depressed and massive infrastructure spending is needed to bring the country back. There is also a lot of pent-up demand for luxury goods. Sri Lanka is probably a great buy as it emerges from years of civil war. Malaysia is a major supplier of palm oil and is also liberalizing its economy. The Philippines is another emerging Asian nation. Thailand will probably end up being a great tourist destination in Asia, with beautiful beaches and great nightlife. Thailand seems to thrive despite its government. Marc Faber, who lives in Thailand, states that he will not do business there but has mentioned a few great leisure stock opportunities.

Cambodia, like Vietnam, is emerging. Laos and East Timor and Myanmar remain poor and backwards and war-torn, but you have to think they will open their borders as areas of cheap labor as the rest of Asia advances.

Cities such as Hong Kong and Singapore should remain large financial centers that supply Asia with capital and benefit from future Asian prosperity.

Finally, we have Russia. Russia is still a rogue market. I don't like the long-term outlook of Russia due to its lack of democratic institutions. However, it is a great market to trade as a bet on oil. When oil collapsed in 1998 and 2008, Russia collapsed with it. Russia, ironically, has become a huge, volatile market, a sort of Wild West capitalism. The market often rallies thousands of percent to be followed by 90 percent meltdowns. These meltdowns represent great trading opportunities. If Russia sees another one of these meltdowns, the tool to play the market is the Templeton Russian Fund (ticker: TRF). I do not like Russia as a long-term hold, but on extreme weakness, such as we saw in 1998 and 2008, it is a good trade.

All in all, I believe that the shift toward prosperity in Asia should result in many of the abovementioned Asian nations becoming strong investments.

Latin America

In the past half-century, Latin America has had a violent history of coups, communism, and government overthrows. It is only in recent years that we have seen the return of many democratic governments in Latin America. However, many Latin American countries still possess socialist policies. Recent socialist party wins in elections in Ecuador and Bolivia have really hindered the advancement of those economies. Chavez is all but bringing the economy of Venezuela to its knees. However, with that said, much of Latin America is still great for investing because they have a huge exposure to the natural resource boom as many Latin American countries produce a variety of commodities, including copper, gold, silver, oil and gas, and agricultural products. Chile and Brazil currently possess the most favorable climate for investment potential and my review of Latin America will focus mainly on these two countries. In fact, I will examine Chile in greater detail than Brazil, as Chile (unlike Brazil) rarely gets any attention in the North American investment community.

Chile

As I write in 2010, a massive earthquake has ravaged much of southern Chile. However, the experience of many countries emerging from war and natural disaster is that, despite their great short-term human suffering, these disasters can actually help a country in the long term. Building codes are strengthened (in the cases of hurricanes and earthquakes) and infrastructure is rebuilt in a much more modern way. I would like to begin this section on Chile by thanking my friend Victor Riesco, a broker and analyst and my source on the ground from Chile, who helped me with much of my research.

Chile is a country located in the southwest region of South America. Chile is a very long and thin country with an extended coastline of about 4,000 miles. The country neighbors Peru and Bolivia in the north and Argentina through the west, separated by the Andes Mountains.

Because of its extended length that crosses latitudes from 17 to 56 degrees south, Chile possesses a variety of climates and diverse natural resources. Natural resources and agricultural products are a major component of the Chilean economy. Chile is a major exporter of copper, molybdenum, iron ore, nitrates, precious metals, wine, grapes, and timber. Its nutrient-rich currents also make it an important producer of fishmeal, fish oil, and salmon. Chile exports about one-third of the global copper supply.

Asia is one of Chile's main trading partners and thus the Chilean economy's performance is much correlated to growth in that region and the price of commodities (CRB Index).

Chile is characterized by a strong democratic tradition (briefly interrupted during the Cold War era) that has given the country high political stability and consistent economic progress. From 1990 to 2008, Chile's GDP grew on average 5.3 percent while per-capita income has tripled in the same timeframe. Chile is somewhat famous for implementing the advice of Nobel Prize—winning economist Milton Friedman. Chile is very disciplined, running up surpluses during times of high copper prices, saving that money, and then using those reserves to keep the economy afloat during times when copper prices fall and the economy weakens. The country also has a private pension system that prevents it from entertaining the under- and unfunded problems that public pension systems in other western democracies could run into.

Throughout the past 20 years, Chile has striven to maintain constant fiscal and trade surpluses, low levels of external debt, high credit ratings, controlled inflation, and expanding currency reserves. Chile is also one of the best foreign mining jurisdictions in the world.

Chilean Stock Market The Chilean stock market has been operating since 1893 when the main exchange, Bolsa de Santiago, was established. It is a medium-sized market with moderate liquidity and with a total market cap of approximately $210 billion. Its two main indices are the IPSA and the IGPA.

The IPSA index consists of the 40 securities that have the largest trading volume and a market cap over $200 million. The IGPA is a broader index that includes all stocks that have a market cap over $400,000 that are traded more than 5 percent of all the possible trading days.

From 2005 to 2009, the IPSA has gained approximately 99 percent, giving it an average yearly return of 19.8 percent. During the past two years, the IPSA has shown great relative strength against the S&P 500. In 2008, amid the financial crisis, the IPSA only lost 22 percent. In 2009, it gained 50.7 percent, recovering all the losses from 2008 and reaching new historical highs. I should note that as we go to press in 2010, the Chilean market has become overheated and overvalued. Therefore, I recommend that you look at the following stocks only when the Chilean market pulls back from these lofty levels.

Investing in Chile There are various ways that you can invest in Chile. ETFs and Chilean ADRs are the best ways.

ETFs The easiest way to invest in Chile is through ETFs or closed-end funds, which give a similar performance to the IPSA index. There are two trading vehicles that try to accomplish this goal:

1. The iShares MSCI Chile Investable Market Index Fund (ticker: ECH) is a free float–adjusted market capitalization index that is designed to measure broad-based equity market performance in Chile. This fund is run by Blackrock Fund Advisors.
2. The Chile Fund (ticker: CH) is a nondiversified, closed-end investment company that seeks total return investing in Chilean equities and debt securities. Credit Suisse and the Chilean investment bank, Celfin Capital, run this fund.

Chilean ADRs If you want to purchase individual Chilean equities instead of a broad-based index, there are a series of ADRs of Chilean stocks that trade on the NYSE.

Beverage Industry

- Embotelladora Andina SA (ticker: AKO-A): Embotelladora Andina is a Chilean company that produces and bottles Coca-Cola products such as soft drinks, juices, and waters in Chile, Brazil, and Argentina. It is a solid and well-run company that has consistent profit growth and high return on equity and pays off good dividends. It is a conservative, low-beta play in the South American economy.
- Viña Concha Toro SA (ticker: VCO): Viña Concha Toro is a Chilean wine producer, bottler, and exporter. It is Chile's biggest wine producer and exporter, selling its products to over 131 countries around the world. The company has built a strong brand name around the world thanks to its excellent wines and innovative products.
- Compañia Cervecerias Unidas SA (ticker: CCU): Compañía Cervecerias Unidas is a Chilean beverage company that operates in Chile and Argentina. It produces a variety of soft drinks licensed by Pepsi, mineral waters, and beers from proprietary and licensed brands. It also produces wines thanks to its investment in Viña San Pedro, being Chile's second biggest exporter in this segment. In Argentina, it is involved in wine production due to its investment in "Finca la Celia."

   The company also produces a typical Chilean spirit called "Pisco" and is also involved in producing snacks and cereals through one of its subsidiaries.

Banks and Financials

- Corpbanca (ticker: BCA): Corpbanca is a Chilean conglomerate that offers an ample variety of retail and commercial banking to people and business. It also offers insurance brokerage, securities brokerage, mutual fund management, and financial advisory services. It is a medium-sized banking conglomerate.
- Banco de Chile (ticker: BCH): One of the largest Chilean banking conglomerates, this company offers a variety of services to retail and large corporations. It also deals in mutual funds, brokerage services, securitization, insurance, and factoring. It recently had a fusion with Citibank in Chile. It offers a high dividend.

- Banco Santander (ticker: SAN): This is another big banking conglomerate in Chile that offers a variety of services to commercial and retail clients. Insurance, securities brokerage, mutual fund management, and loans in foreign currency are some of its services. It operates over 480 banks around the country.
- Administradora de Fondo de Pensiones Provida (ticker: PVD): PVD is a private pension fund administrator. By law, all workers with a legal contract must deposit part of their funds in a private fund administrator in order to have money to finance their retirement. This measure has also helped to add liquidity to the Chilean stock market. Provida is one of the largest and most prestigious fund administrators. It pays a high dividend yield.

Utilities
- Empresa Nacional de Electricidad (ticker: EOC) and Enersis SA (ticker: ENI): These are two sister companies that produce, transmit, and distribute electricity in Chile, Colombia, Argentina, Colombia, and Peru. They produce electric power using hydroelectric, thermal, and wind power technologies. These companies have outstanding profit margins, ROE, plus decent dividend yields.

Airlines
- LAN Airlines SA (ticker: LFL): This is the biggest commercial and cargo airline in South America. During the past decade, with an aggressive growth plan, competent management, and great service, LAN expanded its operations and became a major player in the airline industry. LAN recently announced a multibillion-dollar takeover of Brazilean counterpart TAM, which will make this the largest Airline in South America.

Chemicals
- Sociedad Quimica y Minera SA (ticker: SQM): SQM produces plant nutrients and commodity fertilizer. It also possesses one of the largest lithium mines in the world. With the low global food inventories, diminishing agricultural plots, and money-printing policies around the world, the price of both food and fertilizers should tend to go up. SQM is priced like a growth company with high P/E ratios. The company has displayed aggressive earnings growth and excellent profit ratios.

As you can see, Chile offers some fantastic companies. It has become the jewel of South America as its GDP per capita has outperformed the rest of the continent by 60 percent since the late eighties. I feel that Chile, on any weakness, especially if you believe in the long-term growth of commodity prices, is a great buy. It also ranks tenth in terms of the economic freedom index, easily the highest of any of the South American countries.

Brazil

Brazil is an all-important part of the *BRIC* (Brazil, Russia, India, and China), which represent the largest of the developing economies.

For years, like many Latin American countries, Brazil was an economic basket case. It had high inflation and a stagnant economy. However, Brazil has somewhat opened up and is benefitting from higher commodity prices. Petro Bras, the giant oil company, recently had a huge find off the coast of Brazil. It has also made many strategic deals in selling commodities to China and, interestingly enough, many of the deals are a mix of buying these commodities in yuan and reals in an attempt to get away from the declining U.S. dollar.

After stagnant growth in the early nineties, Brazil has seen its GDP per capita nearly double from $5,496.99 in 1992 to $10,455.59 in 2009. It does not enjoy the high single-digit growth rates of India and China but it is a bit more advanced having a GDP per capita about twice that of China and four times of India.

Brazil will benefit from the commodities demand of Asia. It has seen a more than tripling in exports from just over $59 billion in 2003 to nearly $200 billion in 2009. Brazil has become the twenty-second largest exporter in the world during this timeframe. In addition, after the oil crisis of the seventies adversely affected Brazil, the country made a conscious decision to turn to ethanol so that such a crisis could never again hinder the country in the future. Many of the vehicles and gas stations in Brazil rely on ethanol. Brazilian ethanol is sugar-based ethanol. Sugar is six times more effective in producing ethanol than corn. This fact illustrates why the U.S. plan of producing ethanol by corn is inefficient and ridiculous and is basically a political sellout to appease U.S. corn farmers and the agricultural lobby.

In 2009, Brazil actually enacted some excess taxes on foreign investment to prevent excess speculation in its currency and stock market, which saw strong rebounds in 2009. I think that Brazil may be vulnerable to a correction; however, it should be kept in mind that Brazil has strategically placed itself as a major natural resource exporter to Asia. In addition, Brazil is one of the largest agricultural economies in the world. This means that if grain and agriculture prices rise, Brazil will be destined to benefit.

Brazil has many issues to overcome, such as large slums, high crime, and the deforestation of its rain forests. It must overcome these problems to dispel the famous quote about Brazil: "It is the country of the future and it always will be."

How to Invest in Brazil The ETF for Brazil Ishares (ticker: EWZ) is a simple, nondiversified overview of the Brazilian economy.

The largest and probably best company in Brazil is Peteoleo Brasile (ticker: PBR). This company is one of the largest oil producers in the world and is reaping the benefits of some large finds in recent years. Petro Brazil produced over 2.06 million barrels per day of oil in 2008, representing over 80 percent of Brazilian production.

Large telecom companies should be good investments—such as Telecomincanoes De Sao Paulo (ticker: TSP), which has a yield of over 4.40 percent. CFPL Energies (Ticker: CPL) is another top-tier energy company that yields a high dividend.

Other Nations in Latin America

Having the benefit of a lot of connections in the mining industry, the main way I plan to play Latin America is through mining. It fits into an industry I know and also fits nicely with my long-term bullish view on commodities. For example, in my newsletter I recommended a stock run by a group out of Toronto, Ontario, Desert Sun Mining, a mining company that eventually sold out a mine in Brazil to Yamana Gold for north $7.00 a share (Desert Sun was put together at $0.25 a share). Many nations that I am not a huge fan of on a macro front, such as Mexico, Argentina, and Columbia, have great mining sectors, and I feel that that is the best way to play those countries. Of the smaller nations I am very bullish on Peru. It has emerged from its socialist past, is rapidly growing and seeing huge investment in its mining sector and other areas of its economy.

In South America, many countries are going through another failed experiment with socialism. Venezuela is seeing massive inflation and muzzling of the press under Chavez. Bolivia and Ecuador also have some not-so-mining-friendly governments and have paid the price after trying to nationalize some mines (there was a huge negative reaction and those plans were put on hold).

Many Central American countries are slowly on the mend. However, they are small, and while some, such as Honduras and Guatemala, have large agricultural sectors, you really have to know the market. Central America may benefit from tourism; many of these nations' east coast borders are on the Caribbean and possess pristine beaches that are still small fishing towns and are undeveloped. Compared to the overpriced and overbuilt beaches of Florida, they represent great value.

Panama City has become notorious as a drug-money-laundering center. However, its buildup of financial infrastructure should lead to it becoming a venture center for the rest of Latin and Central and South America.

Finally, the Caribbean is small, but has some interesting opportunities, not so much from a stock investing perspective but from one of real estate and agriculture. The Caribbean was once the center of the sugar world and if we see spikes again in those prices, a sugar plantation in the Caribbean could very well make sense, especially if ethanol takes off. Also, if western governments continue to overtax their citizens, developed financial centers such as the Cayman Islands, Bahamas, Barbados, and British Virgin Islands may be a great place for an expat to set up shop. Again, these countries have their problems with crime and lack of infrastructure, but they also have many benefits such as great weather and low taxes. I can tell you that the small family islands of the Bahamas are still unpopulated, have great infrastructure, and are still the types of communities where you can you leave your door open at night.

Africa

There is an old phrase: *low-hanging fruit*. Low-hanging fruit is easier to reach. It is found on a tree that has not been explored. This is Africa. After years of civil unrest and wars, Africa is in the early stages of stabilizing. China and India are making huge investments in Africa to secure imports of commodities. However, Africa is not quite there yet. As Jim Dines, editor of the *Dines Letter*, has stated, prosperity has moved west from Europe to North America, now to Asia, and will eventually make its way to Africa. Therefore, prosperity will probably take a while to reach Africa.

There are still great opportunities but again you will have to know the local markets. Some African countries such as Zambia and Botswana have started to open up, but most remain riddled with red tape. Angola ended a 20-year-plus civil war and has huge reserves in oil and diamonds. Zambia has the continent's first cell phone company. Ghana is one of the continent's most stable nations; its residents speak English and it has a booming mining industry. In addition, if African nations can stabilize, much of Africa has beautiful coasts and pristine beaches that could be developed into prime vacation property and resorts.

I do like Africa; it has the potential to become a huge natural resource producer like South America. However, it still has a way to go; corruption is still high and transparency low. I would not recommend it unless you really know the inside of these markets.

International Investing Is a Must for Your Portfolio

I hope this chapter has given you a nice overview of global investment opportunities. Although my next book will probably be primarily devoted to international investing, for the purpose of this book, I wanted to give you a glimpse into this world. My mentor, John Templeton, was one of the first people to discover these types of opportunities. The United States is still the most liquid and the largest market in the world. However, the U.S. investment industry has not made many Americans aware of opportunities that exist beyond their borders. You will never see anything about these opportunities in much of the U.S. financial media. With the U.S. Super Bubble ending, cash is going to flow around the world. This will help many of the overseas markets I have mentioned, and it is my hope that my suggestions will provide food for thought for investing in the numerous opportunities that exist outside of mainstream U.S. securities.

Conclusion

This book will end like it began. I will again state that I am not some doom-and-gloom wacko. If you attend any resource and gold conferences, you will find these types of people. They are always predicting the end of the world; they predict that the United States will become a third-world country and call for everything to collapse. Many of these types gained fame during the crash of 2008 and 2009 because in that environment of panic, their extreme views seemed to be realized. Of course, many of these individuals predicted a continuation of the crash in 2009, but the stock market saw a huge rally. In *Addicted to Profits*, in March 2009, we actually produced a report entitled "Eleven Investment Trends for 2009," which called for investors to aggressively buy stocks right near the markets' low. We stated in this report that beaten-up sectors such as banks and casinos and emerging markets would lead the way in the coming market rally, which they did.

One of the things I hope to show in this book is that you have to have a long-term, flexible view on the markets. There are times to buy and times to sell. You sell greed and buy pessimism. You aggressively buy on what John Templeton would call "maximum pessimism." While it was not the start of a long-term bull market, March 2009 saw massive fear and pessimism and was a great intermediate trading opportunity. However, because of where we are in the cycle and the policies instituted by the U.S. federal government, we see this as a false bull market that might go up for one year, maybe two, but will not lead to a long-term bull market in the United States.

As indicated in this book, I am actually very bullish on much of the global economy. Yes, if there is a run on U.S. bonds and the U.S. government teeters on bankruptcy, this will have a short-term negative effect on the economies of Asia. However, more and more in the future, the economies of Asia and South America will become less dependent on the United States and more intertwined with each other. It is just a natural progression of economic power. In the nineteenth century, the United States was dependent on Britain (the economic and political superpower of the time) for financing and gold. However, by the time World War II was finished in the mid-twentieth century, the United States had little to no dependency on the British.

In the decades to come, Asia will have a declining dependence on the western world. Already there are higher car sales in the emerging world than in the first world. Maybe one day India will be setting up call centers in the United States, so maybe Americans should be learning Hindi!

I spent considerable time on emerging economies in this book because I find that many investors in the United States do not know the impact that they are having or that they even exist. This is not the fault of many Americans; their country has been the global superpower and the largest economy in the world for decades. However, sometimes watching the media in the United States, you wonder if there is even a world outside the United States. If you watch the BBC, you get a totally different take; they have outstanding shows such as the *Africa, India, and Middle Eastern Business Reports*, all of which show what is happening in those areas. You will learn about industrial companies in Gujarat, India or cell phone companies in Zambia. As the United States will have a decreasing role in the global economy, it is important for the average investor to take a more global view. That does not mean that you have to go out and dive into emerging markets today. However, it means that, if we have panics or bear markets like 2009 again, you should use such weakness to buy emerging markets.

One also must be a realist. Everything that can be gleaned from the historical similarities regarding the decline and fall of the Roman Empire, British Empire, and other superpowers tells us that the United States is an empire in decline. Judging by the U.S. charts of debt to GDP and the coming unfunded liabilities of Medicare and Medicaid, the United States is about to enter a debt bubble that many of these other superpowers saw near their declines. With much of U.S. debt (over 70 percent) short-term in nature, it will be very difficult for the government to just inflate it away. Within my lifetime and probably much sooner than that (more probably by my fiftieth birthday—I am presently 33), the U.S. dollar will cease to become the reserve currency of the world.

This means inflation, and investors seeking to protect themselves should look to commodities and gold and inflation hedges in addition to investments in non-U.S. markets. Sometimes gold and commodities are portrayed as out-of-date investments. However, as we have illustrated in this book, there are Super Cycles in which commodities outperform equities.

This book seeks to cover ground that exists nowhere else in the investment literature but at the same time I must confess that a review of history shows that the more things change, the more things stay the same. Superpowers rise and fall. Stocks and commodities each have their cycles and days in the sun. I hope that this book will help you to take advantage of the coming cycles and trends in the markets and help you on your way to your financial independence!

Recommended Reading

M y experience has been that most financial reporting and writing will not get you anywhere. I find that the best books and newsletters are written by so-called *contrarian* writers.

Books

I recommend that you read anything by Harvard professor Niall Ferguson; his books *Empire* (Basic Books, 2004), *The Cash Nexus* (Basic Books, 2002), and *The Ascent of Money* (Penguin, 2009) give you a great overview of the history of superpowers and money.

Peter Schiff's two books, *Crash Proof* (2007) and *Crash Proof 2.0* (2009), both published by John Wiley & Sons, Inc., are a great overview of the U.S. debt bubble and consumption bubble and show why the dollar will fall in the coming years.

George Soros's *The New Paradigm for Financial Markets* (Public Affairs, 2008) gives a great detailed analysis of the Super Bubble and why we saw a blow-off in the U.S. mortgage market and the collapse of leverage in the U.S. market. Robert Slater's biography *Soros* (McGraw-Hill, 2008) is a great overview of this great speculator's career.

Jim Rogers' investment journey books *Investment Biker* (Random House, 2003) and *Adventure Capitalist* (Random House, 2004) give a nice introduction to global investing. His book *Hot Commodities* (Random House, 2007) is also a must-read for any commodities bull.

Anything about or by Peter Lynch, Warren Buffett, and John Templeton [*Beating the Street* (Simon & Schuster, 1994) and *One Up on Wall Street* (Simon & Schuster, 2000) and *Investing the Templeton Way* (McGraw-Hill, 2008)] will show a great way to invest from a value/contrarian point of view. Also many of the trading strategies outlined in Martin Zweig's *Winning on Wall Street* (Warner Books, 1997) are still valid today.

Books such as *The Great Reckoning* (Fireside, 1994) by James Davidson and *Bankruptcy 1995* (Little Brown, 1993) by Harry Figgie were just about 20 years ahead of their time. They are must-reads in the debt bubble; just add about 20 years to the dates!

Stan Weinstein's *How to Profit in Bull and Bear Markets* (McGraw-Hill, 1988) is a classic on trading markets from a technical perspective.

Mass Psychology (James Dines & Company, 1996) by Jim Dines is a classic on investment psychology, not just market psychology but how your own psychology can affect your trading.

One of the greatest books on cycles and economic history and the coming emergence of Asia is *Tomorrow's Gold* (CLSA Books, 2010) by Dr. Marc Faber.

I have also had two previous books published: *Stock Market Panic!*, and *The Contrarian Who Saved the World*. *Stock Market Panic!* was published in 1998 and predicted the bear market of the 2000s and commodities and gold boom of the decade. *The Contrarian Who Saved the World* explains market cycles and booms and busts in an easy-to-read fun story. It may be helpful if you are trying to get a young person interested in the stock market.

Investment Newsletters

I write four newsletters, including www.addictedtoprofits.net and *Gold Stock Adviser*. *Addicted to Profits* covers markets using my macro trend view, psychology, fundamentals, and technicals. We give monthly and weekly commentary, stock picks, and much more. The cost is $349 per year; there are about 10 to 12 updates monthly. I also write www.stockchartoftheday.com, which covers markets from a technical point of view, and www.internationalcontrarian.com, which takes a look at global investment opportunities with dozens of commentators from all over the globe.

Gold Stock Adviser is published through www.newsmax.com. It is a more focused newsletter on gold and gold stocks. In it, we give a detailed overview of the gold market and gold stocks. It is a monthly newsletter and retails for only $99 per year.

I do not subscribe to a lot of newsletters. I do not like to read a lot of opinions as they can distract from my own research. However, I can recommend a few that I do read.

From a technical point of view, the best is my good friend Mike Swanson's www.wallstreetwindow.com. Mike is a very disciplined and even more honest trader. He called the bear markets of 2000–2002 and 2009. It retails for $399 per year.

From a fundamental point of view *The Dividend Investor*, written by my friend Bill Spetrino and administered by www.moneynews.com, is a great overview into value and dividend investing.

The newsletter that is my personal favorite (as if you could not tell from the number of times I quoted him in this book) is Marc Faber's www.gloomboomdoom.com. It is in a monthly format and retails for $200 per year.

If you are interested in junior mining, Victor Glonclaves' *Equities and Economics* report (www.enereport.com) is a great read. Victor visits many of the companies himself and his stock picking in 2009 was superb.

Finally, another great newsletter is www.morganreport.com by David Morgan. He is a foremost expert on the silver market.

I also contribute to www.moneynews.com, a web site which gives a great, diversified commentary for numerous experts.

There are many other great books and newsletters, but those are some of my favorites.

References

Chapter 1 Explosion of Debt and the End of the Super Bubble

Bartlett, Bruce. 2004. Warriors against inflation—Volcker and Reagan got the job done. *NRO Financial*, June 14. http://old.nationalreview.com/nrof_bartlett/bartlett200406140846.asp.

Internal Revenue Service. www.irs.gov/businesses/small/international/article/0,,id=97245,00.htm; www.irs.gov/publications/p519/ch04.html#en_US_publink1000222396.

International Monetary Fund. 2009. GDP per capita France. World Bank, 2008. International Monetary Fund. www.measuringworth.org/datasets/japandata/.

Statistics Bureau. 1996–2008. Ministry of Internal Affairs and Communications. www.stat.go.jp/english/data/chouki/03.htm.

Chapter 2 The Money Printers and the Coming Inflation

Bankwatch. 2008. www.thebankwatch.com; http://thebankwatch.com/2008/07/14/fannie-and-freddie-double-the-us-national-debt/.

Barrington, Garrett. 2006. *The pocket money book: A monetary chronology of the United States*. Great Barrington, MA: American Institute for Economic Research.

Boles, Tracy. 2008. IMF puts billion in pot to bail out world. *Daily Express*, October 26. www.dailyexpress.co.uk/posts/view/68011.

Browne, Harry. 1995. *Why government doesn't work pages*. Great Falls, MT: Liamworks, December 1.

Cauchon, Dennis. 2009. Taxpayers on the hook for $59 trillion. *USA Today*, May 28. www.usatoday.com/news/washington/2007-05-28-federal-budget_N.htm.

Chantrill, Christopher. 2010. U.S. government spending. www.usgovern mentspending.com.

Dayen, David. 2010. Health care bill expenditures being $940 billion. CBO from Fire Dog Lake, March 18. http://news.firedoglake.com/2010/03/18/cbo-health-care-bill-costs-940b-lowers-deficit-130b/.

Ferguson, Niall. 2009. An empire at risk. *Newsweek*, November 27. www .newsweek.com/2009/11/27/an-empire-at-risk.html.

Money and Markets. 2008. Fannie and Freddie bailout destined to fail as US debt doubles. *Market Oracle*, September 9. www.marketoracle.co.uk/Article6184.html.

No Nonsense Economics. 2004. UK debt bombshell. www.debtbombshell. com/history-of-national-debt.htm.

Orszag, Peter R. 2007. Trends in earnings variability over the past 20 years. Congressional Budget Office, April 17. http://docs.google.com/viewer?a=v&q=cache:9S7pz3LrUMMJ:www.cbo.gov/doc.cfm%3Findex%3 D8007+CBO+increases+in+wages+since+1980&hl=en&gl= bs&pid=bl&srcid=ADGEESgohDA2jsNrVo0hetH6paiefN-GD1BuVZ-WwUlIRah95EM-lRJgz7IcEEpFDsUpqIiZNYZS-dG4P9sVldWcbdgAOrdm7WYYEEHu0I4TQR72D_KFAcnr0yp-9I CDju7SB3DFj1_iH&sig=AHIEtbQn_B9ydSByvFdoR6dy8IMuvtziEw.

Progressive Policy Institute. 2008. $700 billion—Largest U.S. bailout ever. September 24. www.ppionline.org/ppi_ci.cfm?knlgAreaID=108&subsec ID=900003&contentID=254752.

Soros, George. 2008. Super Bubble Thesis from *A new paradigm for financial markets: The credit crisis and what it means*, Chapter 4. New York: PublicAffairs.

Chapter 3 You Cannot Fight the Power of Cycles

Ferguson, Niall. 2008. *The ascent of money: A financial history of the world*. London: Allen Lane.

Friedman, Milt. Posted to YouTube 2007. *Milton Friedman explains the role in the Great Depression*. Video. www.youtube.com/watch?v=O7pnjzCuSv8.

Friedman, Milton, and Rose Friedman. 1999. *Two lucky people: Memoirs*. Chicago: University of Chicago Press.

Gold standard: Evolution of international monetary systems. http://econ2 .econ.iastate.edu/classes/econ355/choi/golds.htm.

Indexmundi.com. http://indexmundi.com/.

Institute of Latin American Studies. 1986. *The debt crisis in Latin America*, p. 69.

Schwartz, Anna. 2008. Bernanke is fighting the last war. *Wall Street Journal*, October 18. http://online.wsj.com/article/SB122428279231046053.html.

U.S. Census Bureau. 2010. U.S. international trade in goods and services highlights. August 11. www.census.gov/indicator/www/ustrade.html.

Chapter 4 The Fake Bull Market

Bloomberg—*BusinessWeek*. 2009. The death of equities, *BusinessWeek*, August 1979. March 10. www.businessweek.com/investor/content/mar2009/ pi20090310_263462.htm.

Chapter 5 Gold and Silver

Hirsch, Jeffrey A. 2007. *Stock trader's almanac 2008*. Hoboken, NJ: John Wiley & Sons, 131–132.

Norma. 2009. Morgenthau diary, May 9, 1939, Franklin Roosevelt Presidential Library. From Collectingmythoughts.blogspot.com, February 21. http://collectingmythoughts.blogspot.com/2009/02/ sourcing-morgenthau-1939-quote-at.html.

Rogers, Jim. 2009. CNBC quote courtesy of YouTube. www.youtube.com/ watch?v=4HkbS4aDCU0.

The White House. 2009. President Obama delivers remarks on job creation and the economy. *Washington Post*, December 8. www.washingtonpost.com/ wp-dyn/content/article/2009/12/08/AR2009120801695.html.

Chapter 6 Commodities

Life after People, Season 1. 2009. TV documentary. April 21.

Chapter 7 Value and Contrarian Investing

BBC News. 2010. Russia to build nuclear reactors for India. March 12. http://news.bbc.co.uk/2/hi/8561365.stm.

Beeland Management Company, LLC. 2010. Rogers International Commodity Index. www.rogersrawmaterials.com/page1.html.

Burrowes, Andy, Rick Marsh, Nehru Ramdin, and Curtis Evans. 2007. Alberta's energy reserves 2006 and supply/demand outlook 2007–2016. Alberta Energy and Utilities Board. www.ercb.ca/docs/products/STs/st98_current.pdf.

Clarke, Darrell. 2008. Oil prices. June 18. http://lavisions.blogspot.com/2008_06_01_archive.html.

Gupta, Indrajit, and R. Sriram, TNN. 2008. Interview with Ratan Tata: Making of Nano. *Economic Times*, January 11. http://economictimes.indiatimes.com/articleshow/2690794.cms.

Investopedia. Definition of the VIX. 2010. www.investopedia.com/terms/v/vix.asp.

Penoir Inc. 1998–2010. Platinum: The most precious metal. www.penoir.com/platinum.htm.

Templeton, Lauren, and Scott Phillips. 2008. *Investing the Templeton way: The market-beating strategies of value investing's legendary bargain hunter.* New York: McGraw-Hill.

Chapter 8 China

China Venture News. 2009. China investment to GDP ratio. August 31. Data Courtesy Chinese Board of National Statistics. www.chinaventurenews.com/50226711/chinas_investmenttogdp_ratio.php.

History Learning Site. The Suez crisis of 1956. www.historylearningsite.co.uk/suez_crisis_1956.htm.

Kritzer, Adam. 2010. Archive for the Chinese yuan (RMB) category—China currency revaluation: More than just the yuan at stake. August 9. www.forexblog.org/category/chinese-yuan-rmb.

Wierner, Calla. 2008. China's economic stimulus is good news for global markets. *UCLA Today*, November 13. www.today.ucla.edu/portal/ut/china-s-economic-stimulus-is-good-71857.aspx.

Chapter 9 India

Bajaj, Vikas, and Heather Simmons. 2009. India to raise spending and cut taxes. *New York Times*, July 6. www.nytimes.com/2009/07/07/business/global/07rupee.html.

Bloomberg—*BusinessWeek*. 2007. The trouble with India. March 19. www.businessweek.com/magazine/content/07_12/b4026001.htm.

Cerra, Valerie, and Saxena Sweta Chaman. 2002. What caused the 1991 currency crisis in India? IMF Working Papers. www.webcitation.org/5gcvZFemX.

Financial Express. 2004. From the ivory tower: Redefining the Hindu rate of growth. April 12. www.financialexpress.com/news/redefining-the-hindu-rate-of-growth/104268/.

Index Mundi. Indian Economic Stats 2010. http://indexmundi.com/.

Sen, Ronojoy. 2010. India's model of growth is more viable than China's because it's more chaotic. *Times of India*, January 30. http://timesofindia.indiatimes.com/india/Indias-model-of-growth-is-more-viable-than-Chinas-because-its-more-chaotic/articleshow/5516428.cms.

U.S. Energy Information Administration. 2010. India: Oil imports. www.eia.doe.gov/cabs/India/Oil.html.

Wax, Emily. 2008. With Indian politics, the bad gets worse. *Washington Post*, July 24. www.washingtonpost.com/wp-dyn/content/article/2008/07/23/AR2008072303390.html.

Chapter 10 Investing in Other Emerging Global Markets

Australian Bureau of Statistics. 2010. Australian unemployment rate: 6202.0—Labour force, Australia. July. www.abs.gov.au/ausstats/abs@.nsf/mf/6202.0.

CIA World Factbook. Mostly 2009 estimates. www.cia.gov/library/publications/the-world-factbook/rankorder/2186rank.html.

Index Mundi. 2010. Indonesian stats on economy. http://indexmundi.com/.

Japan Today. 2009. Housing starts in Japan plunge 27.9% in 2009. January 30. www.japantoday.com/category/business/view/housing-starts-in-japan-plunge-279-in-2009.

U.S. Energy Information Administration. 2010. Crude oil and total petroleum imports top 15 countries. July 29. www.eia.doe.gov/pub/oil_gas/petroleum/data_publications/company_level_imports/current/import.html.

VOV News. 2010. UK's *Economist* ups Vietnam's growth forecast. July 24. http://english.vovnews.vn/Home/UKs-Economist-ups-Vietnams-growth-forecast/20107/117827.vov.

Acknowledgements

I would like to begin by thanking Chris Ruddy, founder of Newsmax and Moneynews. If we had not had the fortune to meet, this book would not be possible! Thank you, Chris, for believing in me from start to end of this project. I still find it amazing that I met Chris at the memorial for John Templeton. It had to be more than just a coincidence.

I would like to thank Debra Englander, Kelly O'Connor, Adrianna Johnson, and Stacey Fischkelta at Wiley for their help in putting together the project. Thanks also to my father, Toni Skarica, the "greatest" Crown Attorney in history and pseudo-editor, for taking time to edit my work, even after long hours in the court room. And my heartfelt thanks to Mike Swanson who has helped me throughout the years.

I am grateful to all of my loyal subscribers at *Addicted to Profits* and *Gold Stock Adviser* who have supported me the past few years. I would also like to thank Victor Riesco and Genoa O'Brien who helped me with research in the China and Emerging Market chapters. I would like to thank, as well, Aaron Dehoog and Greg Brown at Newsmax for their patience and help since I joined Newsmax. Finally, I would like to acknowledge my new home, the Bahamas, for providing me a wonderful, beautiful setting in which to write. In addition, you will see this book has an international theme. Fittingly, parts of the editing and research were done in the Bahamas, the United States, Canada, Chile, Peru, Panama, Honduras, England, and Monaco. Finally, as always I want to thank you, the reader, without whom this book would not be possible. Hopefully, it will open your eyes to new trends and opportunities and will help you think outside the box.

About the Author

D avid Skarica was born in Toronto, Ontario on September 27th, 1977. He is a Canadian and British citizen. As a child he was obsessed with numbers, NFL films, and videos, and was convinced he would become the next Howard Cosell. At the tender age of 18 David became the youngest person on record to pass the Canadian Securities Course. In 1998 at the age of 21 his first book *Stock Market Panic! How to Prosper in the Coming Bear Market* was published. This book predicted the bear market of the 2000s along with the boom in oil and gold prices and the real estate bust. Also in 1998, he started *Addicted to Profits* (www .addictedtoprofits.net) a newsletter focusing on technical analysis and psychology of markets. From 2001 to 2003 Stockfocus.com ranked *Addicted to Profits* third out of over 300 newsletters in terms of performance. In 2003 David finished second in the Globe and Mail Stock Picking contest with his pick Eldorado Gold gaining over 95 percent that year. David's second book, *The Contrarian Who Saved the World*, was published in 2004. He is also the editor of *Gold Stock Adviser* and *The International Contrarian Services*, which focus on gold and global investing. David is also an avid sports fan who supports the Oakland Raiders, the Los Angeles Lakers, the New York Yankees, the Hamilton Tiger Cats, and the English National Football Team.

Index